Chess Training for Candidat

Alexander Kalinin

Chess Training for Candidate Masters

Accelerate Your Progress by Thinking for Yourself

New In Chess 2017

© 2017 New In Chess

Published by New In Chess, Alkmaar, The Netherlands
www.newinchess.com

Cover design: Volken Beck
Supervision: Peter Boel
Translation: Steve Giddins
Editing and typesetting: Frank Erwich
Proofreading: Maaike Keetman
Production: Anton Schermer

Have you found any errors in this book?
Please send your remarks to editors@newinchess.com. We will
collect all relevant corrections on the Errata page of our website
www.newinchess.com and implement them in a possible next edition.

ISBN: 978-90-5691-715-9

Contents

Foreword

November 28, 2007 is a day that I will remember fondly for the rest of my time on this earth. It was the day I won my final round game at the under-12 World Youth Chess Championship in Antalya, Turkey, securing the gold medal. Every moment from the second I woke up to the instant I went to sleep on that day is seared into my mind, but one episode stands out among the others.

After my opponent – Ivan Bukavshin, who would go on to become one of Russia's strongest young grandmasters before tragically succumbing to a premature death in January 2016 – extended his hand in resignation, I could barely contain my excitement. I wanted to jump on every table, yell in unbridled excitement, hug everything that resembled a human being. Upon exiting the tournament hall, I was met by my mother and my coach, GM Alexander (Sasha) Kalinin, who was helping me at the tournament and whose book you now hold in your hands. After the obligatory embraces and words of congratulations, Sasha and I made eye contact. Following every previous game – win, lose or draw – we had made it a ritual to return to my hotel room and briefly analyse the game before going out to dinner. The dilemma here was obvious: every part of my brain wanted to jump on the bed and celebrate. I had just won the World Youth, who cares about analysing the game?!

But you can probably guess what happened. The three of us returned to my room, my mother took out her phone to text the good news to friends and relatives (most of whom, including my math teacher, were wide awake despite the ungodly hour), and Sasha and I set up the pieces. Then, we analysed my game just like we had analysed the 10 previous ones, concentrating on my inaccuracies and delving deep into the complex opening. Only after we finished our ritual did the bed-jumping begin!

As this episode demonstrates, Alexander Kalinin is a consummate chess professional. Do not be fooled by his (relatively) modest rating or his fairly unknown status in the western chess community: his chess understanding, coupled with his ability to verbalize this understanding in eloquent and concise fashion, is virtually unequalled in the chess world. I worked with Sasha for approximately 4 years, from early 2005 to late 2008, and during this time I grew immeasurably both as a chess player and as a human being. On my ChessBase screen, I still have a database called 'Kalinin Lessons' that I consult very frequently. In this database are more than 500 instructive games that we went over during our lessons; more than half of them are underrated treasures from obscure Soviet tournaments. You will find many of those games in this volume.

Most importantly, Sasha is perfectly in tune with the strengths, tendencies, and weaknesses of the modern generation, as well as the general direction in which the chess world is heading (think chess computers, and how our own thinking has changed as a result). His approach to chess pedagogy is grounded in a classic understanding of the game, but he does not cling to outmoded chess concepts in a kind of misguided Luddism that has become fashionable with some coaches nowadays. Rather, he seamlessly interweaves his chess philosophy with an acute understanding of what modern chess players struggle with and what they must do in order to improve.

But you should not take my word for it; turn the page, and see for yourself! The thoughts and positions laid out in this work are pure gold; I firmly believe that a close reading of the wisdom contained within this volume will immensely benefit a chess player of virtually any strength. This is not just another entry into the ever-growing mass of chess literature. It tackles a litany of crucial themes that one simply has to master in order to become a serious chess player. Both chess players and chess teachers will find this work a treasure trove.

Before I sign off and hand over the reins to Sasha, I will share one more episode from my collaboration with Kalinin that I remember very fondly. In August 2006, Sasha came to the United States to train with me for a month. One evening, my parents' close friends came over for dinner. I knew that a long conversation on non-chess themes was forthcoming. Sasha knew this as well, and just before we came downstairs, he set up the following position, which you will find on page 64 of this book:

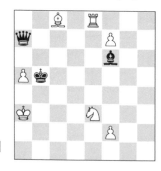

Kalinin's Study (Magadanskaya Pravda 1985)

I ruminated over this position all dinner long, casting furtive smiles Kalinin's way as I began to work out the main line. When I finally came up with the solution – in between mouthfuls of salad – I flashed a big grin that surprised everyone at the table. So many years later, I still remember this moment (and Kalinin's visit as a whole) with more than a measure of fondness. Reading this book has allowed me the rare pleasure of reliving some of my experiences, and it will allow you, dear reader, to broaden your perspective and improve your understanding of our beloved game in a way that you never thought possible. Happy reading!

GM Daniel Naroditsky
San Francisco, California
November 22, 2016

Alexander Kalinin (left) and the author of the Foreword, Daniel Naroditsky, around the time of the World Youth.

How to train the masters of the future

Dedicated to my chess teacher

'Everything is new that has been long forgotten.' Today's young players, growing up with the computer, know little of the methods of improvement used in the 20th century, and regard them as hopelessly outdated. But it is within these methods, in which is concentrated the precious experience of past generations of masters and trainers, that the secrets of the development of chess creativity resides.

There is no question that in our computerised age, a mass of possibilities have opened up before chess lovers! With the aid of the internet, despite being located thousands of kilometres away, we can follow live all the significant tournaments of the day, can try to guess the grandmasters' moves, and have the benefit of expert commentary. Such 'live' participation in strong tournaments has long been considered a highly effective method of training. We can play against opponents from all round the world, at different time controls, not only solving concrete chess tasks, but also interacting with players from other countries. We have at our disposal computer courses in different aspects of the game, whilst powerful playing programs are there to correct our mistakes and suggest improvements in our games and analyses. Those wishing to study endgames can make use of the famous Nalimov tablebases. One can go on indefinitely, listing the benefits of technical progress. Instead, we will limit ourselves to acknowledging openly that the use of the computer has significantly enlarged and deepened our understanding of the ancient game.

However, this process also has its negative side. It is obvious that 'artificial intelligence' is having an effect on the way people think. Many treat the computer as an all-seeing guru, which can give reliable answers to any question. As a result, we have gradually stopped thinking and analysing for ourselves, preferring most of the time to accept as gospel the computer's recommendations. But the most effective way of learning is, and always has been, personal interaction. Humans think in general terms, and find it hard to learn from a computer, which speaks only in the language of bare variations. Everything we see on the computer – lines of variations from Houdini or Rybka, mathematically confirmed variations on Nalimov, etc – is just information, which needs to be translated into the language of emotions and pictures, and built into a logical whole. Only in this way can we take what we have seen and use it in practice, making it a part of ourselves. But to achieve such a level of work with information it is essential to learn a great deal and develop within oneself the habit of using one's own brain.

In the summer of 2008, I was witness to a conversation between the young American player Daniel Naroditsky (with whom I worked at that time) and Yuri Sergeevich Razuvaev, which took place at the former Central Chess Club on Gogolevsky Bulvar in Moscow. The famous grandmaster and trainer expressed a deep thought: 'An intelligent book helps one to understand chess better. One can learn tactics just from a computer, but to develop understanding, one needs contact, whether by reading or listening. Every phrase can be key to understanding a position. You, Dan, need now to learn to understand chess, which requires contact with good books.'

I should also mention the nowadays widespread habit of computer analysis, which is seen as an apparently easy way to find the truth in any position. One needs to be very careful with such 'analysis', because such non-systematic work militates against the formation of the single most important quality in a chess player, namely independent thinking.

In trying to balance the computer thinking with the human decision-making process, I consider it important to explain to our rising generation how their predecessors in the pre-computer era discovered the secrets of chess. In thinking about the sources of the growth of knowledge and strength among young players of that seemingly far-off era, I identified the following directions of independent work, which retain their universal significance today:

1) Forming a relationship with chess as an art;
2) Perfecting analytical mastery, which allows one to study critically your own play and the games of others;
3) Study of the classical heritage;
4) Drawing the lessons from interaction with one's competitors and with more experienced players.

The attempt to reveal the above areas is the main aim of the present book. I decided to show the process of study from inside, i.e. from the pupil's viewpoint. I hope the reader will find it interesting to see how concrete knowledge influences the overall 'world view' of a young player and helps him to take decisions at the board. It is clear that I, the author, could only draw such psychological lessons from my own experience and also from those competitors whom I know especially well. I covered the period from the start of my serious study of chess, until the point when I fulfilled the USSR Master of Sport title norms. This also underlines the aim of the book, which is to provide advice to players seeking to achieve the master title. I began serious chess study at the age of seven, and became a master only at the age of 21, after my army service. Why did it take me so long to achieve the title? By delving into this book, the reader will be able to see the mistakes I made on my way and, I hope, will be able to draw useful lessons for themselves.

A few words about the structure of the book. Its first part ('General questions of chess pedagogy') consists of a short survey of the development of chess pedagogy and acquaints the reader with some general principles and methods of training. This also covers the currently important topic of the interaction of man and computer.

The second part ('How a chess player develops') illustrates the influence of the classical methods of improvement on a young player's development. As I have already said, the role of 'raw youth' will be taken by the author himself. Here I will also give portraits of my mentors and speak about the methods they used in their work. The main source of material in the second part is taken from my own youthful games and analyses and also the games of my contemporaries, many of whom went on to become well-known players. These examples will acquaint the reader with the real picture of how young players think and react during tournament battles, how they acquire and use important information, converting it into forms which they find useful.

The main content of the book comprises material which has not been published elsewhere before. Well-known examples have been used only where they are indispensable in illustrating the way a certain decision is taken with the help of the relevant thought process. The author's task in selecting material has been an extremely responsible one, since the majority of positions are taken from the games of players who were only just setting out on their journey to chess mastery. Therefore, firstly I have used only those games which I recall as especially striking, hoping that they will also provoke an emotional response in the reader. Secondly, tactical examples have been computer-checked (one cannot avoid this – it is a mark of the times!). A portion of the examples failed to survive this process, but the remainder are presented to the reader. In each case, it will be made clear what the human player himself found and what are the suggestions of the computer. A large number of the diagrams in the text are accompanied by questions, which allows them to be used as exercises for independent solving.

The author also hopes that seeing so many interesting ideas in the games of 'ordinary' players will help the reader to develop belief in his own creative possibilities!

Alexander Kalinin
Moscow, March 2017

PART 1

General questions of chess pedagogy

CHAPTER 1

Historical overview

'I want to develop pupils who will be able to think for themselves and treat material critically.' – Emanuel Lasker

Mankind has been playing our present form of chess for close to 500 years, following the European reforms of shatranj in the middle of the XVI century. But chess pedagogy is a topic that is still relatively young. The question of a fundamental basic approach to teaching chess was first raised by Emanuel Lasker in his *Manual of Chess* in 1925. This can be explained as follows. The second World Champion's predecessors, beginning with the Italian masters of the XVI century, had been concerned with researching the game itself and its basic laws and principles, and its internal beauty. Nobody really thought about chess teaching, because the subject matter – chess itself – was something of a 'family secret'. In the works of the strongest masters of the time, we can find only fragmentary, one-off comments on methods of studying chess:

1) From the manuscripts and books of the Italian masters of the XVII-XVIII centuries, the main connecting thread is wonder at the aesthetic beauty of chess. In demonstrating composed positions and beautiful (by the standards of the day) combinations, the authors tried to attract readers to the beauty of chess. One only has to look at the titles of some of the chess books of the time, such as *The Incomparable Game of Chess* (D.Ponziani, 1769)!

2) Philidor's great work *The Analysis of the Game of Chess* (1749) demonstrated that the analysis of a game of chess and explanation of what is happening in it can be based on logical understanding, and not just the detailed breakdown of variations.

3) Labourdonnais in *A New Treatment of the Game of Chess* (1833) was the first to give advice on how to work independently with chess literature: *'In order to learn to calculate variations in one's head, one should follow annotations to games, initially without moving the pieces on the board.'*

4) William Steinitz in the *Modern Chess Instructor* (1889) covered the topic of chess education in the chapter 'Chess as an exercise of the mind and

how to improve at it'. The first World Champion considered it useful to play regularly against an opponent who slightly exceeds one in strength; to replay one's own games from memory, and, even better, the games of masters, reprinted with good annotations in books and magazines; and improve one's playing strength by solving chess compositions. The following comment of Steinitz's is especially instructive: '*Regular study and practice significantly helps with the achievement of rapid success. The person who only does such work occasionally is unlikely to get very far. It is far better to spend an hour a day on chess, six days in a row, than to spend six hours at a stretch, once a week.*'

The period of formulating the basic laws of chess ended at the close of the 19th century, after the work of Steinitz in his major work *The Modern Chess Instructor* (1889). '*Chess rose to its highest level, once masters developed a complete positional understanding. Only then did players begin to produce games which were recognised as true works of art, even by the strictest critics*' (Mikhail Botvinnik). There also arose an audience of observers, who accepted the aesthetic side of the game and respected it. These processes led to the growth in popularity of chess in the world and its gradual transformation into an indispensable part of general culture. The number of international tournaments in Europe and the US grew, the World Championship title began to be played for officially and all of this led to the appearance of increasing numbers of chess books and magazines. A successful synthesis of the sporting and artistic sides of the game led to the growth of an army of masters and chess amateurs. Each group, at its own level, began to be concerned with improving their practical results and their understanding of the game. Thus, people began to develop thoughts about how to improve at chess at all levels, from beginner to master.

5) As already mentioned, a significant moment in the development of chess education was the publication of Emanuel Lasker's *Manual of Chess* (1925). The second World Champion expressed an idea which remains to this day the fundamental basis for chess trainers and their pupils: '*Education in chess should be about developing the ability to think independently!*'

Let us cite several quotations from this work, which give an idea of the second World Champion's pedagogical method:

– *the ability to play chess should not be exclusively a matter of memory, simply because remembering variations is not sufficiently important;*

– *retain in your memory not results, but methods. The method is elastic and may be used in all areas of life;*

– he who wants to develop in himself the ability to think independently about chess should avoid everything in it that is dead: unthinking theory, based on just a few examples and a great many inventions; the habit of playing with weaker opponents; the habit of avoiding danger; the habit of uncritically accepting and following variations and rules, developed by others; smug vanity; unwillingness to admit mistakes – in short, everything that leads to routine or anarchy.

Lasker was the first to suggest in chess literature a timed graphic of study (what we would nowadays called a study plan), the fulfilment of which would enable a beginner to reach a level where he could play against masters without receiving odds (something roughly corresponding to a modern-day first category player, about 2000 Elo). This programme consisted of 200 hours, which nowadays looks rather optimistic. Practice shows that the path from beginner to first category takes about three years. But the general principles of education proposed by Lasker have stood the test of time, and underpin the modern-day view of chess pedagogy.

The wise ex-champion also spoke of the need for professional chess teachers: *'This path requires good chess teachers – masters, who also have teaching skill. How should such teachers fulfil their task? – By introducing youngsters to the game with lectures, good books and by playing against their pupils. On the other hand, they must also annotate games played by their pupils, identifying their strong points and pointing out mistakes, so as to assist the work of the students, without in any way reducing the independence of their thinking. The methods a teacher can use are many and varied. The chess world faces the task of developing such teachers and, having developed them, supporting their efforts.'*

As we have seen, Lasker not only foresaw the establishment of chess specialists in modern institutes of physical culture, but also pointed out the sort of thing they should be concerned with.

In the first half of the 20th century, the leading trainers saw it as their duty to write books. In these, we can also find numerous recommendations and methodological devices, regarding the improvement of chess players.

6) Siegbert Tarrasch, known as 'Germany's chess teacher', employed in his books the method of aphoristic explanations of chess truths, expressing them (for educational purposes) in a very categorical form. Thus, his expressions, such as 'A knight on the rim is always dim!', 'Place a rook behind

a passed pawn, whether your own or the opponent's', 'A cramped position contains within it the seeds of defeat', 'He who has the bishops has the future!' and others, are things one remembers one's whole life! Tarrasch's notes are generously interspersed with Latin sayings, demonstrating the doctor's excellent education and, undoubtedly, enticing the reader into the world of chess creativity.

7) José Raul Capablanca in *Chess Fundamentals* (1923) pointed out that: *'Those wishing to study chess should start with the endgame and then, only after the endgame has been studied, they can go onto studying the opening and middlegame, in connection with the endgame.'* And here too, the Cuban genius adds a very deep observation: *'However, if one approaches chess as an intellectual relaxation of an artistic or scientific type, then the question takes on a different aspect. The majority of players are attracted first of all by combinations and direct attacks on the king. Since this type of play requires imagination above all, efforts should be concentrated on developing this.'*

This small contradiction between the endgame and combinations was brilliantly solved by Capablanca in his book. He employs a method of 'concentric circles', periodically returning to studying different topics (the opening, middlegame and endgame), but each time at a higher level of complexity.

8) Richard Réti in *Modern Ideas in Chess* (1929) employs a historicist method, tracing the development of chess through the ages, via its greatest exponents: *'Modern chess technique is built on the experience of the past and, therefore, the latest games may only be correctly understood by means of a study of the play of the old masters.'*

9) In Max Euwe's works, again much emphasis is placed on a historicist method of presenting material. *'An acquaintance with the history of the game, as well as being of interest in itself, is of great practical significance, since the development of every individual player repeats the stages of the general development of chess art'* – wrote the Dutch champion in his *Course of Chess Lectures* (1930).

In Euwe's *Chess Self-Tutor* (1927, written with G. den Hertog) and *Chess Lessons* (1930) the reader for the first time in chess literature was presented with numerous exercises, after the introduction of each new topic.

10) In his essay 'How I became a grandmaster' , Aron Nimzowitsch introduced the idea of analysing typical positions (e.g. IQP structures, positions

with an open file, etc.) as an effective method of training: 'The process of studying one position of a certain type has the aim of not only discovering the secrets of that concrete position, but also improving one's positional feeling as a whole!'

Nimzowitsch also suggested an original method of developing independent thinking. In analysing games, he suggested first thinking about each move oneself and deciding what to play, and only then looking to see what the master played and what moves are considered in the annotations.

Nimzowitsch's recommendations on the form of lessons with complete beginners are also interesting. The great grandmaster considered that these lessons should emphasis the playing side of things: 'From the very beginning, we should play, fight, compete, and not on any account allow the session to become an academic one of passing on formal knowledge. The pupil needs to be kept interested, and should immediately feel that this is a game, in which victory is both possible and enchanting.' In support of his ideas, Nimzowitsch offers a plan for the first three lessons, which even in our day looks very original and deserves every attention.

We would also emphasis the following observation by Nimzowitsch, which ties in with Capablanca's recommendation: 'From the very beginning, the endgame should be given special attention; the ability to realise a material advantage in the endgame should never been allowed to slip from view.'

It is also worth pointing out that all of the authors of the above works stressed the value of practice in improving a player. This view was beautifully summed up by Réti: 'Nobody has yet managed to learn the art of chess purely from books. Just has one has to get into the water in order to learn to swim, so, in order to become a chessplayer, one has to play chess.'

The next stage in the development of chess education began with the Moscow international tournament of 1925. The capital and indeed the whole country was seized with 'chess fever'. The latter was the title of the film, shot at the tournament. Those taking part in it included Capablanca, playing the role of himself! This event gave a great boost to the growth of popularity of chess in the USSR. For the first time in history, chess received state support.

The task facing Soviet masters was to create a training programme and materials to satisfy the needs of the many thousands of chess lovers in the country. In the early days of the USSR, translations were published of textbooks by foreign writers, but soon, similar manuals by Soviet authors began to appear.

11) One original source of material was *The Chessplayer's First Book* by Grigory Levenfish (1925), which subsequently reappeared in a form revised by the author as *The Book for the Chess Beginner* (1957). In these books, a large place was devoted to exercises, and at the end of several chapters, some pages were added, presenting interesting stories from the history of chess, examples of chess humour, etc. In the opinion of the author, *'a small diversion from sometimes dry technical subjects will be of benefit to the reader.'*

A particularly interesting chapter is 'The methodology of instructing beginners'. In it, Levenfish expresses the thought that *'despite the specifics of chess, its study should be carried out in accordance with the generally accepted principles of educational science.'* Among the qualities which should be developed in a novice player, Levenfish identifies the following: 1) chess vision – the automatic seeing of all one-move threats, both of one's own and of the opponent, and also quick perception of all pinned pieces and pawns; 2) memory; 3) the ability to concentrate all of one's attention on the process of battle; 4) knowledge of the chessboard geometry; 5) a clear impression in one's mind of the position after the next few moves.

To improve one's knowledge of chessboard geometry, he recommends identifying the colour of certain squares, without looking at the board.

To train at mastering pins, the author recommends solving two-move chess problems. *'The pin mechanism has been widely developed and used in many problems, and so solving problems is undoubtedly useful in developing vision.'*

To develop the reflex ability to spot one-move threats (fighting against 'blunders'), Levenfish recommends having pupils play games against one another with the chess pieces, but using checkers rules, with obligatory capturing. The speed of play can be gradually increased. It is also important to develop the habit of recording games as they are played, which improves a player's concentration during play.

12) Another who thoroughly explored chess education was Pyotr Romanovsky, the author of many books and articles on the subject. His book *The Middlegame* (1925) was one of the first systematic explorations of this stage of the game. But greater pedagogic impact was made by his

book *Paths to chess mastery* (1929). Based on his own sporting and creative experience, the author looked at various aspects of chess improvement. A particular hobby-horse of Romanovsky's as a method of improvement was the annotation of one's own games and the games of masters. The weaknesses identified by such annotation could be corrected by means of, for example, preparing reports on the topics concerned and delivering these as lectures before a qualified audience. Romanovsky suggested that analysis of games should be carried out in accordance with a definite scheme, including repeated examinations to identify the turning points of the game. These critical positions would then be subjected to detailed analysis, which allows an objective picture of the game to be built up. Only after such analysis should the annotations be brought together, with consideration also of the opening stage of the game. All of these steps are calculated to develop independent thinking.

13) In 1939, Mikhail Botvinnik published his article 'Concerning my method of preparation for tournaments'. The future World Champion had developed a whole programme of preparation for an event, including chess-related, physical and psychological aspects. In speaking of the chess aspects, Botvinnik advised that it was essential for a player to develop an opening repertoire that was bound up with plans for the middlegame. It was also important that the lines one intended to use in the tournament should have been tested beforehand in special training games.

Botvinnik recommended using training games not only for opening preparation, but also to cure other weaknesses, such as overcoming a habit of time-trouble, gaining experience in playing endgames, etc.

But the cornerstone of Botvinnik's system for preparation (as with Romanovsky's) was analytical work: '*In what does a chess master's art consist? Fundamentally, in the ability to analyse chess positions. Admittedly, at the board, a master has to be able to analyse quickly and without moving the pieces, but at the end of the day, calculating variations and assessing the positions is just the art of analysis. The conclusion follows from this of its own accord: anyone who wishes to become an outstanding chess player must aim to master the art of analysis*'.

The analytical method was also used by Botvinnik as the basis for his famous chess school (which ran, with various interruptions, from 1963 to 1988). By analysing the games of his pupils, he was able to diagnose their strong and weak points, after which each was given a tailored homework exercise. To fulfil this latter task, the pupil had to analyse a great deal. At the next session, each pupil would present the results of his work to the assembled class, being assessed and criticised by not only the teachers, but also by his fellow pupils. All of this led to a significant improvement in the young players' analytical capabilities.

14) A unique leap from first category player to grandmaster was achieved by Alexander Kotov at the USSR Championship in 1939, which made a great impression on the chess world. In 1940 (in the magazine *Chess in the USSR*), Kotov wrote in detail about his methods of work. As usual, the future grandmaster began with the analysis of his own games, which reveals the main weaknesses in his play – poor calculation of variations. To remedy this, Kotov undertook the following exercises:

a) Calculation of complicated positions, taken from annotated games, for 30 minutes, followed by comparing his results with the analysis given by the masters and grandmasters;

b) solving endgame studies from the diagram, without putting the position on the board;

c) reading chess books 'blindfold', i.e. without a chessboard;

d) 'blindfold' analysis of positions.

These methods were supplemented by developing an 'algorithm' for the calculation of variations, distinguished by strict restrictions and economy: *'Candidate moves (i.e. moves deserving calculation) should be identified at once and listed in one's mind. This work must not be done bit by bit – calculate one move, then look for another candidate, etc. This leads to disorder... In calculating complicated variations, one must cover each branch of the tree of variations once only. Never get distracted or waste time going back over the same variations and re-checking one's calculations, the main cause of which is lack of self-confidence'.* In this way, Kotov created a system for training a player's calculating abilities, which for a long time enjoyed unquestioned authority.

15) Starting in 1951, the USSR began to publish a series of booklets, containing a programme of study for players of different categories (starting from beginner to first category). Among the authors were Levenfish, Rokhlin, Zak, Golennikov and others. In order to develop massed ranks of qualified players, the programme was built on annual study plans (following Lasker's ideas). These programmes contain not only

a list of training topics, with details of the hours needed to cover them, but also a mass of instructional material, summarised as brief snapshots. This provided a unified programme for chess study at all national chess groups and physical culture collectives.

This course represented a method of concentrated study which accorded with the requirements of modern educational science. These requirements were based on the following: 1. The principle of conscious and active study; 2. The principle of clarity; 3. The principle of systematic and consequential work; 4. The principle of accessibility; 5. The principle of strengthening fundamental knowledge; 6. The principle of developing the educational programme further over time. The programmes apply and interpret these principles in a chess context.

16) A significant effect on chess education and the perfection of training methods was made by Nikolay Krogius' *Man and chess* (1967), *Personality in conflict* (1976), *The Psychology of Chess* (1981) and others.

Discussing the tasks for psychological research in the area of chess education, Krogius identified the following principal areas: identifying the optimal age at which to begin studying chess; forming a lasting and stable interest in chess; working out effective methods of studying with the very young.

From the point of view of psychology, studies were made of the thought processes of a player during a game. Introducing such concepts as 'the image of chess', 'dynamic thinking' and 'broadening thinking', practical recommendations were made and training exercises developed, aimed at optimising the thinking process during a tension of a tournament battle.

For example, it is interesting to see Krogius' take on Kotov's method of calculating variations: 'Kotov's striving to achieve a disciplined thinking process is understandable and creditable. In the main, his recommendations are useful, but they should not be set in stone. Constant checking and re-checking of variations, and switching the zone of one's thoughts, is characteristic for every chess player. The well-known Soviet psychologist O.Tikomirov did experimental research on the decision-making process during a chess game. He pointed out that many computer programs operate by reducing the number of variations examined. The human thinks differently. At first, he also rejects lines he does not like the look of, but if he is not satisfied with his candidate moves, he will widen the search zone and start analysing new possibilities. Another human characteristic is to return again and again to the* same variations, extending them with new ideas based on additional characteristics of the position.'

17) A significant role in perfecting methods of study with young players was played by the work of Vladimir Zak, in particularly his article 'On methods of teaching chess to beginners – children from aged 12 upwards' (1959), and his books *From small to large* (1973) and *Paths to improvement* (1981).

Let us present a few of the great trainer's thoughts:

'It is extremely important from the very first lessons to develop an interest in chess amongst the pupils. One matter of great importance is sorting the children correctly into groups and sub-groups. One must not put strong players in with weak ones, else the latter, constantly losing, will quickly lose interest in chess.'

'The first lessons with any chess player should be devoted to chess notation. As practice shows, this does not cause any difficulties, even with kids as young as 7-8.' To teach notation, Zak recommended an interesting idea – playing 'Battleships' on the chessboard.

'The younger the pupils, the more one must limit dry theoretical matter. This baggage can come to them gradually, as they get older. The normal balance to observe is one lesson of theory to two lessons of practice.'

'It is absolutely essential that each of your pupils, even the very weakest, should occasionally experience the joy of victory. Therefore, I do not run rated events, based on formal achievements of category titles. The tournaments run throughout a whole year, and are composed of players of roughly equal strength, and are thematic tournaments, in terms of openings. Only at the end do pupils achieve categories – from IV to III, depending on results.'

'Usually, lessons on the endgame should not last more than one hour. However, the children's interest will generally grow, if they are shown not just dry, technical positions, but more practical, entertaining endgame examples. This kind of entertainment should not be feared. It is often as a result of a very striking, spectacular example that it is easier to understand and remember a general rule.'

'Concrete thinking is one of the typical peculiarities of childhood. And it is only when the child has managed to progress from making separate concrete threats to solving the general task posed by the position that one can regard his play as having become stable. Only then can the trainer be justified in drawing conclusions about the pupil's potential and whether it is time to put him in for serious competitions, exploiting his fast development.'

We would also point out that Zak was the first to use children's play in demonstrating theoretical material. This device definitely helps children to accept textbook themes more readily.

18) The final quarter of the 20th century is inescapably dominated by the training and educational activity of Mark Dvoretsky. Accumulating all that was valuable from his predecessors, Mark Israelevich has created his own system for preparing top-class players, forming their creative outlook as follows: 'All-round development of the personality, fighting not only against chess weaknesses, but also personal weaknesses as well. A rejection of the all-too-common modern tendency to concentrate all efforts on one opening only; all-round preparation and high chess culture. Developing the player's strong sides and creating his own style, whilst at the same time fighting to liquidate weaknesses. A maximum of activity and independence in the approach to every problem. Constant training, solving special exercises, aimed at developing the necessary areas of thinking. Perfecting analytical mastery, in particular detailed analysis of one's own games. Sporting behaviour...'

All of these principles were known before, but Dvoretsky, by collecting them into one unified whole, has intensified to a maximum the training process. The leitmotiv of this process is the systematic and planned elimination of the player's weaknesses. One of the principal means used to achieve this is the solving of specially-selected exercises, which is a development of the so-called 'diagram method'. In his famous card index, Dvoretsky has built up numerous exercises, grouped into the various elements of chess mastery. His method of playing out training exercises is also original and remarkable. His approach and the various 'trade secrets' of his method have been set out in detail in his series of books, which appeared in the 1990s.

These then are the main epochs in the development of chess education in the pre-computer era. Thanks to the efforts of their predecessors, modern trainers do not have to reinvent the wheel – the basic principles, methods and devices in chess training are already well-known, but one needs a creative approach to adapt these to the constantly changing chess world and the individuality of each pupil.

'Educational mastery is more of an art than a science' – I should like to end this survey with these words of Konstantin Ushinsky.

CHAPTER 2

Man and computer

'Human chess is blind, a man cannot see the whole board which the universe has placed before him.' – Milan Vidmar

In the 21st century, the face of the chess world has changed sharply, thanks to the emergence into the ancient game of the latest computer technology. Humans started losing games against machines and it soon became clear that a man could not hope to compete with the computer in positions depending on calculation. Many famous games and chessboard achievements suddenly lost their lustre and faultlessness under the gaze of the computer. The computer had gradually encroached on the space of free human thought and is already able to give definite assessments and analyses of any position with seven or fewer men on the board. One involuntarily begins to have doubts as to whether the old methods of training will still be effective in this brave new world. Is it still worth studying classic games and annotations, when the computer so often points out tactical oversights in them? Is it still worth doing one's own analytical research, or should one just pass this job entirely over to our 'silicon friends'?

By way of an answer to these questions, it is useful to consider the subtle observations of the grandmaster and trainer Vladimir Tukmakov from his book *The Key to Victory* (2012), which portrays the relationship between the player and the computer, at the highest level of chess: 'The study, search for and assessment of opening variations takes a massive amount of time and energy for the modern grandmaster. The relationship between home preparation and play is shifting more and more in favour of the former. Whereas in older times, home preparation was just a prelude to real action over the board, nowadays, independent play and improvisation at the board tends to be seen as a sign of an annoying failure of home preparation. A player frequently comes to the board tired and worn out, with barely enough energy to recall and execute the complicated computer analyses. The modern player also faces one other danger. The ease with which one can obtain the all-knowing computer's suggestions tends to foster an illusion of simplicity. In the pre-computer era, every new idea, every quality piece of analysis, required great effort and hard work. The process was no less valuable than the result. In the search for the answer, much that was new was discovered and, even if the ultimate search proved fruitless, the work done was not in vain. These days, the unexpected departure over the board from the anticipated line of preparation frequently produces something akin to shock, because the line being followed was not governed by the player's logic or understanding, but was simply the opinion of the computer. As a result, we see a widening gap between faultless opening play, satisfactory middlegame play and then very often a flop in the endgame. At this stage of the development of chess it is not so much about the absolute harmony of all these elements, as about some sort of harmony between them. Here there is also great scope for improvement. And for a young player who notes this modern tendency it will be significantly easier to achieve a new level of mastery.'

I should like to reassure the young reader – the problems of grandmasters (many created by the GMs themselves) need not be taken to heart. For the present, childhood, when so many new worlds are opened up and so many striking impressions are revealed, remains the happiest time of one's life. The same is true in chess – this is when we accumulate knowledge, discover the beauty of the game, fantasise, argue, search for the truth, play, risk, etc. We should by no means compare our every move with that of the computer. Later, once having gained experience and formed our understanding of chess, we can engage with the computer, secure against its hypnotic influence on our own independence of thought. In this chapter, I want to discuss in simple terms the successes and failures in the 'thinking' of the electronic GM.

Probably, dear reader, you have had moments of disappointment, when the computer has solved in seconds an endgame study or immediately found a combination which you yourself played over the board, only after long thought and with the aid of a great piece of creative imagination. The electronic GM, thanks to its enormous speed of processing, has replaced the intuitive searching of a human with what the programmers call 'brute force'. Pessimists believe that in the future, all the secrets of chess will be revealed by the computer (i.e. it will succeed in analysing out all of the game's possibilities) and it will become a game where the result is known. In opposition to this view the optimists believe that these gloomy predictions will not come true and that the ancient legend of the invention of the game and of the grains of wheat will be fully realised. Personally, I am sympathetic to the words of Boris Vainshtein in his booklet *Ferzberi's Traps* (1990): 'Chess is not inexhaustible purely because of a very large number of possibilities, a number too great for us even to imagine. Rather, chess is inexhaustible in the same way as music! Music does not consist of numerous variations on the possible combinations of notes, but of something internal, its emotional content. Chess is the same: the size of his cosmic library of possibilities means nothing to us, as far as our conception of it is concerned as an artistic competition, based on knowledge, logic, ideas, etc. And the inexhaustibility of chess is not in numbers of variations, but in an inexhaustible idea, resulting from the collision of intellects.'

Now let us move on from general discussions to questions of concrete practice interest. There is no question that in matters of calculation, the computer is extraordinarily accurate and far-seeing. The tactical resources pointed out by the computer can be extremely hard for the carbon-based chess player to see and require special chess/psychological thought processes. As a rule, the human will overlook ideas which breach established principles and it is useful to pay attention to this issue.

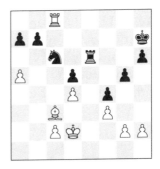

By way of illustration, let us look at a simple example. Not so long ago, in search for exercises for a training programme, I looked through a collection of Smyslov's *Best Games*. My attention was attracted by the following position:

Vasily Smyslov
René Letelier Martner

Venice 1950

White has just played 27.♘d3-b4, and after 27...♘xb4 28.♖xe6 ♖xe6 29.♖xc8 ♘c6

30.a6! bxa6 31.♖c7+ ♔g6 32.♖d7 ♘e7 33.♗b4 ♘f5 34.♖xd5 he obtained a strong passed pawn in the centre. In his notes to the game, Smyslov points out that 'the continuation 27...♘e7 allows an effective combinational blow: 28.♘xd5! ♘xd5 29.♖xe6! ♖xc5 30.♖xf6 ♘xf6 (or 30...♖xc3 31.♖d6, and White regains the piece, keeping an extra pawn) 31.dxc5 ♘d7 32.♔d3! ♘xc5+ 33.♔c4, and the white king goes after the black queenside pawns.'

Is the ex-World Champion's variation correct?

29

In his notes, Smyslov committed an error. After the moves 27...♘e7 28.♘xd5 ♘xd5 29.♖xe6 ♖xc5 30.♖xf6

Viswanathan Anand   2783
Vladimir Kramnik   2772
Bonn Wch-match 2008 (7)

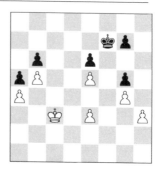

the computer immediately points out the unexpected (for the human player) refusal of all captures – 30...♖c7!!, and Black wins a piece. And yet how many players (myself included) have studied this classical game without anyone noticing this resource!

However, one must also note that the electronic GM also has its weaknesses. There is an interesting comment by Alekseeva and Razuvaev (in the article 'School, the computer and chess' 2003): 'In terms of depth and accuracy of calculation, the human is helpless before the 'silicon beast'. But nature has endowed the human with a wonderful panorama of vision and at the present moment, he still exceeds the computer in that respect.'

Let me illustrate this with some examples.

In this position, taken from a World Championship match, the players agreed a draw. In his commentary, Alexander Khalifman noted that 'It is surprising that all the best computer programs assess the final, dead-drawn position as clearly in White's favour. It seems their programmers still have some work to do.'
How could this happen? The fact is that the human is able to assess this position very quickly, because his general strategic grasp tells him that the white material advantage is of no use, because there are no squares in the black camp to which he can penetrate.
The computer, however, does not think in such 'general' terms – it simply calculates variations. After penetrating 18 moves deep into the position, the computer still sees an extra pawn and a space advantage for White!

That the computer has trouble with positional fortresses has long been known, but it is inconceivable that it should also be weaker than a human in calculating combinative complications. However, look at the following game. Vaiser's comments on the key moment made a great impression on me at the time:

Grünfeld Indian Defence
Anatoly Vaisser   2576
Maxime Vachier-Lagrave   2527

Chartres ch-FRA 2005 (7)

'With the help of the computer, my young opponent had prepared an interesting novelty in a long theoretical variation, which is considered to be dubious for Black. When after a long think, Fritz pronounces a large advantage, then in 9 cases out of 10, it is indeed a large advantage. Maxime's mistake was that the deep position arising in the game was incorrectly assessed by the computer. The reason is very unusual – zugzwang in the middlegame.'

After the well-known moves
1.d4 ♘f6 2.c4 g6 3.♘c3 d5 4.cxd5 ♘xd5 5.e4 ♘xc3 6.bxc3 ♗g7 7.♘f3 c5 8.♖b1 0-0 9.♗e2 ♘c6 10.d5 ♗xc3+ 11.♗d2 ♗xd2+ 12.♕xd2 ♘a5 13.h4 ♗g4 14.♘g5 ♗xe2 15.♔xe2 h6 16.♘f3 ♔h7 17.♕c3 b6 18.♘g5+ ♔g8 19.h5 hxg5 20.hxg6 fxg6 21.♖h8+ ♔f7 22.♖h7+ ♔e8 23.♕g7 ♔d7 24.d6 ♕e8 25.dxe7 ♖g8 26.♕e5

the following position arose:

26...♔c8
'Finally the novelty. Vachier had played all 26 moves at blitz pace. In the stem game Chernin-Stohl (Austria Bundesliga 1993) there followed 26...♘c6? 27.♖d1+ ♘d4+ 28.♖xd4+! cxd4 29.♕d5+ ♔c7 30.♕xa8! ♕b5+ 31.♔f3 ♖e8 32.g3!, and White eventually won.'
27.♕d5!!
A powerful move, which decides the outcome of the game. The silicon beast considers it to be bad, clearly preferring 27.♖d1?, which allows 27...♕b5+ and 28...♖e8.
27...♘c6 28.♖bh1 ♘d4+ 29.♔e3 ♖b8

30.g4!
'A most unlikely position! The black pieces turn out to be in zugzwang in the middle of the game. But this move is already outside the

computer's horizon. This explains why Fritz mistakenly assesses Vachier's novelty at move 26.'

30...♖b7

Or 30...a5 31.a4 ♘c2+ 32.♔f3 ♘d4+ 33.♔g2.

31.♕xg8! ♕xg8 32.♖h8 ♖xe7 33.♖xg8+ ♔b7 34.♖xg6 ♖f7 35.♖h3 ♘c2+ 36.♔e2 ♘d4+ 37.♔f1 1-0

Some time later, I had a case in my own experience, which confirmed the computer's vulnerability in judging positions at the end of long tactical variations.

King's Indian Defence
Edward Duliba
Alexander Kalinin
XXI cr 2007 (7)

In 2006 I gave up playing tournaments, to concentrate on training work. From time to time, I quench my craving for competition by playing in postal chess tournaments. I should add that I had played successfully in several such events at the end of the 1980s, during my army service. Sadly, I soon realised that over the intervening 20 years, postal chess had changed beyond recognition. Now one is playing against a computer and can oneself also make use of its help. In my view, such play has no relation to chess and is more like a scientific experiment aimed at finding the best way to fight against the computer.

1.d4 ♘f6 2.c4 g6 3.♘c3 ♗g7 4.e4 d6 5.f3 0-0 6.♘ge2 c5 7.d5 e6 8.♘g3 exd5 9.cxd5 h5 10.♗g5 ♕b6 11.♕b3 ♕c7 12.♗e2 a6 13.a4 ♘h7 14.♗e3 ♕e7

In the game Dreev-Topalov (Elista 1998) there followed 14...♕e7 15.0-0 ♘d7 16.f4 ♗d4 17.♗f2 h4 18.♘h1 g5 with mutual chances.

15.♘f1 ♘d7 16.♘d2 f5 17.a5 f4 18.♗f2 ♘g5

This knight is aiming at the e5-square, whilst its colleague remains on d7 for the time being, restricting possible enemy entry to b6.

19.♘a4 ♘f7 20.0-0 ♘fe5

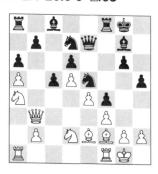

The white pieces, to my mind, are quite clearly being conducted by a computer. He has allowed his opponent to achieve everything a KID player can dream of – an open diagonal for the ♗g7, a knight secured on the blockading e5-square, and the kingside pawns ready to go in motion. But the machine does not bother with such general considerations. The 'calculations' show a clear advantage... to White! Think of it for yourself – the threatening ♘e5 and ♗g7 are not so strong, the kingside pawn advance does not threaten anything yet, and the black queenside pieces are not fully developed. At the same time, the excellently developed white army is ready to break through on the queenside with b2-b4... But which side would you rather play in this position, dear reader?

21.♕a3 g5 22.b4 c4

The pawn on c4 is dropping off, but I did not wish to allow the opening of all the queenside lines, that would follow after 22...cxb4. However, the computer advises Black to keep material equality.

23.♗d4 g4 24.♕c3 g3 25.h3 ♕h4 26.♖fe1 ♘f6 27.♗f1 ♘h7 28.♘b6

28...♗xh3

I did not even look at playing with material equality after 28...♘g5 29.♘xc8. A KID player knows very well that without the light-squared bishop, he has practically no chances of breaking through the enemy king's defences. As you have probably guessed, the computer recommends refraining from the bishop sacrifice.

29.gxh3 ♘g5 30.♗g2 ♘xh3+ 31.♔f1 ♘f2

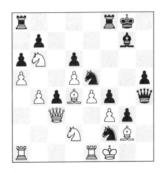

32.♘dxc4

White does not expend time taking the ♖a8, the priority instead being to take action to neutralise the activity of the ♘e5 and ♗g7.

32...♕h2 33.♗xe5 dxe5 34.♘xa8 h4 35.♖e2 ♖xa8 36.♘b6 ♖d8

After 36...h3 37.♖xf2 gxf2 38.♗xh3 ♕xh3+ 39.♔e2 Black has a strategically lost position, with a 'dead' bishop on g7.

The retreat of the black rook to d8 is explained by the fact that after the more natural 36.♖f8 it will later come under attack from the white knight on d7.

37.♖xf2 gxf2 38.♔xf2 h3 39.♖g1 ♗f6 40.♘d7

If 40.♔f1 ♔h7 41.♗h1 ♔h6!? White's extra piece is not of any special significance.

40...♗h4+ 41.♔f1 ♔h7

42.♕xe5!

White does not lag behind his opponent in sacrifices! By clearing the pawns from the centre, White initiates a counterattack against the black king. I was reluctantly forced to realise that the sharp advance of the black kingside pawns was not only an attack on the white king, but also exposed Black's own monarch!

42...hxg2+ 43.♔e2 ♕xg1

To this day I do not know if 43...♕g3, recommended by the computer, leads to a draw, because I have not especially analysed it. My attention was immediately attracted by the text move, which the computer considers a serious mistake and leads to a position where the machine gives the unprecedented assessment of +5.00 in White's favour.

44.♕h5+ ♔g7 45.♕g4+ ♔h8 46.♕xh4+ ♔g7 47.♕g5+ ♔h8 48.♕xd8+

By giving endless checks, White has more than regained the sacrificed material. The whole question now is whether the passed pawn on g2 will compensate Black for his large

material deficit, or whether White will succeed in weaving a mating net around the black king. To the human, the essence of the problem is clear, but the computer does not realise it, even in the course of 20-30 moves! This happens because White has an enormous number of checks, none of which, however, change things, and the real assessment of the position remains hidden behind the computer's horizon.

48...♔g7 49.♕f8+ ♔h7 50.♘f6+ ♔g6 51.♘g4 ♕f1+ 52.♔d2 ♔h7!

The only defence, but sufficient.

53.♕e7+ ♔h8 54.♕d8+ ♔g7 55.♕c7+ ♔h8 56.♕c8+ ♔g7 57.♕xb7+

With the disappearance of the b7-pawn, the position changes and White obtains another 'million' checks.

57...♔h8 58.♕c8+

Perpetual check, but this time to the white king, follows after 58.♘f6 ♕f2+. An interesting situation arises after 58.♕b8+ ♔h7 59.♕a7+ ♔h8 60.♘f6.

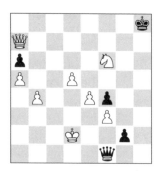

It seems as though Black is in trouble, since after 60...♕h1 White decides

things with 61.♕b8+ ♔g7 62.♕g8+!
♔xf6 63.e5+! ♔xe5 (Black also loses
after 63...♔e7 64.♕g7+ ♔e8 65.e6)
64.♕e6+ ♔d4 65.♕e4#. But Black
has a saving combination: 60...♕c1+!
61.♔xc1 g1♕+! 62.♕xg1 – stalemate!
In the game, things ended more
prosaically.
**58...♔g7 59.♕d7+ ♔h8 60.♕e8+
♔g7 61.♕e7+ ♔h8 62.♕f8+ ♔h7
63.♘f6+ ♔g6 64.♕g8+ ♔xf6 65.e5+
♔e7 66.d6+ ♔d7 67.♕d5 ♕f2+
68.♔c3 ♕e3+ ½-½**

So, how should we assess the
position arising after 20 moves in
this game? Maybe the computer was
right, since Black had to sacrifice
material and only saved himself
by a miracle? I will not hide the
fact that I believed the position
was clearly better for Black and
was extremely optimistic. But
even now, I am convinced that in
a practical game between humans,
Black's position is easier to play.
The computer, even when its king
is under strong attack, can never
lose its head, which can hardly
be said of a human player. The
assessment of complicated positions
often depends on the personal
characteristics of the players.
Another interesting question is:
how far, in these days of computers,
should a player calculate variations,
before deciding on a sacrificial
combination over the board?
Let us consider the next example.

Garry Kasparov   2810
Veselin Topalov   2700
Wijk aan Zee 1999 (4)

The unexpected blow **24.♖xd4!!?**
served as the start of a grandiose
sacrificial idea by the 13th World
Champion. Topalov accepted the
sacrifice, but later it was discovered
that 24...♔b6!! would have allowed
the white attack to be beaten off.
Alexander Beliavsky and Adrian
Mikhalchisin, in their book *Intuition
in chess* (2003), commented as follows
on the events of the game: 'Here
Kasparov had the chance to choose
between 24.♘c6+ ♗xc6 25.♕xd6
♖xd6 26.dxc6 ♔b6 27.♖e7 ♔xc6
28.♖de1 with the threat of 29.♖a7
♔b6 30.♖ee7 with at least a draw, and
the active 24.♖xd4?!. As Kasparov
himself put it: 'For the first time
in my life, I calculated a variation
18 moves deep!' (further than the
computer – AB and AM.). But this
calculation hardly made sense for
either player – after 24.♖xd4?! ♔b6!
25.♘b3 ♗xd5! 26.♕xd6+ ♖xd6
27.♖d2 ♖hd8 28.♖ed1 c4 29.♘c1 ♔c7
and the further exchange of rooks,
it is very hard for White to save

the endgame. This variation was intuitively rejected by both players and Black instead plunged into the complications.'

24...cxd4 25.♖e7+! ♔b6 26.♕xd4+ ♔xa5 27.b4+ ♔a4 28.♕c3 ♕xd5 29.♖a7! ♗b7 30.♖xb7 ♕c4 31.♕xf6 ♔xa3 32.♕xa6+ ♔xb4 33.c3+ ♔xc3 34.♕a1+ ♔d2 35.♕b2+ ♔d1 36.♗f1! ♖d2

37.♖d7! ♖xd7 38.♗xc4 bxc4 39.♕xh8
In playing his 24th move, White had calculated the main line up to this moment. Black's position is lost and he soon resigned. 'Much ado about nothing!' concluded Beliavsky and Mikhalchisin.

I think that most chess lovers, thankful for the present of the beautiful combination presented to them by the 13th World Champion, would not agree with the esteemed grandmasters. By sacrificing the rook, White posed his opponent a difficult problem, which the latter failed to solve successfully in the conditions of a complicated and tense game over the board. In such a case, it is appropriate to remember Alekhine's words: 'At the end of the

day, chess is not just knowledge and logic!'

In this last example, as well as Kasparov's fantastically deep calculation, I was also astonished by his comment in his annotations, that if, in the start position, the black rook had stood not on h8 but g8, then the entire combination would have been unsound! It turns out that the fate of such a brilliant idea depends on a seemingly insignificant detail, revealed only some 20 moves later in the combination.

It is obvious that not every player, even of the highest class, could perform such lengthy and detailed calculation. So what should one do – refrain from the combination because one cannot calculate everything out to the very end, or go for the sacrifice anyway, trusting one's judgement of the position? The answer to this question has already been provided by the play and writings of such creative attacking players as Spielmann, Tal and Shirov. The fact that the powerful modern-day computers occasionally find a hole in the analyses of such intuitive human combinations does not change anything fundamental. Humans always make mistakes and all the while chess is played by humans, it is a battle, in which there is an element of risk!

Let us quote a few observations by Rudolf Spielmann, from his famous book *The Art of Sacrifice*:

'If you require from every sacrifice undoubted, analytically-demonstrable proof of correctness, then you will strip all elements of risk out of chess. But this would effectively eliminate all real sacrifices, leaving only those which, strictly speaking, cannot really be regarded as sacrifices at all.' [...] 'At the critical moment, it is only possible to calculate that for the piece, White obtains two pawns and an ongoing attack. Whether it will end in victory is a matter of judgement... As a rule, it is extremely difficult to analyse sacrifices fully, covering every possible variation, even just a few moves; more often, such an expenditure of precious time and energy leads to nervous exhaustion, time trouble and an undeserved defeat... A good chess player should be able to calculate, but should not do so to excess. My comments, of course, apply to tournament games over the board, with limited thinking time. For postal play, one must have a different approach and here one can strive for accurate and complete analysis.'

The attempt over the board to calculate a long and complicated set of variations to the very end is a fruitless endeavour, as such a thing is beyond human capability. There are some cases, however, where even unlimited home analysis, with the computer's help, fails to reveal the definitive answer to a position.

By way of illustration, I offer another of my correspondence games.

Slav Defence
Alexander Kalinin
Vladimir Napalkov
cr Abramov Memorial 2006/2007

1.d4 d5 2.c4 c6 3.♘f3 ♘f6 4.♘c3 a6 5.e3 b5 6.b3 ♗g4 7.♗e2 e6 8.0-0 ♘bd7 9.h3 ♗f5 10.♗d3 ♗b4 11.♗b2 ♗xd3 12.♕xd3 0-0 13.♖fc1
In this quiet variation, White retains a minimal advantage, thanks to his growing pressure on the c-file.
13...bxc4 14.bxc4 ♕e7 15.♖c2 ♘b6 16.♘e5 ♖fc8 17.♘e2 ♘fd7 18.♘xd7 ♘xd7 19.cxd5 exd5 20.♖ac1 ♘b6!
The defence of the c6-pawn hangs on this manoeuvre. After 20...♘b6 21.♖xc6 ♖xc6 22.♖xc6 ♘c4 the white rook is trapped and the exchange sacrifice for two pawns with 23.♖xc4 dxc4 24.♕xc4 ♕b7 does not offer any special prospects.
21.♘g3
Preparing for active operations on the kingside.
21...♘c4

The critical position, in which White must either settle for empty equality or head for irrational complications.

22.♖xc4

The emergence of the ♗b2 and the transfer of the theatre of operations to the kingside emphasises the distance of the black pieces from their king. I was sure that this dynamic decision was the natural one and answered to the logical requirements of the position, and went in for the following sacrifices in defiance of the recommendations of the computer.

22...dxc4 23.♖xc4 ♕b7!

A precise reply. The black bishop will manage to occupy a good defensive post on f8.

24.d5 ♗f8

Black collapses after 24...cxd5? 25.♖g4 ♗f8 26.♗xg7 ♗xg7 27.♘h5.

25.♖h4 h6

26.♗xg7!

Here time is more valuable than a bishop! The tame 26.♗c3 would allow Black to bring his queenside pieces into the game. Furthermore, if the white bishop is not sacrificed on g7, then it is practically useless for the attack.

This idea was suggested to me by Kasparov's notes to the following famous game:

Garry Kasparov
Lajos Portisch
Niksic 1983

'At this moment I had a think. White's pieces stand ideally, but nothing concrete is apparent. I felt that it was important to play actively, but how? It is tempting to play ♘f3-g5 or ♘f3-e5. However, on g5, the knight does nothing. 21.♘e5 looks good, but then the bishop on b2 is doing nothing. But what if we sacrifice it? Yes, sacrifice it!

21.♗xg7!! ♔xg7 22.♘e5

A surprising thing – White has no direct threats and he is a piece down, but he stands superbly! However, there is an explanation for this – the black knight is completely out of the game on a5...' (G.Kasparov).

To complete the picture, we will give the rest of the game:

22...♖fd8 23.♕g4+ ♔f8 24.♕f5 f6 25.♘d7+ ♖xd7 26.♖xd7 ♕c5 27.♕h7 ♖c7 28.♕h8+ ♔f7 29.♖d3

♘c4 30.♖fd1 ♘e5 31.♕h7+ ♔e6
32.♕g8+ ♔f5 33.g4+ ♔f4 34.♖d4+
♔f3 35.♕b3+, and Black resigned.

26...♗xg7 27.♘f5

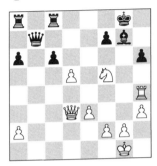

I had studied this position prior to
sacrificing the exchange. Black's
extra rook is slumbering on a8,
whilst White is attacking the king
with greatly superior forces. But
the computer assesses the position
as clearly better for Black, who has
a wide choice of continuations, the
combination not being forcing. In
an over the board game, I would
have headed for this position
without any qualms, but given the
possibility of computer defence, I
needed additional comfort.
What was that? The fact that I
myself also used the computer to
help did not solve the problem, as
the net of variations was too wide.
But here I recalled a device which
Mark Dvoretsky pointed out was
used by Mikhail Tal. In deciding on
an irrational sacrifice, the magician
from Riga would convince himself
by calculating a few spectacular
variations (not necessarily always
correct), where the attacking side

triumphs, and which would give
him confidence that the sacrifice
will succeed in practice. I followed
a similar path. Using the computer
quickly (not giving it extensive time
to think), I went through several
lines and reached a satisfactory
result, which convinced me of the
correctness of the sacrifice.
Speaking of the concrete position
before us, we can note first of all
that the black king cannot flee the
danger zone: 27...♔f8 28.♘xg7 ♔xg7
29.♕d4+ f6 30.♕g4+ ♔f8 31.♖xh6
♕g7 32.♖g6 ♕f7 33.♕f5 ♔e7 34.d6+,
and White wins.
However, Black does have at his
disposal the solid defence 27...♖ab8
28.♖g4 ♕b1+ 29.♕xb1 ♖xb1+
30.♔h2 ♔f8 31.♖xg7 cxd5, which
would force his opponent to take
a draw by repetition: 32.♖h7 ♔g8
33.♖g7+ ♔f8 34.♖h7=.
One might reasonably pose the
question why White would take
such risks to move from an equal
position to another equal one,
where Black can force an immediate
draw with such a logical and
sensible move as 27...♖ab8 ? Of
course, I was under no illusions
about the sacrifice, but I still felt
it was the most logical way of
revealing the resources contained in
the position. The white pieces seem
to spring into life and I felt I did
not have the right to condemn them
to a boring future, marking time.
27...♗f6
An illustration of the laws of
combat, even with computers

around the place! Being a rook up, with his opponent apparently having no immediate threats, Black decides to continue the fight.

28.♖g4+ ♚h8

If 28...♚f8? 29.♘xh6 cxd5 30.♕a3+ ♚e8 31.♕d6, White's attack achieves its aim.

29.♘xh6

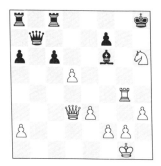

Planning to bring the queen over via d3-f5-h5.

29...♖ab8

In the variation 29...cxd5? 30.♕f5 ♕e7 31.♖g3 Black is defenceless against the threat of 32.♕h5.

30.♚h2 ♕d7 31.♕e4 cxd5

Black loses after 31...♕xd5? 32.♕f4 ♗g7 33.♖h4 etc.

32.♕f4 ♖b6

The extra rook finally comes into play and White must force a draw.

33.♘xf7+ ♕xf7 34.♖h4+ ♚g7 35.♕h6+ ♚g8 36.♖g4+ ♗g7 37.♕xb6 ♕c7+ 38.♕xc7 ♖xc7

White has three connected passed pawns for the piece in the endgame,

but in this instance, it does not give him real winning chances.

39.♖a4 ♖c6 40.♖a5 d4 41.exd4 ♗xd4 42.f3 ♗c3 43.♖a4 a5 44.h4 ♗b4 ½-½

In summarising the results of the discussion above, I should like to wish the reader courageous creative play, not hampered by doubts or uncertainties over computers refuting your ideas. At the end of the day, to paraphrase Lasker's well-known saying, chess is played by living people, not computers. Let us go back once again to the game Kasparov-Topalov and imagine the game was played by two machines. Without a doubt, White would have seen the resource 24...♚b6, and so would not have sacrificed the rook, preferring instead 24.♘c6+. As a result, the game would have been an unremarkable draw and chess culture deprived of one of its greatest works of art.

Of course, I am not recommending that the reader deliberately play sub-optimal moves, but as Xavier Tartakower wittily pointed out, 'real chess only arises as a result of real mistakes!'

PART 2

How chess players are formed

My chess childhood occurred at the end of the 1970s and early 80s, a rich period for the development of children's and junior chess in the Soviet Union. Every major town had chess sections at the Pioneer Palaces, where the children were coached by experienced masters. The growing need for qualified trainers led to Grigory Goldberg establishing a chess specialisation at the main state university for physical culture and youth activities. Television started showing 'The Chess School', which had a number of programmes aimed at beginners, qualified players and even schoolchildren. In the traditional schoolchildren's national event 'The White Guard' some 1 million (!) children took part.

From such a vast number of children it was easy to pick out the most promising for further training at specialised sports schools. In Moscow, for example, a special chess section was opened at sports school no.9, to which many talented pupils were invited. Following the example of Botvinnik, the ex-World Champions Vasily Smyslov and Tigran Petrosian both opened their own chess schools. The idea of bringing together junior talents with top players was promoted by the tournament sponsored by the newspaper *Komsomolskaya Pravda*, in which children obtained the opportunity to play against well-known GMs in clock simuls. Periodically, events were organised along the Scheveningen system, 'youngsters versus masters', where the young players could get essential experience of facing masters in one-to-one games. Thus, I managed to be at all the main student events. My experiences at these will be discussed in the second half of the book. I hope that Russia will soon be able to establish these various forms of junior event, which so recommended themselves in the former USSR.

As already pointed out in the Introduction, among the many methods of improving the mastery of young players, I would single out four main directions for independent work:

1. Forming a relationship to chess as an art.

2. Analytical work (annotating one's own games and those of masters; independent analysis of the typical positions arising at different stages of the game).

3. Study of the classical heritage.

4. Creative relations with one's competitors and with more experienced players.

Below I try to reveal as much as possible the contents of the areas listed above.

CHAPTER 3

The aesthetics of chess

'Like love, like music, chess has the power to make men happy.' – Siegbert Tarrasch

A newcomer, scoring his first victories in skittles games, starts to become interested in chess, but a real attraction only develops when he discovers the inherent beauty of the ancient game. The best productions of chess masters, like those of artists and musicians, have the ability to provide men with minutes of happiness and creative delight. But we experience even greater pleasure when we ourselves are able to be creative. And it does not matter whether we are talking about a grand conception worthy of a master, or a simple beginner's combination. Chess helps to uncover a person's creativity and this is perhaps its main attraction.

My teachers gave special attention to the creative side of chess, drawing their pupils' attention in the first instance to the quality of play, rather than its result. They introduced us to the world of chess art, demonstrating the best of its examples and interesting us in further, independent explorations.

I remember the very first session of the Smyslov chess school. At the beginning, it had not yet assembled its full trainer list (later Dvoretsky, Razuvaev and the ex-World Champion himself) and the opening lecture was given by Victor Alexandrovich Liublinsky, a participant in the first post-war USSR Championship finals. The subject of this experienced master's lecture was 'Beauty in a chess game', which seems highly symbolic. Among the examples he demonstrated were two from his own practice. They are not to be found in databases, nor have I ever found them in old magazines. It would be a shame if games which Victor Alexandrovich prized so much should sink into oblivion, and so I give them both below.

French Defence
Viktor Liublinsky
Dmitry Rovner
Moscow 1955

**1.e4 e6 2.d4 d5 3.♘c3 ♘f6 4.♗g5
♗e7 5.e5 ♘fd7 6.♗xe7 ♕xe7 7.f4
a6 8.♘f3 c5 9.dxc5 ♘xc5 10.♗d3
♘xd3+**

The immediate 10...0-0? is bad
because of 11.♗xh7+ ♚xh7 12.♘g5+
♚g6 13.♕g4 f6 14.exf6 ♖xf6 15.0-0
with a winning attack for White.
**11.cxd3 0-0 12.0-0 ♕c5+ 13.♖f2
♘c6 14.♕d2 ♗d7 15.♖c1 ♕a7
16.d4 ♖ac8 17.g4 ♘e7 18.♖d1 ♖c4
19.♕d3 ♖fc8 20.♘g5 ♘g6**

21.♕e3

Preparing the advance f4-f5, which
does not work at once because of
the counter-blow 21...♘xe5!.
However, White could already
sacrifice with 21.♘xf7! ♚xf7 22.f5,
which White carries out on the
following move.
21...h6 22.♘xf7! ♚xf7 23.f5
The white pawn phalanx sweeps
away everything before it.
**23...♘e7 24.fxe6+ ♚xe6 25.♕xh6+!
gxh6 26.♖f6#**

Benoni Defence
Vladimir Zagorovsky
Viktor Liublinsky
Moscow 1952 (6)

**1.d4 ♘f6 2.c4 c5 3.d5 e5 4.♘c3 d6
5.♘f3 ♗e7 6.♕c2 0-0 7.♗d2 a6 8.a4
♘e8 9.e4 g6 10.♗h6 ♘g7 11.h4 ♘d7
12.h5 ♘f6 13.hxg6 fxg6 14.♘d1 ♘g4
15.♗d2 ♘h5 16.♘e3 ♘f4 17.♘h2?**

White's last move is like a toreador,
waving a red flag before a bull.
17...♘xf2! 18.♚xf2 ♗h4+ 19.♚g1
The variations 19.g3 ♗xg3+ 20.♚xg3
♘h5+ 21.♚g2 ♕h4 22.♗e1 ♕h3+
23.♚g1 ♕xe3+ 24.♗f2 ♕g5+ 25.♗g2
♘f4 or 19.♚f3 ♘e6+ 20.♚e2 ♘d4+
are also fatal for White.
**19...♘h3+! 20.gxh3 ♗f2+ 21.♚g2
♗xh3+! 22.♚xh3 ♕h4+ 0-1**

It is no secret that for beginners,
beauty in chess tends to mean
combinations above all. I recall one
example when theoretical knowledge
and practical occurrence were
realised together, before my very
eyes. It was in an event at a Moscow
Pioneer Palace. At a session for
second category players, our trainer,

Alexander Nikolaevich Kostyev, showed a famous old combination.

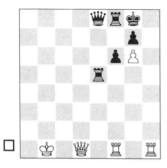

Damiano (XVI century)

Here White wins by sacrificing two rooks, with the idea of freeing a path for his queen to reach h1: **1.♖h8+! ♔xh8 2.♖h1+ ♔g8 3.♖h8+! ♔xh8 4.♕h1+ ♔g8 5.♕h7#**
Among the eager students following the lecture was Alyosha Gromov, my close schoolfriend and chess comrade. Remarkably, just a few hours later, playing a tournament game in the evening, Alyosha found a way to carry out the same idea!

Alexander Evdokimov
Alexander Gromov

Moscow 1978

At this moment, Alyosha shot me a momentary glance (I was playing

on the next board) and played the move **1...♖d2!?**, immediately thinking of several combinational blows. The attack on the d4-pawn provoked his opponent into the natural **2.♕e3**, simultaneously attacking both the rook and the e6-pawn. Now in the game there triumphantly followed Damiano's combination **2...♖h1+! 3.♔xh1 ♕h8+ 4.♔g1 ♕h2#**. At that moment, Alyosha was the happiest man alive and spent the whole of the next week beaming from the effects of his combination!
I would just add that the move 1...♖d2 is rather more cunning than it appears at first sight. If the opponent had seen the main idea and stopped it by leaving the queen on f3, he might well instead have played the blow 2.♘xe6. But after this, Black had prepared the stunning counter 2...♖h1+!! with an even more effective realisation of Damiano's idea!
For the sake of objectivity, we should point out that after 2.♖ad1! White retains a solid advantage, and therefore Black should have preferred the solid positional continuation 1...♗f6 2.♖ad1 ♕g8! with good attacking possibilities. But at this stage of his career, the black player deserves no criticism. In this context, one can recall Emanuel Lasker's words in his *Manual of Chess*: 'The beginner should strive above all that in a practical game, he feels the possibility of combinations and executes them'.

I will tell you of my first 'real' combination. I started serious chess study in my first class at school and after ending it as a third category player, I completely failed to progress for the whole of the following year. I recall one game where I had a good knight versus bad bishop. I worked ceaselessly to get my knight to a certain weak square, and no sooner did it land there than it was taken by the enemy queen – the latter turned out to be immune because of a back-rank mate!

It became obvious that I had become too carried away with general considerations and overlooked the tactical possibilities in the position. During the summer holidays, I studied master Georgy Lisitsyn's remarkable book *The Strategy and Tactics of Chess* and in general solved several thousand (!) exercises on positional and tactical themes. This work was not in vain. Even so, when the new year started and I sat down at the board again, still as a third category player, I was very worried – would my new-found knowledge translate into practical play...?

Queen's Pawn Game
A. Anosov
Alexander Kalinin
Moscow 1978

1.d4 ♘f6 2.♘f3 e6 3.♗g5 d5 4.♘c3 ♗b4 5.♕d3 c6 6.a3 ♗xc3+ 7.♕xc3 0-0 8.♘e5 ♘bd7 9.♕h3

Here and later White plays very illogically and fully in the style of a third category player, preferring one-move threats to solid development. Now he is ready to attack h7 with e2-e3 and ♗d3.

9...♕b6 10.♘xd7 ♘xd7

The 'developing' recapture 10...♗xd7 could have led after 11.♗xf6 ♕xb2 12.♕g3 ♕xa1+ 13.♔d2 g6 14.♕e3 e5 15.dxe5 d4 16.♕h6 ♕c3+ to perpetual check. However, as the reader may suspect, I did not even dream of the existence of this variation during the game.

11.0-0-0 c5 12.♕c3 c4 13.♕g3

More logical was 13.e4, after which 13...♕c6 is possible, followed by ...b7-b5 or ...♘d7-b6-a4.

13...♔h8 14.♕f3 ♕c6

Here again, my old illness struck. Thinking White's last move was connected with the preparation of the advance e2-e4, I took the decision to take control of e4, at the same time opening the path of the b7-pawn. My thoughts would be perfectly logical, were it not for having overlooked a one-move threat from the opponent.

15.♗e7 ♖g8 16.♕xf7

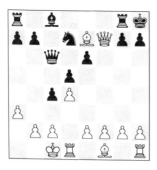

Black loses a pawn, but I did not worry for long, as the prospect of a pawn storm against the white monarch seemed very attractive. I even started to convince myself that the blundering of the f7-pawn was a deliberate sacrifice, aimed at luring the white queen into my camp!

16...b5 17.c3 a5 18.g4

White finally remembers to develop and prepares the move ♗g2. But more was offered by the manoeuvre 18.h4 and then ♖h3, including the king's rook in the defence of the queenside.

18...b4

This pawn was sacrificed without any qualms, since I had mastered well the principles of attacking in positions with opposite-side castling.

19.axb4 axb4 20.♗xb4 ♕a4 21.♗a3 ♕b3

I did not even occur to me to play 21...♘f6!, underlining the unfortunate position of the white queen – I only had eyes for the white king.

22.♕e7

Black to move. What would you play?

The ♗a3 stops the black attack, but its invulnerability is dependent on being guarded by the white queen. Therefore, I found a combination, based on deflecting the queen away from its protection of the bishop.

22...♘b8! 23.♗g2

Nothing is changed by 23.♕b4 ♕a2 followed by ...♘c6.

23...♘c6 24.♕c5

Or 24.♕d6 ♖d8!.

24...♖a5 25.♕d6 ♖d8

Finally forcing the queen to take the knight and give up protection of the ♗a3!

26.♕xc6

If 26.♕g3 (during the game I had not seen this way of protecting the c3-pawn) Black decides with 26...e5! 27.dxe5 ♖xa3 28.bxa3 ♗xg4! with irresistible threats.

26...♖xa3 27.bxa3 ♕xc3+ 28.♔b1 ♕b3+ 29.♔c1 c3 30.♖d2 ♕xa3+ 31.♔d1 ♕a1+ 32.♔c2 ♕b2+ 33.♔d3 ♕xd2#

I was in seventh heaven. It seemed to me then that I had sacrificed a great many pieces! The game had great psychological significance, and gave me confidence. In this tournament, I finally fulfilled the norm for second category and in the following one I became a first category player.

Remembering the combinations played by my opponents, I would choose the following from a first category tournament.

Queen's Indian Defence
Vadim Hvostov
Alexander Kalinin
Moscow 1981

1.d4 ♘f6 2.c4 e6 3.♘f3 ♗b4+ 4.♘bd2 0-0 5.a3 ♗xd2+ 6.♗xd2 d6 7.♗g5 ♘bd7 8.e3 b6 9.♕c2 ♗b7 10.♗d3 ♕e8 11.♖d1 a5 12.0-0 e5 13.dxe5 dxe5 14.♗f5!

14...h6 15.♗h4 g6 16.♗h3 ♔g7
The attempt to eliminate the pressure with 16...g5 allows various piece sacrifices: 17.♘xg5 hxg5 18.♕f5 gxh4 19.♖xd7 or 17.♗xd7 ♘xd7 18.♕f5 ♗xf3 19.gxf3 ♘c5 20.♗xg5 with a dangerous attack for White. With the text, Black decides to strengthen the vulnerable points in

his position. This aim could have been achieved more effectively, however, by means of 16...♗c6.

White to move. What should he play?

The pressure against d7 and f6 is considerable, but it seems that Black has everything defended. The following combination came like lightning from a clear sky to me. **17.♘xe5!! ♘xe5 18.♗xf6+ ♔xf6 19.♕c3!**

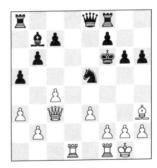

This quiet move gives the combination special merit. The pin on the long diagonal allows White to regain the piece, with an extra (albeit doubled) pawn in the centre and a weakened enemy king position. The combination played by Vadim Hvostov (my friend, with whom I played many times on the team of the Moscow Pioneer Palace) is especially nice, because it arises logically from his previous purposeful action.

19...♔g7 20.f4 ♗c8

Now White keeps a healthy extra pawn. Preferable was 20...f5 21.fxe5 ♔h7 (a further combinative explosion would occur after 21...♕e6 22.♖d7+! ♖f7 23.♖xf5!! gxf5 24.♗xf5, winning), although White's advantage is not in doubt here either.

21.♗xc8 ♖xc8 22.♖d5! ♔g8 23.♖xe5 ♕c6 24.f5

And White went on confidently to realise his material and positional advantage.

It must be said that a player's tactical mastery is also closely bound up with his positional understanding. This is not surprising, since in a tournament game, the ability to sense when a combination is possible depends on the ability to assess the position objectively. It sometimes happens that we get caught up in combinative fever and fail to play according to the objective spirit of the position. There are examples of this in my own practice too.

Alexander Kalinin
Sirotin

Moscow 1979

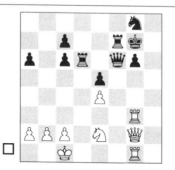

Assess the position. What should White play?

Thinking about my move, I reasoned roughly as follows: 'The black king's position is weakened, but g6 is well defended and it is not clear how to strengthen the white attack. The inactive knight on e2 is particularly regrettable. Meanwhile, Black has an extra pawn. Admittedly, his pawn structure is broken, but it is not easy for White to attack the queenside pawns, whilst the extra pawn on g6 could become a dangerous passed pawn in the event of queens being exchanged. White is no better and is a pawn down.' And now I spotted the surprising knight jump to d4!

26.♘d4?!

The knight comes into play, under attack from two pieces! Black must accept the sacrifice, which leads to a forced draw. Such a development of affairs seemed to me to be an entirely logical outcome of the position, because it solves White's main problem, the passivity of the knight on e2.

26...exd4 27.e5 ♕xe5 28.♖xg6+ ♖xg6 29.♕xg6+ ♔f8 30.♕xg8+ ♔e7 31.♕g5+ ♕xg5+ 32.♖xg5 ½-½

For a long time, I was very proud of my 26th move, but when I came to prepare the example for publication, I looked at the initial position once again and came to the conclusion that in fact, it clearly favours White!

Judge for yourself: as well as a direct attack on the g6-pawn, White can also threaten the enemy king by penetrating with his major pieces on the h-file. The exchange of queens is not currently realistic for Black, because of the weakness of g6, and defending the pawn with ...♘g8-e7 improves White's attacking chances on the h-file. In the long run, the weakness of the black queenside pawns may tell; for example, one cannot exclude the rook on g3 transferring to c3 or a3. And finally, the most important thing of all, White can bring the ♘e2 into play without sacrificing it! He has available the manoeuvre 26.♔b1! and then ♘e2-c1-d3, underlining the vulnerability of the pawn on e5. In case of necessity, he can also flick in the unhurried move a2-a3, making luft for the king. I will not give any variations here, to prove White's advantage – it

will be more useful for the reader to satisfy himself of this with a small independent analysis.

I think the decision to play 26.♘d4, as well as being based on a misassessment of the position, also had a psychological motive. Firstly, sub-consciously I very much wanted to play the spectacular move, and secondly, as Tigran Petrosian once pointed out, 'many people, after sacrificing a pawn, lose because they play as though they had lost the pawn, rather than consciously parted with it.'

In forming my attitude to chess as an art, a great role was played by my father. He had an outstanding library and developed in me a taste for the books of the old masters, who could write sublimely about our ancient game.

One episode remains forever in my memory. It was in Zvenigorod. A Saturday morning in summer, I had just woken up, and my father dragged myself and my mother to his chessboard, and began emotionally to demonstrate a combination, which he had brought off the evening before, in a skittles game against a friend. I should add that I was just five years old at the time and had only recently learned the moves, whilst my mother did not play chess at all!

Let us have a look at this combination:

Vladimir Kalinin
G. Skripnik
Moscow 1973

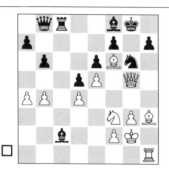

Vladimir Kalinin
Sheremetievsky
Zvenigorod 1956

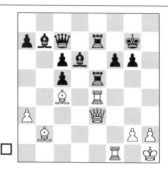

What should White play in this position?

White's pressure on the kingside is obvious, but the ♗c2 allows Black to hold the defence. Now the direct 33.♕h5 h6 or 33.♗g4 ♗e4, pinning the ♘f3, get nowhere.

33.♗f5!!

A problem-like move, combining ideas of interference and line-opening.

33...♗xf5

In the event of 33...♗e4 White wins by 34.♕xg6+! (34.♖xh7? ♗xf3+) 34...fxg6 (34...hxg6 35.♖h8 mate) 35.♗xe6 mate.

34.♖xh7! ♔xh7 35.♕h5+ ♗h6

Or 35...♔g8 36.♘g5 mating.

36.♘g5+

Black resigned.

Here are a few more combinative fragments from my father's archive (he was a first category player), acquaintance with which stimulated my love of chess.

Show an effective way to develop the attack.

Black's extra pawns on the c-file are of no significance, and the assessment of the position is decided by the activity of the white bishops. Black is already offering to buy White off with the exchange sacrifice on e5.

29.♖xf6!?

This rook sacrifice destroys the black king's pawn cover. At the time this game was played, my father was studying at a student chess circle, the leader of which was international Master Oleg Moiseev. Oleg Leonidovich, whilst approving of the young player's combinative talent, pointed out that a rather simpler solution was offered by the equally strong 29.♖h4! g5 (29...♖xe3 30.♗xf6+ ♔f8 31.♖h8#) 30.♕h3! gxh4 31.♕g4+ ♔h7 32.♕g8+ mating.

29...♔xf6 30.♖g4

In his notes, my father pointed out that after 30.♖f4+ ♔g5 (the game continuation is reached after 30...♔g7 31.♖h4) White has to repeat the position after 31.♖e4+ ♔f6. However, here too, Moiseev found something stronger: 31.g3!! ♖xe3 32.♗f6+ ♔h6 33.♖h4#.

30...♔g7 31.♖h4 ♖e8 32.♕h3!

Less accurate is 32.♕h6+ ♔f6 33.♖f4+ ♔e7 34.♗xe5 ♔d8, and the black king escapes from the danger zone.

32...♔f8

Or 32...♔f6 33.♖h7 winning.

33.♖h8+ ♔e7 34.♗xe5 ♖xh8 35.♕e6+ ♔d8 36.♗xd6 ♕h7 37.♗e5 ♖f8 38.♕d6+ ♔e8 39.♕b8+

Black resigned.

Vladimir Baranov
Vladimir Kalinin

Moscow 1969

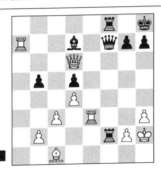

What should Black play?

Black forces a simple but attractive mating finish:

29...♖xg2+! 30.♔xg2 ♕f1+ 31.♔h2 ♖f2+ 32.♔g3 ♖g2+ 33.♔h4 g5+ 34.♔h5 ♕f7+ 35.♔h6 ♕g7+ 36.♔h5 ♗g4+! 37.hxg4 ♖h2+! 38.♕xh2 ♕g6#

Two Knights Defence
Leonid Bass
Vladimir Kalinin

Moscow 1968

1.e4 e5 2.♘f3 ♘c6 3.♗c4 ♘f6 4.♘g5 d5 5.exd5 ♘a5 6.♗b5+ c6 7.dxc6 bxc6 8.♗e2 h6 9.♘f3 ♗d6

The main continuation here is 9...e4. The text allows Black to get off the beaten track quickly, but allows White more easily to establish a firm central position.

10.d3 0-0 11.♘c3 ♘d5 12.♘e4 ♗c7 13.0-0 f5 14.♘g3 c5 15.♗d2 ♘c6

The transfer of the white knight from the good square c3 to the poor location on g3 has wasted time and allowed Black, who has placed his pieces actively, to secure compensation for the sacrificed pawn.

16.c3 ♗e6 17.♖e1 ♕d7 18.♗f1 a5 19.a3 a4 20.c4

This move aims at creating pressure against the e5-pawn.

20...♘de7 21.♗c3 ♘g6 22.h4 ♘d4 23.h5 ♘xf3+ 24.♕xf3 ♘h4 25.♕d1 f4

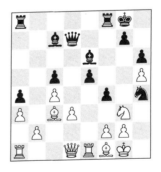

A standard device. The strong pawn on f4 opens chances for Black to attack the kingside. The price of this activity is the e4-square, which becomes White's property. However, when the white knight comes to e4, it will shield the black e5-pawn from attack.

26.♘e4 ♗g4 27.f3 ♗xh5 28.♘xc5 ♕c6 29.♘e4 ♕g6 30.♔h2 ♖f5! 31.c5

Black to play. How would you continue?

The outcome is decided by the inclusion of the rook on f5.

31...♗xf3! 32.gxf3 ♖h5 33.♗h3 ♕g2+! 34.♗xg2 ♘xf3#

King's Gambit
L. Elinzon
Vladimir Kalinin
Moscow 1968

1.e4 e5 2.f4 exf4 3.♘f3 d5 4.exd5 ♘f6 5.c4
The spirit of this energetic opening is better suited by 5.♗b5+.
5...c6 6.dxc6 ♘xc6 7.d4 ♗b4+ 8.♗d2?
White needed to play 8.♘c3.
8...0-0 9.♗xb4 ♘xb4 10.♗e2 ♘g4 11.♕d2 ♘e3! 12.♘a3 ♕e7 13.♔f2 ♗f5 14.g3 ♖fe8 15.gxf4 ♖ad8 16.h3

Black to move. What would you play?

A series of effective blows allows Black to shatter the opponent's centre and get through to the white king:

16...♘d3+! 17.♗xd3
Or 17.♔g3 ♘xf4! 18.♔xf4 ♕d6+ 19.♘e5 ♖xe5, and Black wins.
17...♖xd4! 18.♘xd4 ♕h4+ 19.♔f3 ♗g4+! 20.hxg4 ♕xg4+ 21.♔f2 ♕g2+ 22.♔e1 ♕xh1+ 23.♔e2 ♕g2+ 24.♔e1 ♘xc4+ 25.♘e2 ♕g1#

Incidentally, the aesthetic side of chess does not only find its expression in combinations. With experience, we start to appreciate the pristine logic of strategic plans, the subtlety of prophylactic manoeuvres and the depth of the endgame. 'Teaching an understanding of beauty in chess is one of the trainer's tasks, – wrote Vladimir Zak – and the following game can help with this. It completely lacks striking tactics or sacrifices, but even so, it unquestionably belongs amongst the greatest productions of chess art.'

José Raul Capablanca
Dawid Janowsky

St Petersburg 1914

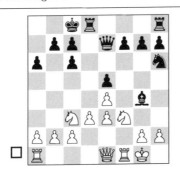

11.♖b1!!

'This is the move, the elusive beauty of which is hard to explain. It is the start of a plan which wins the game for White. This consists in organising the advance b2-b4-b5, breaking up Black's castled position. The beauty of the unremarkable-looking move 11.♖b1 is that this plan immediately makes the whole position clear. It is already hard for Black to do anything against this' – Zak.

There followed 11...f6 12.b4 ♘f7 13.a4 ♗xf3 14.♖xf3 b6 15.b5 cxb5 16.axb5 a5 17.♘d5 ♕c5 18.c4, and White obtained a decisive advantage.

Let us momentarily return to the game Liublinsky-Rovner. The final attack was nice, but to an experienced player, it rather plays itself. He will probably be more interested in the position after Black's 12th move:

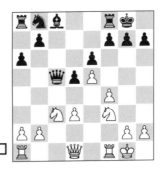

Both the king retreat to h1 and the move d3-d4 are tempting. However, Liublinsky played 13.♖f2!?, voluntarily pinning his own rook. What is the point of this at first sight strange-looking decision? The truth is that after 13.d4, White loses the chance to use the d4-square as a piece outpost, and the black queen can retreat to e7. By leaving the d4-square open, White forces his opponent to reckon with the possibility of ♘c3-e2-d4. Therefore, after the moves 13...♘c6 14.♕d2 ♗d7 15.♖c1 the black queen retreated to a7 – 15...♕a7, keeping guard over d4, but also moving far away from the kingside. Then White immediately played 16.d4 ♖ac8 17.g4, transferring the weight of the struggle to the kingside. At the same time, the move ♖f2 becomes extremely useful, because White's rooks are already prepared to double on the f- or c-files, should circumstances permit.

Thus, the 'strange' move 13.♖f2 has a definite point. It is useful to focus on such decisions, since they are very much bound up with developing a feeling for the key moments of a game.

And did you, dear reader, take a particular note of the move 13.♖f2 when you first saw this game?

However, it sometimes happens that a positional decision makes as great an impression on the spectator as a sacrificial combination.

José Raul Capablanca
L. Molina, L. Ruis
Buenos Aires 1914

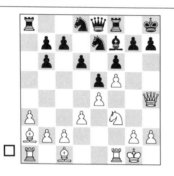

It seems that White has no other sensible move than 17.♗xf7, exchanging the opponent's 'good' bishop (based on the pawn position). When, as a youngster, I first saw Capablanca's move, it made a staggering impression on me!

17.c4!!

I simply could not believe my eyes! Is this really possible?! Capablanca not only refuses to exchange off his opponent's good bishop, but, horror of horrors, he shuts in his own bishop with his pawns, making it into a 'bad' bishop! We have what is effectively a sacrifice

– not a material one, but in terms of positional factors. After calming down, I started to understand the motives for this unusual decision. The truth is that Black's position on the kingside is extremely cramped. White threatens an attack on this wing with the advance g2-g4-g5. If we refuse to exchange off the black bishop, it will get under the feet of its own pieces, as well as potentially itself coming under attack from a white pawn reaching g6 (one can see such a motif, with colours reversed, in the KID). Thus we see that there is nothing 'supernatural' about the move 17.c4 – it is simply that, after breaking one positional rule (i.e. that concerning good and bad bishops), White follows another (avoiding exchanges when one's opponent is cramped).

In the game there followed:
17...c5 18.g4 ♞g8 19.♗d2 b5 20.g5 fxg5 21.♞xg5 ♞f6 22.♖f3 bxc4 23.♞xh7! ♞xh7 24.♖h3 ♗g8 25.♗xc4 ♖f7 26.♔h1 b5 27.♗d5 ♖aa7 28.♖g1 ♖f6 29.♗g5 ♖af7

30.b3!

After tying up his opponent hand and foot on the kingside, White decides the game by creating a passed pawn on the a-file.

30...♕f8 31.a4 bxa4 32.bxa4 ♕e8 33.a5 ♘c6 34.a6 ♘b4 35.♗xf6 ♘xd5 36.♗xg7+ ♖xg7 37.♖xg7 ♔xg7 38.♕h6+ ♔h8 39.♕xd6

Black resigned.

It is remarkable that, in his book *My Chess Career*, Capablanca does not even comment on the move 17.c4. Evidently, for the great Cuban, this was a move that virtually played itself!

In the following example, White's strategic idea combines at the same time a deep move and a 'sacrifice' of positional assets.

French Defence
Vasily Prokofiev
Igor Glek
Moscow (rapid) 1989

The white player in this game was Vasya Prokofiev. We studied together from the first year at school, played for the school team together and for the Moscow Pioneer Palace and then the Moscow city youth team. We both studied in the group led by Alexander Kostyev and then, as we got older, that by Abram Khasin. Vasily twice became Moscow youth champion. In 1982, he represented the city well in the strongest-ever USSR junior championship (among

the participants were Khalifman, Bareev, Dreev, Epishin, Oll, Dautov, Shabalov and many others who later became well-known players), sharing 11th-16th places together with Gelfand. Vasily never became a master, though – sadly, after army service, he stopped playing seriously. His life tragically ended at just 27 years of age...
I should add that even after giving up serious chess, Vasya never quite rid himself of its pull. He could often be seen at the famous Central Chess Club on Gogolevsky Boulevard, where at the end of the 1980s, there were frequent rapid tournaments. This game was played in one such.

1.e4 e6 2.d4 d5 3.♘c3 ♘f6 4.e5 ♘fd7 5.f4 c5 6.♘f3 ♘c6 7.♗e3 a6 8.♕d2 b5

This system with ...a7-a6 and ...b7-b5 became popular in the 1990s, in considerable measure thanks to the efforts of Igor Glek. As we see, the Moscow GM used rapid tournaments to test and develop his opening ideas.

9.dxc5 ♗xc5 10.♘e2 ♕b6

11.♘ed4

Not wishing to allow the ♞d7 into e4, White refrains from the strategically favourable exchange of dark-squared bishops.

Nowadays, the battle for an opening advantage revolves exclusively round the continuation 11.♗xc5, e.g.: 11...♞xc5 12.♞ed4 ♞e4 13.♕e3 b4 14.♗d3 ♗b7 15.0-0 0-0 16.♖ae1, and White's chances are slightly preferable (Leko-M.Gurevich, Elista 2007).

11...f6 12.0-0-0

The logical development of the idea of the previous move – White keeps his pawn outpost on e5, by tactical means.

In the game Van Mil-Hergott (Groningen 1988), White chose 12.exf6 ♞xf6 13.0-0-0 ♞e4 14.♕e1 0-0 with an excellent game for Black.

12...fxe5 13.fxe5 0-0

After the immediate capture of the pawn with 13...♞dxe5 14.♞xe5 ♞xe5 there could follow 15.b4! ♗f8 16.♖e1 ♞g4 17.♞xe6! ♞xe3 18.♞c5 ♗xc5 19.bxc5 ♕xc5 20.♖xe3+ ♚d7 21.♗e2, and the black king is very uncomfortable in the centre of the board.

14.♖e1!

This 'quiet' rook shift adds to the energy of the white set-up – the positions of the ♗e3 and the e5-pawn are strengthened. The move also contains some tactical poison.

Can Black take the e5-pawn now?

14...♞dxe5?

Black cannot resist the chance to eliminate the cramping e5-pawn, but this turns out to be a serious mistake. Correct was 14...♞xd4 15.♗xd4 b4 followed by ...a6-a5 and ...♗a6, which gives Black a good game.

15.♞xe5 ♞xe5

The least of the evils was 15...♗xd4 16.♞xc6 ♗xe3 17.♞e7+ ♚f7 18.♖xe3 ♚xe7 19.♗d3 with advantage to White.

16.b4!

This move has a degree of unexpectedness and, hence, aesthetic value. Players frequently fail to consider sharp pawn advances in front of the king!

16...♗e7 17.♞f5 ♕d8 18.♞xe7+ ♕xe7 19.♗c5 ♕f6

Hoping for 20.♗xf8? ♞c4, and Black wins.

20.♗d4!
Perhaps in the madness of a
rapid game, it was this pendulum
manoeuvre by the white bishop
which the GM had missed?
Black resigned.

Beauty in chess has many forms,
but even so, the majority of players
(and not only amateurs) are most
attracted by sacrifices, made on the
altar of attack. How is this to be
explained?
The best way to answer this
question, it seems to me, is
to compare two quotes, made
centuries apart:

Ercole del Rio (XVIII century):
'In chess, the human spirit is attracted
most of all by the poetry of the game and
in this respect chess should be considered
a precious part of world culture. The
poetry of the game consists in the
battle of pieces, many of which sacrifice
themselves to achieve the desired goal.
What would a man not sacrifice for the
sake of his favourite lady? Mating the
king is the aim, for which no sacrifice is
too great.'

Alexander Alekhine (XX century):
'The difference between chess and other
popular games, where the aim is to seize
space or win material, is that chess has a
unique idea, the mating of the king. At the
beginning of the game, the opponents also
try to win material or gain space, but once
the idea of mating the enemy king becomes
real, the player will sacrifice any amount
of space, time and material to achieve this.

This is why chess is useful and why it is
attractive, because deep down, it embodies
the human ideas of striving towards a
goal and of the pleasure of self-sacrifice to
achieve that goal. This is also why chess
gives rise to such aesthetic feelings and
why it gives us a feeling of beauty, as the
internal nature of the game fully accords
with our concept of striving towards self-
sacrifice.'

To finish this chapter, here are two
more examples from the play of my
peers. In my schooldays, I had the
habit of writing down games that
interested me, which allows me now
to present them for your attention.

Yakov Nesterov
Vladimir Chuchelov

Moscow 1982

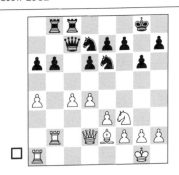

This game between two first
category players was played in the
Moscow youth championship.
The white pieces were played by
Yasha Nesterov, who even then
was distinguished for his subtle
positional understanding. Later,
Yakov became a grandmaster
and represented the colours of
Kazakhstan at the Olympiads. Black

was Vladimir Chuchelov, now a well-known Belgian GM and a top trainer.

What plan should White choose?

White's position is superior – he has a freer position and the black king's cover is somewhat weakened. But how can we exploit this? The b6-square is well-defended and the consequences of activating the central pawns are unclear. One could consider a4-a5, but this idea too is not very clear.

22.h4!

A favourite device of the Danish GM Bent Larsen – the advance of a rook's pawn to disturb the balance of the enemy position.

22...h5

This response with the black h-pawn further weakens his kingside.

Maybe the advance should have been stopped by less radical methods, e.g. 22...♘f6 23.♖ab1 ♘f8, bringing the other knight to d7 to defend the b6-pawn.

23.♖ab1 ♔g7 24.♕d3

Freeing the d2-square for the knight, which increases the flexibility of the white pieces.

24...♕a7 25.♘d2 ♘c7 26.♕a3

Forcing the opponent to reckon with the advance a4-a5.

26...a5

Revealing the idea of Black's previous move – he is preparing to bring the knight to b4, shutting off the pressure along the b-file, at the cost of weakening b5.

27.♘e4 ♘a6

White to play. What would you do?

28.♖b5!

The appearance of the rook on the 5th rank underlines the distance of the black pieces from the kingside. The stereotyped transfer of the white knight to b5 (28.♘c3 ♘f6 29.♘b5 ♕d7) was less effective.

28...♘b4 29.♖g5

Given that the long-range rook affects the kingside even from its distant post on b5, it was also worth considering 29.♘g5.

29...♔h7

He had to play 29...♘f6.

White to play. What would you choose?

30.f4?!

White is ready to smash the enemy kingside with the battering ram f2-f4-f5, but he slows up the tempo of his attack. He had at his disposal an energetic combination: 30.♗xh5! gxh5 31.♖xb4! axb4 32.♕d3 ♚h8 33.♘xd6! exd6 34.♕f5, and the black king succumbs.

30...♘f6 31.♗d3 ♘xe4 32.♗xe4 f5?

The classical rule of defence is to avoid pawn moves on the side of the board where you stand worse. By continuing 32...e6!, Black could defend successfully.

White to play. What should he do?

33.♗xf5! gxf5 34.e4!

'War is about communication!' said Napoleon. The sudden appearance of the white queen on the kingside decides the outcome of the game.
34...♖g8 35.♖xh5+ ♚g6 36.♖xf5 e6 37.♕g3+ ♚h6 38.♖f6+ ♚h7 39.♕f3 ♖xg2+ 40.♕xg2 ♖g8 41.♖h6+ ♚xh6 42.♕xg8
Black resigned.

French Defence
Yuri Piskov
Igor Khenkin
Dnepropetrovsk 1984

This game was played in the junior championship of the sports society Burevestnik and won the best game prize. The two future GMs were both Candidate Masters at the time.
1.e4 e6 2.d4 d5 3.♘c3 dxe4 4.♘xe4 ♗d7 5.♘f3 ♗c6 6.♗d3 ♘d7 7.♕e2 ♗e7 8.0-0 ♘gf6 9.♘g3 ♗xf3 10.♕xf3 c6
Black has chosen a somewhat passive, but extremely solid line of the French, which results in a structure more reminiscent of the Caro-Kann.
11.b3 0-0 12.♗b2 a5 13.a3 ♘b6 14.c4 a4 15.b4 ♘c8

By transferring the knight to d6, Black hopes to fight for the d5-square, with the advance ...b7-b5. Even so, this manoeuvre, begun by his 13th move, looks somewhat artificial. In such positions, the black queen's knight is usually more flexibly placed on d7.

16.♖fe1 ♘d6 17.♖e5!

In this game, thanks to the availability of e5, the white rook exploits the 5th rank as a 'trampoline', to jump to the kingside.

17...♕d7

Completing the final preparations for the advance ...b7-b5, but he should have preferred 17...g6, strengthening the kingside bastions.

18.♘h5

The exchange of the ♘f6 opens the way for the 'Horwitz bishops' and the white major pieces to the kingside.

18...♘de8 19.♖ae1

What happens after 19...♘xh5?

19...♘xh5

Allowing a combinative solution to the position. However, the concentration of white pieces in the attack is so great that Black can hardly hope to defend. For example, 19...♗d6 20.♖g5 ♘xh5 21.♕xh5 g6 (or 21...♘f6 22.♖xg7+ ♔xg7 23.♕g5+) 22.d5! e5 (22...cxd5 23.♕xh7+! ♔xh7 24.♖h5+ ♔g8 25.♖h8#) 23.c5, and Black is in a bad way.

20.♗xh7+! ♔xh7 21.♖xh5+ ♔g8 22.♕h3 f6

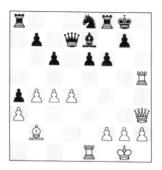

23.d5!

The final point to the combination – the black king won't find a peaceful haven in the centre of the board.

23...cxd5 24.cxd5 ♘c7 25.♖h8+

The endgame a pawn down after 25.dxe6 ♘xe6 26.♕xe6+ ♕xe6 27.♖xe6 ♖fd8 28.g4 ♔f7 would be a considerable relief for Black.

25...♔f7 26.♕h5+ g6 27.♕h7+ ♔e8 28.♕xg6+ ♔d8 29.♖xf8+ ♗xf8 30.dxe6 ♕d2 31.♗xf6+ ♔c8 32.♔f1 ♖a6 33.♕f5

And because of the inevitable 34.e7, Black resigned.

CHAPTER 4

The benefits of solving endgame studies

'Analysing the so-called technical endgames of Capablanca and Smyslov, I realised that they all hang on combinational elements and far-seeing, accurate calculation.'

David Bronstein

'If a master is weak in the endgame, he should analyse endgame studies more.'

Mikhail Botvinnik

Young players love to play combinations and carry out attacks on the king. At the same time, they are frequently at sea in the endgame. It is claimed that young players find studying endgames boring, but I think this just means that we need to make the process of such study more attractive!

When I was seven years old, my father interested me in solving studies. I carried out this task with pleasure, first with simple studies and later with more difficult ones. As I got older, I even tried my hand at composing studies. The love of studies extended itself to all aspects of the endgame. Thanks to the presence of a combinational element in the ending, I developed my imagination and never found endgames boring!

Incidentally, study ideas can be useful to a player not just in the endgame itself, but also in the middlegame. Here are a couple of examples from my childhood games:

Alexander Kalinin
Mikhail Postovsky

Tuapse 1979

What follows after 1...♞d8 ?

While Misha Postovsky (the son of the well-known trainer Boris Naumovich Postovsky) was considering his move, I spotted a beautiful combinative idea. Holding my breath, I awaited the typical Spanish manoeuvre ...♞b7-d8-f7, bringing the knight to the defence of the kingside.

On **1...♞d8** I had prepared the effective **2.♗xh6! gxh6 3.♞g6+!** (not 3.♕xh6 ♖g8) **3...♔g8 4.♕xh6 ♖f7 5.♕g7+! ♖xg7 6.♞h6#.**

In the game, all this beauty remained behind the curtain, however, as Black played 1...♗d8.

In this combination, we see the old Arab motif, such a mate with two knights having been featured in the ancient Arab Mansuba manuscript! Below, we see the same mate in a striking endgame study form:

M. Mikhailov

Shakmatny Misl 1955

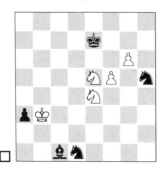

Win!

1.g7! ♘xg7 2.f6+ ♔f8 3.♘c5!
Threatening to promote the pawn after ♘c5-d7+.
3...a2! 4.♔xa2
If 4.♘cd7+ ♔g8 5.f7+ ♔h7 6.f8♕ a1♕ White is the first to promote, but this does not bring any particular dividends, e.g. 7.♘f6+ ♔h6 8.♕h8+ ♔g5 9.♕xg7+ ♔f5 etc.
4...♘c3+ 5.♔b3 ♗a3! 6.♔xa3 ♘b5+ 7.♔b4 ♘d6
It seems Black has managed to stop the opponent's passed pawn, but now there follows a lovely finish!
8.♘cd7+ ♔g8 9.f7+! ♘xf7 10.♘f6+ ♔f8 11.♘g6#!

I once managed to save a very difficult position with the aid

of a beautiful combination, of which I was very proud. On closer examination, however, the study-like idea had a flaw. So as to preserve this interesting idea, at least as an exercise, I have composed a study specially for this book, containing the idea in question.

Alexander Kalinin

2013

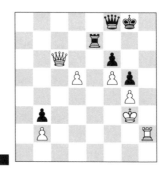

How should Black defend?

1...♔g7!
Preparing counterplay on the h-file against the white king. The immediate 1...♖e3+ 2.♔f2 ♕e7 fails to 3.♕c8+.
2.♔f3
After the natural 2.d6 there follows the study-like 2...♖e3+ 3.♔f2 ♖e2+! 4.♔xe2 ♕e8+! 5.♕xe8 – stalemate! He could take control of e3 with 2.♕c5 ♕e8 3.♔f3, but after 3...♖f7! 4.♖e2 ♕a4! the insecure position of his king deprives White of any chances to realise his extra pawn. With the text, White also prevents

the entry of the black rook, but here too, Black has a good reply.
2...♕b8! 3.d6 ♕b4! 4.dxe7 ♕f4+

Lajos Portisch
Garry Kasparov
Moscow 1981

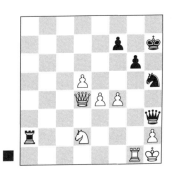

5.♔e2
If 5.♔g2 ♕d2+ 6.♔g3 ♕f4+ 7.♔h3 ♕e3+ 8.♔g2 ♕d2+ the white king cannot escape perpetual check.
5...♕c4+! 6.♕xc4
And it is again stalemate!

I should add that the reader can find the game Novikov-Kalinin (Moscow 1985), which was the prototype for this study, in the chapter 'Lessons at the chessboard'. What was it that helped me find this stalemate idea at the board? Mikhail Tal once observed that 'Although each of us thinks we have created something original, in reality we only ever reproduce, even if subconsciously, what we have already seen before.'

The idea of stalemate in major-piece positions was one I had come across many times in studies and positions, and the preparatory king move was probably prompted by the following example:

What should Black play?

In 1981, as a schoolboy, I visited almost every round of the Moscow international, with my friends. When we saw this adjourned position, we assessed it as better for White, because we could not find a draw in the variation 41...♘xf4 42.♕f6 ♕e3 43.♕xf7+ ♔h6 44.♖f1!. Great was our surprise when, on resumption, the future World Champion demonstrated a precise and effective path to equality!
41...♔g8!!
A brilliant preparatory move, setting up the subsequent combination. This was my first (and, of course, a memorable) acquaintance with the idea of a quiet king move, strengthening the attacking resources of the position. In one of his books, Mark Dvoretsky devoted a whole chapter to this idea, under the title 'Don't get in the way, Your Majesty!'.

42.d6 ♖xd2! 43.♕xd2 ♕f3+ 44.♕g2 ♘g3!+ 45.hxg3 ♕h5+ 46.♕h2 ♕f3+
If the black king were on h7 now, the black queen would be pinned!
47.♖g2 ♕d1+ 48.♕g1 ♕h5+ 49.♖h2 ♕f3+ ½-½

In speaking of striking study ideas, realised in practice, one cannot pass by this Kasparov combination.

Jaime Sunye Neto
Garry Kasparov

Graz 1981

Black's last move was 41...♘h4-f3+. The Brazilian GM replied
42.♔f1
after which there followed the effective 42...♗xe3! 43.fxe3 ♖dxg2! 44.♕c3 ♖h2 45.♘e2 ♔h7! with a winning attack for Black.

How would events develop after 42.♔h1 ?

On 42.♔h1 Kasparov had prepared an even more beautiful variation: 42...♗xe3! 43.fxe3 ♖dxg2!! 44.♘xg2 ♖g3!!

A fantastic domination by two black pieces, against a huge material superiority for the opponent – despite it being his move, White cannot prevent mate!

On the basis of this game, I composed the following study, which was my first entry in an official composing tourney:

Alexander Kalinin

Magadanskaya Pravda 1985

Win!

The immediate 1.f8♕? is impossible because of 1...♕xa5+ 2.♔b3 ♕a4#. Therefore White disrupts the harmony between the black pieces, with the aid of two preliminary checks:

1.♗a6+! ♛xa6 2.♖b8+ ♚xa5 3.f8♛

Black's position looks hopeless, but by the laws of the study genre, he must show his trumps.

3...♗e7+!

Beginning a stalemate combination. In the event of the 'cunning' 3...♛d3+ 4.♚a2! (but not 4.♖b3? ♗e7+! 5.♛xe7 ♛d6+! 6.♛xd6 stalemate – see below!) 4...♛e2+ 5.♚b1 ♛e1+ 6.♚c2 ♛e2+ 7.♚c1 ♛e1+ 8.♘d1 ♗g5+ 9.f4 the white king escapes the checks and Black loses.

4.♛xe7 ♛d6+!

Now a draw seems inevitable, in view of 5.♛xd6 stalemate, but...

5.♚b3! ♛xe7 6.♖b6!!

In the battle against the black king, the two white pieces establish a domination on an open board. At the same time, the white rook is hanging!

6...♛xe3+

Or 6...♚xb6 7.♘d5+.

7.fxe3 ♚xb6 8.♚b4!

And White wins.

I have very sharp memories of a lecture I once heard by IM Oleg Averkin, given at the Smyslov chess school. From the mouth of the remarkable player and experienced trainer, I heard a paradoxical thought: 'Tactics have greater significance in the endgame than in the middlegame!'

At the time I could not believe this. In the endgame, only a few pieces remain on the board, and with exchanges, the combinational possibilities gradually diminish. It was only later that I came to understand the philosophical point that lay behind the master's comment.

Certainly, in the middlegame, where there are plenty of pieces on the board, the relations between them are less tense – if one piece is 'hobbled', another can cover for it. But in the endgame, with fewer pieces on the board, the relations become much more critical. If a particular piece is badly placed, there is not another to replace it, which means that each unit bears a greater weight in the endgame and a greater importance attaches to coordination between the pieces and to tactical considerations. For this reason, a small number of units can control the whole board.

This idea is excellently illustrated by the following remarkable study.

Alexey Troitzky

Shakmatny Listok 1929

Win!

The very idea of a win seems at first sight to be completely unrealistic. However, the two white pieces succeed in controlling the whole board! In what follows, White plays simultaneously against the black king and bishop. It should be pointed out that, if either of the black pawns were not on the board, the position would be a draw.

1.♗h6!

Now play divides into two lines:

A) **1...c5** Freeing the ♗a8. **2.♘b5! ♔g8 3.♘d6!** Placing the black king under arrest.

Then play could unfold along these lines: **3...♗d5 4.♔c2 ♗h1 5.♔d2 ♗d5 6.♔e3 c4 7.♔d4 ♗f7 8.♔e5 c3 9.♔f6 ♗b3 10.♘c8 c2 11.♘e7+ ♔h8 12.♗g7#**;

B) **1...♔g8 2.♘e4! ♔f7** The king gets to freedom. **3.♘c5!** This time the bishop is arrested. There could follow **3...♔g6 4.♗f8 h5 5.♔c2 ♔f5 6.♗d6!** A typical device – the bishop and knight create a barrier

against the black king. **6...♔g4 7.♔d2 ♔f3 8.♔e1 ♔g2 9.♗e7 ♔g3 10.♔f1 ♔f3 11.♗d6 ♔e3 12.♗e5! ♔d2 13.♔g2 ♔c2 14.♔h3 ♔b1 15.♔h4 ♔a2 16.♔xh5 ♔a3 17.♗c3!**, and the black king cannot come to the aid of the bishop on a8. Now White wins simply by bringing his king over to the enemy bishop. A grandiose study! The coordination of the white pieces creates a great impression.

The following game was played in the Pioneer Palace team event 'The White Rook', between the Moscow and Leningrad schoolboy teams.

Vasily Prokofiev
F. Tolmachev

Pervomaisk 1981

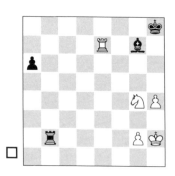

Very few pieces remain on the board, but this does not stop the players engaging in some nice study-like fencing, exploiting some tactical tricks. It is not easy for White to realise his extra pawn, even though he has two connected passed pawns on the kingside. The difficulties are caused firstly by the small amount of material remaining on the board, and secondly, in the resulting play on both flanks (Black has his trump in the form of the passed pawn on a6), the black bishop could prove stronger than the white knight.

47.h5!?

A more fundamental continuation was 47.♖a7 ♖a2 48.♔h3 followed by a gradual advance of the kingside pawns. The brash text move sets a cunning trap.

47...♖b5

Black is tempted by the possibility of winning the h-pawn. Better was 47...a5.

48.h6 ♗xh6?

The fatal slip. By keeping the bishop on the long diagonal, Black could retain chances of a successful defence. The h6-pawn could also have been taken in another way: 48...♖h5+ 49.♔g3 ♗xh6. But then after 50.♘f6 ♗f8 51.♖f7 ♗d6+ (or 51...♖h1 52.♖xf8+ ♔g7 53.♘d7 ♖d1 54.♖d8 a5 55.♘c5! winning) 52.♔g4 ♖h2 53.♔f5 the black king is in a mating net.

Why does the move 48...♗xh6 lead to defeat?

Now the rook and knight pair achieve miracles:

49.♘f6 ♗g7

The mate threat forces Black to part with the bishop, but he hopes to exploit the tangled position of the enemy pieces.

50.♖e8+ ♗f8 51.♘d7!

The hasty 51.♖xf8+ ♔g7 52.♘d7 ♖d5 53.♖d8 ♔f7 leads to a draw.

51...♔g7 52.♘xf8 ♔f7 53.♖d8!

The enemy king must be lured to e7. After 53.♖a8 ♖h5+ 54.♔g3 ♖h8 Black saves himself.

53...♔e7

On 53...♖h5+ 54.♔g3 ♖h8 the plan was 55.♘e6!.

54.♖a8 ♖g5

The threat of 54...♖g8 makes it seem as though the knight is trapped after all. However...

55.♘h7!

Now it turns out that the white knight is invulnerable (55...♖h5+ 56.♔g3 ♖xh7 57.♖a7+) and escapes! After a few moves, Black resigned.

In the following example, a ♖+♗ combination manage to dominate the whole board. It is noteworthy how the energetic endgame reached was a logical outcome from the middlegame.

Ruy Lopez

Alexander Kalinin
S. Tkachuk

Moscow 1987

1.e4 e5 2.♘f3 ♘c6 3.♗b5 a6 4.♗a4 ♘f6 5.0-0 ♗e7 6.♖e1 b5 7.♗b3

0-0 8.d3 d6 9.c3 ♘a5 10.♗c2 c5
11.♘bd2 ♖e8

More flexible is 11...♘c6, firstly
getting the offside knight back into
the game.

12.♘f1 ♗f8 13.♘e3 g6 14.h3

Preparing the manoeuvre
♘f3-h2-g4.

14...♗g7 15.♘h2 d5?!

Black wants to exploit the enemy
knight's departure from f3, but the
opening of lines favours White,
because the poor position of the
♘a5 starts to tell.

16.exd5 ♘xd5 17.♘xd5 ♕xd5 18.d4

A thematic central break. I was
familiar with the method of play
in similar positions from the game
Alekhine-Eliskases (Bad Podebrady
1936).

18...f5

On 18...♗b7 there could have
followed 19.♗e4 ♕d6 20.♗xb7
♘xb7 21.dxe5 ♖xe5 22.♗e3 ♖d5
23.♕f3 ♖ad8 24.♘g4 with pressure
for White.

19.dxe5

The alternative was 19.dxc5 ♕c6
20.♕d6 ♕xd6 21.cxd6 ♗e6,
winning a pawn, but allowing the
activation of the black pieces. The
text continuation seemed clearer to
me.

19...♕xd1 20.♗xd1 ♖xe5 21.♖xe5
♗xe5 22.♗e3

In an apparently simple position,
Black has trouble with the defence
of his queenside pawns.

22...♗d6

On 22...c4 there follows 23.a4!.

23.♗f3 ♗b7

How should White play?

24.♖d1! ♗xh2+ 25.♔xh2 ♗xf3 26.gxf3

After a forcing series of exchanges
we reach an endgame where White's
kingside pawns are broken. But this
latter factor is not currently of great
significance. The assessment of the
position depends on such factors as
the activity of the white rook, the
vulnerability of the black queenside
pawns and the misplaced ♘a5.

26...♘c4 27.♗c1 ♖e8 28.b3 ♘e5
29.f4 ♘f7 30.♗e3 c4?

Defensive chances could have been
retained by 30...♖c8 31.♖d7 ♖c6, not
letting the white bishop onto the
long diagonal.

31.bxc4 bxc4 32.♖d7 ♖c8 33.♖a7 ♖c6

Black has managed to defend his
queenside pawns, but now his king
falls into trouble.

34.♖a8+ ♔g7 35.♗d4+ ♔h6 36.♖a7 ♘d6 37.♗g7+ ♔h5 38.♗f8,

and Black resigned, since after 38...h6 39.♖h7 he is mated.

To conclude this chapter, here are two more studies which are dear to me.

Alexander Kalinin

1984

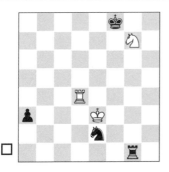

Draw!

1.♘e6+!

White loses after 1.♔xe2? a2 2.♖a4 ♔xg7 or 1.♖a4? ♔xg7 2.♔xe2 a2.

1...♔e7 2.♖a4

The same reply would follow after 1...♔f7.

2...♘c3

In the event of 2...♔xe6 the thematic variation works: 3.♖xa3! ♖g3+ 4.♔e4 ♖xa3 stalemate.

3.♖a7+!

Forcing Black to take the white knight. A mistake is 3.♖xa3? ♖g3+.

3...♔xe6

A draw results after 3...♔f6 4.♘d4 a2 5.♔d3 or 3...♔d6 4.♘d4 a2 5.♘b5+.

4.♖xa3 ♖g3+ 5.♔f4! ♘e2+ 6.♔e4 ♘c3+ 7.♔f4 ♘e2+ 8.♔e4 ♖xa3

Stalemate.

I showed my study to my friends at a gathering of the Moscow Pioneer Palace team and they solved it quickly, of course. I remember that our trainer, Abram Iosovich Khasin, said at the time that composing studies was 'risky', because one could find one's efforts anticipated. He added: 'That's why composers keep a card index of studies.' And, indeed, the stalemate mechanism in this study has been seen in many other studies. I knew this, but considered that my study still had the right to exist, because all of the pieces play and in the starting position, one would not dream of the possibility of stalemate. And, the main thing, this study is my only miniature in my 'amateur' study-composing career!

Alexander Kalinin

Bent-70 tourney 1989

Win!

1.♖h2

The point is that Black has two pieces hanging. White gets nowhere with 1.♗xg5 ♘e6 2.♗f6+ ♔g8 3.♘c8 ♖b8 4.♔xd7 ♔f7 etc.

1...♗xh5+!

The bishop sacrifice allows Black to create counterplay.

The variations 1...♘b3 2.♖xe2 ♖b2 3.♔f7 h6 4.♔g6 or 1...♖b8+ 2.♔e7 ♘e4 3.♖xe2 d5 4.♘c6 ♖b2 5.♖xe4 dxe4 6.♗xg5 lead to a win for White.

2.♖xh5 ♘e4

The double attack on d2 and f6 forces the white bishop to come to g5, where it will soon be pinned.

3.♗xg5

A draw results from 3.♖h2 ♖d1 4.♗e3 ♖e1=.

3...♖b7

The white knight must be driven from the guard of b5, but now it comes closer to the awkwardly-positioned black king.

4.♘c8

If 4.♗f4 ♖xa7 5.♗e5+ ♔g8 6.♖h4 ♘g5 7.♗f6 ♖a5 8.♔e7 d6! Black successfully defends.

4...♖b5

White to play. What should he do?

The introductory play has led to the key position of the study. The pin along the 5th rank is a death sentence for White's extra piece, but the constricted position of the black king allows a winning combination.

5.d5!

Opening the long diagonal to attack the black king.

5...♖xd5 6.♗c1! ♘f6+!

The black knight is prepared to sacrifice its life to defend his own king. An immediate mate follows after 6...♖xh5 7.♗b2+ ♔g8 8.♘e7#.

7.♔f8 ♖xh5 8.♗h6!

A bishop sacrifice to trap the black king in the corner. After 8...♖xh6 9.♘d6 Black's massive extra forces are helpless to prevent mate by a white knight from the f7-square.

8...♖g5!

Both sides show great willingness for self-sacrifices, in the battle over the life of the black king.

9.♗xg5 ♘g4

Now after 10.♘d6 h5 Black manages to free his king from the mating net.

10.♗h6!

A second, and this time decisive, blockading sacrifice by the bishop on h6.

10...♘xh6 11.♘d6

We have a position of reciprocal zugzwang! White's only surviving piece lands a deadly blow against the black king.

11...♘f5 12.♘f7#

I was especially pleased to discover that the well-known Soviet study composer Anatoly Kuznetsov included this study in his anthology *Brilliant Endgame Studies* published in 1998.

CHAPTER 5

Analytical exercises

'Independent thoughts arise only out of independently acquired knowledge.'
Konstantin Ushinsky

One of the best ways of realising the principles of active participation in training sessions is to develop in young players the habit of independent analytical work. Annotating their own games is an excellent way to develop this habit, starting from the attainment of third category level.

When dealing with groups of second category players, in giving homework, one can already start setting them the task of annotating master games, and then comparing their notes with those published by the masters themselves.

In this respect I was lucky – my father and my first trainer both independently of each other were devoted to the method of independent analysis as a tool of self-improvement. A conscientiously performed analysis helps to develop in the pupil independent thinking, objectivity, the ability to draw logical conclusions and to support them.

The following example discusses how the trainer can help to support the pupil's interest in analysis.

Vladimir Kalinin
Alexander Kalinin

Vatutinki 1977 (variation from game)

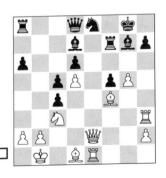

A training game between my father and myself could have reached this position. I, then a nine-year-old third category player, was Black and declined to take the white pawn on c4 (...b5xc4 – this move has already been made in the diagram), fearing the white rook sacrifice on h7. To defend h7, I chose the passive ...♗g7-f8 (instead of ...b5xc4) and later lost. But let us check the consequences of the rook sacrifice.

What happens after the rook sacrifice on h7? Support your answer with variations.

In my notes on the game, I gave the following variation: 1.♖xh7! ♚xh7 2.g6+ (a transposition results from 2.♕h5+) 2...♚g8 3.♕h5! (after 3.gxf7+ ♚xf7 Black's position is fully defensible) 3...♖e7 4.♕h7+ ♚f8 5.♗h6! ♖xe1 6.♗xg7+ ♘xg7 7.♕h8+ ♚e7 8.♕xg7+ ♚e8 9.♕f7#.
After checking this analysis, my trainer Alexander Nikolaevich Kostyev found a mistake:

'The attack is beaten off by 5...♘f6! (instead of 5...♖xe1) 6.♕h8+ ♘g8.' And he concluded: 'The game was played passively by Black, who was afraid of various empty threats from the opponent.'
After encouragement by my father, I explored the line further and found this resource: 5...♘f6 6.♕h8+ ♘g8 7.♘e4!!

7...♗xh6 (on 7...♕b6 or 7...♖b8 White decides with 8.♘f6!!) 8.♘f6 ♖g7 9.♘xg8 ♖xg8 10.♕xh6+ ♖g7 11.♕h8+ ♖g8 12.g7+ ♚f7 13.♗h5+ ♚f6 14.♕h6#
But even this variation was in need of correction. It turns out that the refutation of '7...♕b6 or 7...♖b8 by 8.♘f6!!' is far from indisputable. After 7...♖b8 8.♘f6

Black has a fantastic resource: 8...♖xb2+!! 9.♚xb2 ♖e2+!! 10.♖xe2 ♕xf6+, and it is the white king which is mated!
But even so, I did manage to correct the suggested combination:

The prophylactic move 8.♖e2! wins for White, as is underlined by the following variation: 8...♗xh6 9.♘f6 ♖g7 10.♘h7+! (after 10.♘xg8 ♖xg8 11.♕xh6+ ♖g7 Black defends)

10...☐xh7 11.gxh7 ☐f7 (11...♛g5
12.hxg8♛+ ♛xg8 13.♛xh6+
winning)

Now White gets an irresistible
attack after 12.hxg8♛+ ♛xg8
13.♛xh6. But even stronger is the
striking new blow 12.☐e8!! ♛xe8
13.☐h5+, which immediately ends
Black's resistance.

As modern fashion demands,
it only remains to add that this
analysis survives scrutiny by the
'silicon beast', although the latter
does correct the assessment of the
line 12.hxg8♛+ ♛xg8 13.♛xh6,
in which the reply 13...♛g1! allows
Black to defend successfully!
I would particularly emphasise the
method of 'corrections' used by
my trainer. He just pointed out the
errors to me, leaving me to analyse
the position further on my own. I
should add that it was the creative
discussion of this combination
which stimulated in me a taste for
analytical work.

In my time as a youngster, I gained
invaluable benefit from analysing
adjourned positions. Such analysis
is usually performed to a high
standard, without the player
needing any special incentive –
after all, the result of the game
depends on it! The majority of
adjourned positions are endgames.
This allows one in a natural way
to increase one's knowledge of the
final stage of the game, and forces
one to consult endgame manuals.
Uncovering the secrets of the
following position remains to this
day a particularly striking memory
for me.

Alexander Kalinin
V. Borisov
Moscow 1979

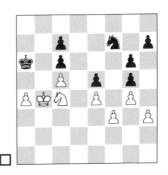

**Does White have any ideas which
might allow him to play for a win?**

The game was adjourned in this
position. Black's broken pawn
structure and the outside passed
pawn on the a-file give White
a clear positional advantage.
However, the position is so blocked
that it is far from clear that White
can break down his opponent's
defences. On 1.♞a5 there follows
1...♞d8. Playing for zugzwang does

not work either, because if it were Black's move, and even assuming he has not got any reserve moves with the h7-pawn, he can just play 1...♚a7 (1...♚b7? 2.♘a5+) and only after 2.♚a5 – 2...♚b7. To me, it was perfectly obvious that the position was drawn, but my father told me that there was still scope to dig down more deeply into the position.

The result of his first researches was the following plan:

1.♚c3 ♚a7 2.♚d3

The white king is heading for g3, to support the advance h3-h4.

2...♚a6 3.♚e3

A) 3...♚a7

Black marks time for the moment.

4.♚f2 ♚a6 5.♚g2! ♚a7 6.♚g3 ♚a6 7.h4

As will become evident from what follows, it is important for White to play h3-h4 at the moment when the black king is on a6. This circumstance explains the white king's triangulation on moves 5 and 6.

7...gxh4+

If 7...h6 8.h5 gxh5 9.gxh5 the white king gets through to the f5-square.

8.♚xh4

Threatening 9.g5, 10.♚g4 and 11.f4.

8...h6

With 8...g5+ 9.♚h5 we reach a position of reciprocal zugzwang, and after 9...♚a7 9.♘a5 Black cannot defend the weaknesses on both flanks.

9.g5! h5

After 9...hxg5+ 10.♚g4 we again have a reciprocal zugzwang and White wins.

10.♚g3

Over the next few moves, White rearranges his forces so they support the advance f3-f4 as effectively as possible. In this case, the fact that Black has a protected passed pawn on the h-file does not play a significant role.

10...♚a7 11.♘a5 ♘d8 12.♚h3 ♚a6 13.♘c4 ♘f7 14.♚h4

This new triangulation drives the black king away from the a4-pawn, in readiness for the transfer of the knight to d3.

14...♚a7 15.♘b2 ♚a6 16.♘d3 ♚a5

17.f4

The decisive break.

17...exf4 18.e5 ♘d8 19.♘xf4 ♚xa4 20.e6 ♘xe6 21.♘xe6

and White wins.

For a while this variation interested me, but once it became clear that by playing ...h7-h5-h4 at a suitable moment, Black could extend the 'no entry' zone on the kingside, I completely lost interest in taking the analysis any further. My father's attempts to interest me in new ideas came to nothing. With the assurance characteristic of a weak player, I declared that there was nothing further to be found in the position and that any further efforts would be a waste of time. My father continued his researches alone and after several days of silence, he handed me an exercise book, with analysis of the second line of defence for Black...

B) 3...h5 4.♔f2

4...h4

If 4...hxg4 5.fxg4 ♔a7 6.♔g3 ♔a6 7.h4 gxh4+ (otherwise 8.h5) 8.♔xh4 ♔a7 9.♘a5 ♘d8 10.♔g5 ♔a6 11.♘b3 White achieves a decisive breakthrough into the enemy position.

After the text move, the kingside is completely blocked and the white king now heads back to the other side of the board.

5.♔e2 ♔a7 6.♔d3 ♔a6 7.♔c3 ♔a7 8.♔b4 ♔a6 9.♘b2 ♘d8 10.♘d3 ♘f7 **11.a5**

Now White pushes his opponent back as far as possible on the queenside.

11...♔a7 12.♔a4 ♔b7 13.♘b4 ♘d8 14.a6+ ♔a7 15.♔a5 ♔b8 16.♘d3 ♘f7 17.♘b2 ♘d8 18.♘c4 ♘f7

All preparations are complete and White effects a breakthrough into the enemy camp via the b6-square.

19.♘b6!! ♔a7

The knight cannot be taken, because after 19...cxb6+ 20.♔xb6 ♘d8 21.a7+ ♔a8 22.♔c7 ♘b7 23.♔xc6 ♔xa7 24.♔d5 ♔b8 25.♔xe5 ♘xc5 26.♔f6 White should win.

20.♘c8+ ♔a8 21.♘e7 ♘d8 22.♘xg6

White has spent 19 moves in 'monetising' the weakness in Black's pawn structure created by the move 3...h5.

22...♘f7 23.♘f8 ♘d8 24.♘d7 ♘f7 25.♘b6+!

The white knight calmly returns to its own camp, again using the 'forbidden' b6-square.

25...♔a7 26.♘c4 ♔a8 27.♘b2 ♘d8 28.♘d3 ♘f7 29.♔a4 ♔a7 30.♘b4 ♘d8 31.♔b3 ♔a8 32.♔c3 ♔a7

33.♔c4 ♔a8 34.♘d3 ♘f7 35.♘e1 ♔a7

36.f4!

After long and painstaking preparatory work on both flanks, White finally achieves the decisive breakthrough!

36...exf4

Or 36...gxf4 37.♘f3 ♔xa6 38.g5 winning.

37.♘f3 ♔xa6 38.e5

And White wins.

This analysis, a product of imagination, determination and total belief in the inexhaustible richness of chess, simply amazed me! I was staggered by the beauty and depth of these analytical researches, and also rather ashamed of my confident declarations about the dead drawn nature of the adjourned position. This was a very good lesson for me. I became convinced that truth in chess rarely lay on the surface and that a great deal of work is required to unearth it.

Almost 30 years later, after checking the analysis with a computer, I realised that White

is not winning by force, after all. Black should accept the first knight sacrifice on b6. As you will recall, the original analysis dismissed this with the claim that the knight could not be taken on account of the variation 19...cxb6+ 20.♔xb6 ♘d8 21.a7+ ♔a8 22.♔c7 ♘b7 23.♔xc6 ♔xa7 24.♔d5 ♔b8 25.♔xe5 ♘xc5 26.♔f6 'and White should win'.

It seems that after the fall of the black pawns on g6, g5 and h4, the armada of white foot-soldiers should easily cope with the black knight. However, if we continue the variation: 26...♔c7 27.♔xg5 ♔d6 28.♔xg6 ♔e5 29.♔g5 ♘e6+ 30.♔xh4 ♔f4 31.♔h5 ♔xf3 32.g5 ♔xe4 33.♔g4 ♘f4 34.h4 ♘g6 35.h5 ♘e5+ 36.♔h4 ♔f5, and the white passed pawns are neutralised!

Incidentally, this correction in no way detracts from the value of White's idea, which reveals the depth of possibilities hidden in the position. In any event, Black would face serious practical problems. In fact, after the resumption, my opponent followed the path of least resistance, refraining from the advance ...h7-h5-h4, which significantly simplified White's task.

Thorough analysis of adjourned positions not only earned me points in the tournament table, but also, much more importantly, helped me to develop a positional feel for the endgame. The ideas found in the knight endgame with Borisov helped me eleven years later, in the following game.

Alexander Kalinin
A. Deitch

Moscow 1990

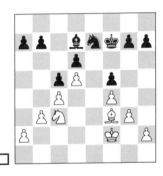

White's position is preferable because of his extra space. However, it is far from clear how he can exploit it, as the position is quite closed and it is not obvious how White's limited forces can achieve a breakthrough. In addition, Black's position does not contain many weaknesses and even his one vulnerable point on d6 is hard to get at. Even so, I decided not to be in a hurry to agree a draw and first set about strengthening my position to the maximum degree.

32.h3 g6 33.g4 h6 34.g5 h5

The pawns on d5 and g5 significantly limit the activity of the enemy knight. In the ending, White also has the 'spare' tempo move h3-h4. But it is still not clear how he can break into Black's more cramped position.

35.a3

White now has the plan of advancing b3-b4 followed by the manoeuvre ♗f3-d1-a4.

35...♔e8 36.♗d1 ♔d8 37.♔e3 ♔c7 38.b4 ♗e8 39.♗a4 ♗xa4 40.♘xa4 b6

The exchange of light-squared bishops has opened a bit of air on the queenside. The white knight can now bother the d6-pawn from the square b5, whilst the white king has the possibility of entering the queenside via b3-a4-b5, although Black can cover b5 with the move ...a7-a6.

In this position, the game was adjourned. I did not know if I had real winning chances, but remembering the previous example, I decided to subject the position to close analysis during the adjournment.

Does White have a plan to play for a win?

In home analysis, and having experience of such positions, I fairly quickly established that Black's position is in fact very difficult. White's winning plan consists of the following stages:

A) Placing the white pieces in their ideal positions for the preparation of the advance a3-a4-a5 (the king goes to c3 and the knight to b3):

41.♘c3 ♘c8 42.♔d3 ♔b7 43.♔c2 ♘e7 44.♔b3 ♘c8 45.♘e2 ♘e7 46.♔c3 ♘c8 47.♘c1 ♘e7 48.♘b3 ♔a6

B) Advancing the pawn from a3 to a5, followed by the exchange a5xb6 – a7xb6, which clears some space for penetration on the queenside and also weakens the b5-square:

49.a4 ♘c8 50.a5 ♘e7 51.axb6 axb6

C) A new regrouping of the white pieces, with the aim of threatening to bring the knight to b5, and thus forcing the enemy knight to take up a defensive post on a7:

52.♘d2 ♘c8 53.♔b3 ♘e7 54.♘b1 ♘c8 55.♘c3 ♘a7

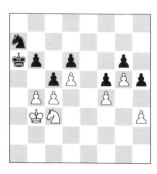

D) By exploiting zugzwang, to break through to a5 with the king:

56.♔a4

The b6-pawn deprives its own king of the valuable 'corresponding square' and forces Black to concede space on the queenside. If it were White's move here, he would place the opponent in zugzwang by a triangulation manoeuvre via a4-b3-a3-a4. In this case, it becomes clear that another corresponding square is blocked by the knight on a7!

56...♔b7 57.bxc5 bxc5 58.♔a5

58.♘b5 ♘xb5 59.♔xb5 h4 with a draw, would be premature.

58...♘c8 59.♘b5

The latest zugzwang forces Black to permit the enemy king onto the sixth rank.

59...♔a8 60.♔a6 ♔b8

61.h4

Only now does White use up his extra reserve tempo move. Yet another zugzwang forces Black to allow the enemy king right into his camp.
61...♚a8 62.♘c7+ ♚b8 63.♘e6 ♚a8 64.♘f8 ♞e7

The need to defend the g6-pawn means that Black has to remove his guard of b6.
65.♚b6 ♚b8
Black holds his final line of defence. Now a further regrouping follows, which sees the white king reach c6, after which the d6-pawn falls.
66.♘e6 ♚c8 67.♘c7 ♚d7
Or 67...♚b8 68.♘b5 ♞c8+ 69.♚c6 winning.
68.♚b7 ♚d8 69.♘a6
And Black resigned, because he has no defence against the manoeuvre ♘a6-b8-c6, leading to a winning king and pawn ending for White.

I played this game during my student years. Analysing it with teammates and the leader of the chess section, Boris Zlotnik, the latter pointed out that White's biggest achievement was in having the confidence to play the position for a win. As the reader will have seen, this confidence was in large measure the result of acquired knowledge.

Adjourned positions can also help in teaching one to analyse not only endgame positions, but also middlegame ones too. I especially remember the following analysis, which was fully realised on resumption:

N. Katkova
Alexander Kalinin

Moscow 1978

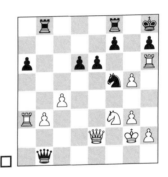

In this sharp position, White sealed his 41st move. Black's chances look superior, mainly thanks to the disunited white rooks. In addition, if the black major pieces manage to break through on the b-file, then the white king will start to feel very uncomfortable, as it lacks pawn protection along the second rank. Retreating the rook to h5 or h3 now looks illogical and so I concentrated my attention on the move
41.♖f6
From here, the rook threatens a possible exchange sacrifice on f5

and also ties Black's rook to the defence of f7.

41...♕c1

The continuation 41...♖xb3 42.♘d2 ♖b2 43.♖d3 did not strike me as very convincing. Black wins a pawn, but White significantly improves his position, bringing his queen's rook into the game, whilst Black's king's rook still plays a very passive role.

After the move in the game, the analysis took two directions:

A) 42.♖xa6 ♖xb3 43.♖a2

Preparing to meet 43...♖e3 with 44.♕b2.

43...♖fb8 44.♔h3 ♖b2

44...♖e3 45.♕f2 ♕xc4 does not achieve the aim because of 46.♖xf7.

45.♖xb2 ♖xb2 46.♕d3 ♔g8!

A quiet move, defending the f7-pawn. Now the ♖f6 turns out to be out of play and White finds it hard to neutralise the pressure from the opponent's greater forces. Furthermore, White is practically in zugzwang, e.g. 47.g4 ♖b3! 48.♕e2 (48.♕xb3 ♕f1#) 48...♕f4 or 47.♘h4 ♕xg5, winning for Black. Meanwhile, after 47.♔g4 ♖c2

followed by ...♖xc4 Black obtains a material and positional advantage.

47.♖xf5

White gives up his passive rook for the knight, in the hope of creating threats against the black king.

47...exf5 48.♕xd6

With the intention of giving perpetual check, but Black is the first to land a decisive blow.

48...♕f1+ 49.♔h4 ♕xc4+ 50.♔h5 ♕g4+ 51.♔h6

51...♖xh2+! 52.♘xh2 ♕h3#

I was very proud of the fact that, from a multi-piece initial position, I had managed to analyse all the way to a study-like finish.

B) 42.♕a2

This move was played in the game.

42...♘e3+ 43.♔h3

In the event of 43.♔f2 Black wins with both 43...♘xc4 and 43...♘g4+.

43...♕f1+ 44.♔h4 ♘f5+ 45.♔g4

Events develop by force. Nor is White helped by 45.♖xf5 exf5 46.♕a1+ ♕xa1 47.♖xa1 ♖xb3 48.♘d4 ♖b2 49.♘xf5 ♖xh2+ 50.♔g4 ♖a8 51.♘xd6 a5 with a winning endgame, although this was the most tenacious continuation.

Black to move. What would you play?

Three pawn blows, one after another, bring Black victory:

45...h5+! 46.♔f4

Or 46.gxh6 ♖g8+ 47.♔f4 e5+ 48.♔e4 ♖g4+ 49.♔d5 ♕xf3#.

46...e5+! 47.♔e4 d5+! 48.cxd5

Mate results from 48.♔xf5 ♕xf3+ 49.♔xe5 ♖fe8+.

48...♖b4+ 49.♔xe5 ♖e8+

Mating.

I would add that the whole of this variation occurred on resumption. The enjoyable work of teasing out the secrets of an adjourned position has now disappeared, of course, with the abolition of adjournments. Nowadays the main method of developing a master's analytical skill is the study of one's own games. It is helpful for young players to develop as early as possible a taste for annotating games. For me, for example, my father specially prepared master games, with questions. Answering these helped to establish the structure of the commentary,

and helped me identify the key moments of the game and to unite concrete variations with general considerations.

At first, my attention was directed to games with simple content, which allowed me to give true answers to the questions posed. I remember the first game of this type was Smyslov-Rudakovsky (Moscow 1945). The fact that my assessments coincided with the annotations by Smyslov himself naturally served as a stimulus for further analytical work.

My first trainer Alexander Kostyev also used such an approach. I remember at the first session of third category players he led, we analysed the game Capablanca-Janowski (St Petersburg 1914), a game noteworthy for the crystal clarity of its ideas.

The art of annotating games is one most of my generation learned from the books of Alekhine, considered the finest analyst of his day. In his annotations, the fourth World Champion precisely combined assessments of the position with concrete calculation. It is not surprising that, in my first attempts at analysing games, I tried to adopt the manner of the great Russian champion. Turning the pages of my school exercise books, in which I wrote out my homework assignments from the Smyslov chess school, I wish to pay particular attention to the analysis of two games – one win and one loss. Incidentally, this pattern of results was an obligatory condition of homework at the school and allowed our trainers to see the pupils' strong and weak points. First I will reproduce without amendments the analysis of those two games and then I will draw the reader's attention to one very important moment.

Ruy Lopez
Alexander Kalinin
V. Baban

Vilnius 1980

1.e4 e5 2.♘f3 ♘c6 3.♗b5 a6 4.♗a4 ♘f6 5.0-0 ♗e7 6.♖e1 b5 7.♗b3 d6 8.c3 0-0 9.h3 ♘d7

The aim of this move is to strengthen control of e5 by means of ♗f6. The idea (in similar form) was first seen in the third game of the Tarrasch-Chigorin match in 1893.

10.d4 ♗f6

The move 10...♘b6 makes the advance a2-a4 more difficult, but allows the manoeuvre ♘b1-d2-f1.

11.a4 ♗b7 12.axb5 axb5 13.♖xa8

13...♕xa8

A nice tactical blow occurred in the game Boleslavsky-Smyslov (Moscow 1950): 13...♗xa8 14.d5 ♘e7 15.♘a3 ♕b8 16.♘xb5!, and White won a pawn.

14.♘a3

This direct move should not bring White any special dividends. Theory prefers the variation 14.d5 ♘a5 15.♗c2, hoping in the subsequent battle to exploit the advanced position of the b5-pawn.

14...♘a7?

An unnatural move – in defending the pawn, the knight moves to a passive position.

By continuing 14...b4 15.♘c4 bxc3 16.bxc3 ♘a5! (during the game I missed this knight jump), Black avoids pawn weaknesses on the queenside, exchanging the active knight on c4 and equalising the game (Matulovic-Gligoric, Titograd 1965).

15.♕d3

15...b4?!

By exploiting the undefended ♘d7, White was threatening to win the b5-pawn. Defending it by 15...♗a6 deprives the bishop of its activity whilst after 15...♖d8 Black must reckon with 16.♘g5. Black also still has problems after 15...♘b6 16.d5. By his temporary pawn sacrifice, Black tries to change the course of events, but the subsequent active operations do not fit in with the passive knight on a7.

16.cxb4 exd4 17.♘xd4 c5 18.♘f5 cxb4 19.♘c4 ♘c5 20.♕g3

The advance ...b5-b4 and opening of the centre has allowed the white knights to take up splendid secure outposts on c4 and f5. The strong position of his pieces, coupled with the absence of most black pieces from the kingside, allows White to start a direct attack on the king.

20...♘xe4

Black has no time to eliminate the Spanish bishop with 20...♘xb3, because after 21.♘xg7 ♘xc1 (or 21...♔h8 22.♘h5 ♕d8 23.♕xb3) 22.♘h5+ ♔h8 23.♘xf6 he has no satisfactory defence against the move 24.♕h4 with an unstoppable mate.

21.♕g4 d5

Nor is 21...♔h8 (defending against 22.♘xg7) any better, as there follows 22.f3 ♘c5 23.♗g5 ♕d8 (or 23...♗xg5 24.♕xg5 ♖g8 25.♘cxd6 ♗d5 26.♗xd5 ♕xd5 27.♘h6 ♕d4+

28.♔h1; 23...♖g8 24.♘cxd6 ♗d5 25.♗xd5 ♕xd5 26.♗xf6 gxf6 27.♕xg8+ ♔xg8 28.♖e8#) 24.♖e7 ♖g8 25.♘cxd6 mating.

And if Black plays 22...d5 (instead of 22...♘c5), then the win is achieved by 23.fxe4 dxc4 24.e5! ♕e8 (or 24...♖e8 25.exf6 ♖xe1+ 26.♔f2 g6 27.♗h6) 25.♗g5 ♗xe5 26.♗f6, and White wins.

White to move. Calculate the consequences of 22.♘b6.

22.♘b6

The simplest continuation of the attack. By exploiting the poor position of the black pieces, White obtains a material advantage.

22...♕d8 23.♘d7 ♔h8

Obviously, after 23...♕xd7 or 23...♖e8 there follows 24.♘h6+, but the intermediate move 23...h7-h5 had to be anticipated by White. In this case, the following variations could arise: 23...h5 24.♘h6+

A) 24...♔h8 25.♘xf8! ♕xf8 (a transposition results from 25...gxh6 26.♕xh5 ♕xf8) 26.♕xh5 gxh6 (or 26...g6 27.♘xf7+ ♔g7 28.♕h6+ ♔xf7 29.♖xe4±) 27.♗xh6 ♗g7 (27...♕a8 28.♖xe4±) 28.♗e3+ ♔g8 29.♗xa7 winning (I remember that I was extremely pleased to find this variation at the board – it seemed to me that I was seeing 'everything');

B) 24...♔h7 25.♕xh5 ♕xd7 (or 25...g6 26.♘xf8+ ♕xf8 27.♕f3±; 25...gxh6 26.♕xh6+ ♔g8 27.♖xe4±)

Analysis diagram

26.♖xe4! (the computer shows an even more effective way to win: 26.♘g4+! ♔g8 27.♖xe4 dxe4 28.♘xf6+ gxf6 29.♗h6!, and Black has no defence against the mating threat 30.♕g6+) 26...g6 (26...dxe4 27.♘xf7+ ♔g8 28.♕h8#) 27.♘g4+! gxh5 28.♘xf6+ ♔g7 29.♘xd7 dxe4 30.♘xf8 ♔xf8 31.♗d1 h4 32.♗g5 – White has a winning endgame.
24.♘xf8 ♕xf8 25.♗e3
White has won the exchange for a pawn, keeping his active pieces, and in addition, Black starts to suffer from the weakness of his back rank.
25...♘b5 26.f3 d4 27.♗f4 ♘c5 28.♗d6 ♘xd6 29.♘xd6 ♗c6 30.♘xf7+
The fall of f7 proves deadly for the black king. There followed:
30...♔g8 31.♘h6+ ♔h8 32.♘f7+ ♔g8 33.♗c4 ♗a4 34.♘h6+ ♔h8 35.♘f7+ ♔g8 36.♕h5 1-0

In the following encounter, my opponent was the first-category player from Odessa, Mikhail Golubev, who later became a well-known grandmaster. Even in his youth, Mikhail was distinguished by his aggressive attacking style.

Sicilian Defence
Mikhail Golubev
Alexander Kalinin
Yaroslavl 1983

1.e4 c5 2.♘f3 e6 3.♘c3 a6 4.d4 cxd4 5.♘xd4 ♕c7
My opponent's favourite weapon against the Sicilian was the Sozin Attack, based on the move ♗c4. The move-order chosen by Black allows him to avoid this set-up.
6.♗e2 d6 7.0-0 ♘f6

8.♗e3
All the while the black knight has not come out to c6, White should refrain from ♗e3, which makes it harder to defend the e4-pawn (for example with ♗f3 and ♕e2), in the event of Black playing ...♘bd7-c5. Consequently, a more flexible move was 8.f4.
8...♗e7 9.f4 0-0 10.♕e1

Faced with a wide choice of continuations (10.g4, 10.a4, 10.♔h1), White opts for the queen transfer to the kingside. From g3, the queen supports the advance f4-f5 and exerts pressure against the enemy castled king.

10...b5 11.♗f3 ♗b7 12.a3

White plays in an unhurried manner, allowing Black to play his pieces comfortably. A more principled continuation was 12.e5 dxe5 13.fxe5 ♘fd7 14.♕g3 ♔h8 with a tense struggle.

12...♘bd7 13.♖d1 ♖ac8 14.♔h1 ♘b6

Black is developing activity, planning to transfer the knight to c4, with the further thematic threat to take on a3.

15.♗c1 ♖fd8 16.♕g3 ♘c4 17.b3

A tempting sacrifice of the a3-pawn, with the idea of quickly bringing the bishop to a strong attacking diagonal. Thus, after 17...♘xa3 18.♗b2 b4 19.♘d5! exd5 20.♘f5 g6 21.exd5 White obtains a strong attack. However, this idea runs into a refutation, although other continuations, such as 17.♖d3 d5 or 17.f5 e5 18.♘de2 ♔h8, leave Black with the initiative.

17...♘a5?

Missing the chance to secure a significant advantage by means of 17...♘e3! 18.♗xe3 ♕xc3 when the weakness of the e4-pawn would deprive White's set-up of all attacking potential. After the text move, the initiative passes to White.

18.♗b2 ♘c6 19.♘f5! g6

It is clear that the ♘f5 cannot be taken because of 20.♘d5.

20.♘xe7+ ♕xe7 21.e5 ♘e8 22.exd6 ♘xd6

Forced, to prevent the white knight coming to e4.

23.♖xd6!

This exchange sacrifice ensures White the transit square for his knight.

23...♖xd6 24.♘e4 ♖d4

The return of the material is practically forced and allows Black to neutralise his opponent's threats on the long diagonal.

25.♘g5 ♖cd8 26.♗xd4 ♖xd4

Worse is 26...♘xd4 on account of 27.♗xb7 ♕xb7 28.♘xh7 ♔xh7 29.♕h4+ ♔g7 30.♕xd8.

27.♖e1

27...h6?

In time-trouble, I decided to kick the white knight away from its attacking position, but I missed a tactical blow. I should have played 27...♘d8, when Black's chances are already slightly preferable.

28.♘xe6! fxe6 29.♕xg6+ ♕g7
30.♕e8+ ♕f8 31.♕xe6+

Of course, not 31.♗xc6 because of 31...♕xe8 32.♗xe8 ♖d2.

31...♕f7 32.♕xh6

White has four pawns for the piece and an unstoppable attack. The exposed position of Black's king means he has no chance of surviving.

32...♘d8

Or 32...♖xf4 33.♗d5 ♕xd5 34.♕g6+ mating.

33.♕g5+ ♔h8 34.♕e5+ ♕g7
35.♕h5+ 1-0

Let us now compare the level of annotation of these two games. The first game is well annotated. Here we have the key moments identified and objectively assessed, and concrete variations are harmoniously combined with general considerations, as well as being quite deep. But the notes to the second game are very weak! It may seem as though Black has pointed out his mistakes (on moves 17 and 21) and suggested improvements, but let me draw your attention to the following:

1) In commenting on the move 17...♘a5?, I wrote that the initiative passes to White. White's next few moves twice attract exclamation marks (moves 19 and 23), but in the notes to 27...h6? it is claimed that with correct play, Black could have obtained a small advantage! Where is the logic in this?

2) The analysis of the position after the capture of the a3-pawn (17...♘xa3) is very superficial. The assessment of the variation 'after 17...♘xa3 18.♗b2 b4 19.♘d5! exd5 20.♘f5 g6 21.exd5 White obtains a strong attack' is based on a purely outward appearance. Analysis is not like an over the board game, and should involve the maximum possible penetration into the critical position. In reality, after 21...♖e8 or 21...♘c2, White has nothing!

3) No attempt has been made to find the strongest continuations for the opponent. Take the position after Black's 18th move:

After **19.♘f5 g6** instead of the game move 20.♘xe7+? White can win with the simple 20.♘d5! exd5 21.exd5.

It was also possible to invert the move-order – 19.♘d5! exd5 20.♘f5 g6 21.exd5±.

OK, let us go further on:

**20.♘xe7+? ♛xe7 21.e5 ♘e8
22.exd6**

Why bring the ♘e8 into play? The
simple 22.♘e4 ensures White a clear
advantage.

22...♘xd6

23.♖xd6

And here too 23.♘e4 ♘xe4 24.♗xe4
retains an advantage for White,
thanks to the strong bishop on b2.

**23...♖xd6 24.♘e4 ♖d4 25.♘g5 ♖cd8
26.♗xd4 ♖xd4 27.♖e1,**

and now the comment 'he should
have played **27...♘d8**, and Black's
chances are even somewhat
preferable' does not survive scrutiny
in the spirit of the position. White is
not even a fraction worse with quiet
play, nor with the energetic **28.♗xb7
♘xb7 29.f5!**. Mutual satisfaction for
both sides follows after the computer
variation **29...♖d5 30.fxe6 ♛xg5
31.exf7+ ♚f8 32.♛c3 ♘d6 33.♛h8+
♚xf7 34.♛xh7+** with perpetual check.

 4) In identifying my errors at
moves 17 and 27, I did not draw any
general conclusions or think about
the weaknesses in my thinking that
gave rise to those mistakes. The
note to 27...h6? is typical – 'Being in
time-trouble, I decided to kick the
knight from its attacking position,
but missed a tactical blow.' A typical
case – without any attempt to delve
into the real, underlying reason
for the mistake, we just blame
everything on time-trouble!
One immediately recalls Alekhine's
famous comment on his game
with Winter at the Nottingham
tournament of 1936: 'The fact that
White was in time-trouble, in my
opinion, can no more be considered
as an excuse than, for example, a
criminal's claim that he was drunk at
the time of the offence. The inability
of an experienced master to cope
with the clock should be considered
as serious as an error in calculation.'
In reality, the move 27...h6? was the
result of a weakness which followed
me around for many years, namely
a tendency to lose my equanimity
when there were threats against
my king. As for falling into time-
trouble, this is already a second
mistake, the causes of which should
have been addressed.

We see that Black played the game
poorly, but by a thorough and
conscientious analysis of it, he could
have drawn some valuable lessons. It
would have become clear to me that
I calculated variations badly, trying
as soon as possible to get away from
concrete calculation and replace it
with general, outward impressions of
the position, whilst my imagination
was lacking and I tended only to
see stereotyped moves (the jump
17...♘e3 did not even enter my head
– my opponent pointed it out after

the game). By making an objective diagnosis, I could have concentrated on battling my weaknesses...
Unfortunately, the difference in quality between my annotations of the game I won and the game I lost shows that I did not like to return to my defeats and put them under the microscope.

It is important to learn to uncover one's mistakes, not only in lost games but even in games one has won. Very often, the favourable result of the game stops the player being objective about his own play. I will tell you about an example, which served as an object lesson for me.

The following simple combination occurred in a team match between the schoolboys of Moscow and Leningrad.

Alexander Kalinin
A. Sidorov

Leningrad 1982

What should White do?

All of the white pieces are pointing at the black king, which means that

we are justified in looking for a tactical solution.

23.♕e5+
Taking the f7-pawn would allow Black to wriggle out: 23.♗xf7 ♗d6 24.♕g4 ♖xe4, and White should force perpetual check: 25.♖xh7+ ♔xh7 26.♕xg6+ ♔h8 27.♕h5+ ♔g7 28.♕g6+.
23...f6
Other continuations also fail to save Black: 23...♔g8 24.♗xf7+ ♔xf7 25.♖xh7+ mating; 23...♘g7 24.♗xf7 ♗d6 25.♘g5! (25.♘f6? ♕xf6) 25...h5 26.♗xe8 ♗xe5 27.♘f7+, and White wins.
24.♘g5! h5 25.♕xf5! gxf5 26.♖xh5+ ♔g7 27.♘e6+ 1-0

Delighted with my combination, I believed the whole game was a great creative achievement and 'analysed' it to the final combination. The earlier moves were as follows
1.e4 e5 2.♘f3 ♘c6 3.♗b5 a6 4.♗a4 ♘f6 5.0-0 ♗e7 6.♖e1 b5 7.♗b3 0-0
Strange as it may seem, at the time of this game, almost everyone played 7...d6.
8.a4
The only thing I knew then about avoiding the Marshall was that I had heard of the possibility of the move a2-a4.
8...♗b7 9.c3 d5
What is that? – I thought. Why is Black again playing the Marshall?
10.exd5 ♘xd5 11.axb5 axb5 12.♖xa8
'Excellent! Now I exchange rooks, which was probably the point of the move a2-a4.'
12...♗xa8 13.♘xe5 ♘xe5 14.♖xe5 ♘f4

Chapter 5 – Analytical exercises

I remember this jump coming as an unpleasant surprise for me.
15.d4 ♘xg2 16.♕g4 ♘h4 17.♘d2 ♗f6 18.♖e3 ♔h8 19.♘e4 ♗e7 20.♖g3 g6 21.♕f4 ♘f5 22.♖h3 ♖e8 and we reached the position of the diagram on the previous page.

After the game, despite the whole caricature of my opening considerations, I did not look this variation up in theoretical sources, nor did I objectively assess the position arising. Soon, I confidently repeated the whole variation for 17 moves, in the following game:

Alexander Kalinin
Semyon Skorodelov

Moscow 1982

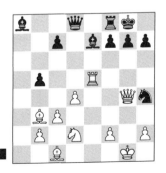

Black was Semyon Skorodelov, my great friend, with whom I had studied at the same chess section and the Smyslov chess school, and played with on the Moscow youth team. Semya had a good positional understanding, but was too peace-loving. It goes without saying that the great majority of games between us ended in draws, even though there was no pre-agreement – at a certain moment, it seemed to me, neither of us wanted to upset the other!

In the diagram position, Semyon sunk into a long think. The longer I waited for his move, the less I liked the white position. After 20 minutes, there came the subtle move

17...♔h8!

and at the same moment, I understood that there would not be a draw between us this time... White cannot stop the deadly advance of the f-pawn! A short agony followed:

18.♗c2 g6 19.f4 f5 20.♕g3 ♗d6 21.♖xb5 g5 22.♘c4 gxf4 23.♕f2 ♖g8+ 24.♔f1 ♖g2

And I stopped the clocks. A drastic, but also fully deserved crush!

Today, it is obvious to me that an insufficiently critical approach to my own play was the main thing that stopped my self-improvement, but at the time, this simple truth never entered my head.

89

CHAPTER 6

The classical heritage

'In general, it is useful for a chess player to have a good memory, because often he will not need to find the best move himself, but can choose something from the store in his memory. But every memory has its limit.' – Viktor Kortchnoi

Studying the play of masters is an indispensable component of improvement. But whilst the play of contemporary grandmasters is a living thing in which young players have considerable interest, the games of the kings of past generations are something with which the majority of young players have a fairly lukewarm relationship. Thirty or so years ago, when I was growing up, children, when ignoring the classics, often justified this by claiming that the older generations of masters did not play as well as modern GMs and the opening variations met with in their games were hopelessly old-fashioned.

In this regard, I remember a speech by Tigran Petrosian, at the jubilee evening of the Polytechnics Museum in 1979. By tradition, the master finished his appearance by taking questions, and my father asked the ex-World Champion: 'How should a young player perfect his strategic mastery?' The ninth World Champion's answer was highly instructive and has subsequently been quoted in many different sources. Tigran Vartanovich recommended studying the classical heritage of the great players, precisely because there was a considerable gulf in class between them and their opponents. Imagine, for example, that Alekhine is playing Tartakower. Alekhine comes up with a strategic plan and is able to carry it out to the letter, as Tartakower does not sense the danger and fails to prevent his opponent's ideas. Thanks to this, the entire plan is laid out like a model before the reader. On the other hand, in games of the modern-day top players, it is much harder to follow a clear plan in pure form, as their opponents know very well what is threatened (thanks to having seen the classical games!) and take steps to prevent the opponent's ideas.

Studying the classics can happen in two forms. Firstly, by playing through the game and the accompanying annotations, we can try to find our own improvements on the play and notes. In this way, we improve our analytical abilities. With this aim, it is useful to work in the manner of Nimzowitsch, playing one side in the game and trying to guess the player's moves. Secondly, we can take into our arsenal surprising strategic ideas

90

and plans, many of which have become typical in our day. In this way, we enrich our understanding of the game and enlarge our baggage of typical ideas.

I will offer a couple of simple, but memorable fragments, in which I managed to find corrections to the conclusions of annotators.

Isaak Boleslavsky
Vladimir Makogonov

Moscow ch-URS 1940 (14)

In time-trouble, the game ended quickly:
34...gxh5? 35.♗h6+! ♔g6 36.gxh5+!
And Black resigned.

In his book *Grandmaster Boleslavsky*, Alexey Suetin wrote:
'There is only one correct defence. Thus, it seems that 34...♖f8 was simple and natural, but then there follows the combinative blow 35.♖xe5! fxe5 36.h6+! winning. Also insufficient is 34...g5? 35.h6+ ♔g6 36.♕h3!. Only by playing 34...♕e7 can Black retain a sufficiently solid position.'

What happens after 34...♕e7 ?

The move 34...♕e7 is refuted with the help of a simple combination: 35.hxg6 hxg6 (or 35...♔xg6 36.♖h1

♖h8 37.♗h6) 36.♗h6+! ♔xh6 37.♖h1+ ♔g7 38.♕h3 ♘f7 39.♕h7+ ♔f8 40.♕xg6 (with the threat of 41.♖h8+! ♘xh8 42.♕g8#) 40...♕d7 41.♖h7, and White wins.

I was proud of this discovery and, in my youthful way, jumped to a categorical conclusion about the impossibility of defending the black position. Nowadays, I see that by means of 34...♘f7! Black can defend his vulnerable points and retain approximate equality.

Isaak Boleslavsky
Alexander Kotov

Moscow 1944 (4)

How should White develop his initiative? Give some possible variations.

In the game there followed
30.♖ad1!

(Boleslavsky's punctuation)
30...♞b3 31.♖xd6 ♛xd6 32.♖d1 ♛b6 33.♖d5

With a large advantage to White. In reply to 30...♖ed8 Boleslavsky gives the variation 31.f6! ♖xf6 32.♖xd8+ ♛xd8 33.♖d1 ♛e8 34.♖d7

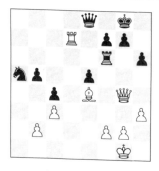

Analysis diagram

34...g6 (or 34...♞c6 35.♛d1 ♞d4 36.♖a7 ♞c6 37.♖b7 g6 38.♖xb5) 35.♛d1 ♚g7 36.♛d5 with a decisive breakthrough.

However, by playing 34...♖f4!, Black emerges intact, since after 35.♛d1? (35.♖e7! ♛d8 36.♖d7 ♛e8 37.♖e7=) 35...♖xe4 36.♖d8 there follows 36...♖e1+!. White has to settle for the modest 34.♖d5 (instead of 34.♖d7) 34...g6 35.♛d1 ♚g7 36.♖d8 ♛e6, and Black manages to cover the entry squares.

Therefore, back at the position of the first diagram, it was more accurate to play 30.♖ed1!. Now on 30...♖ed8 there follows 31.♖xd6 ♖xd6 32.f6, and 32...♖xf6 is impossible because of 33.♖xa5!±, whilst after 32...g6 33.♗xg6 ♖xf6 34.♗c2+ ♚f8 35.♛e4! White has a large advantage.

It may be that these examples will raise a smile from the reader – after all, in these days of computer checking, it would be hard to find such naïve mistakes in annotations. Does this fact reduce the value of working with old books?

I remember one session of the Smyslov school, when I shared a room with Alexey Dreev. Every day, as soon as he got a spare minute, the future strong GM was studying David Bronstein's famous book on the 1953 Zurich Candidates tournament. With great delight, Alyosha told me that, on the advice of his trainer Mark Dvoretsky, he was deliberately using the first edition of the book, because it contained more analytical mistakes and was therefore a better way of training oneself in independent analysis!

Here is an example from my first more or less serious analysis of a GM game. I became interested in a game, which was the subject of a lively discussion in the chess press, and was characteristic of Alekhine's splendid imagination.

Queen's Gambit Accepted
Alexander Alekhine
Eero Böök
Margate 1938

1.d4 d5 2.c4 dxc4 3.♞f3 ♞f6 4.e3 e6 5.♗xc4 c5 6.0-0 ♞c6 7.♛e2 a6 8.♞c3 b5 9.♗b3 b4 10.d5 ♞a5 11.♗a4+ ♗d7 12.dxe6 fxe6

13.♖d1!

'The starting move of a complicated combination, which results in the complete tying up of the entire black force, albeit at the cost of a rook!' (Alekhine)

The World Champion's idea was greeted with general acclamation, but once the strongest defence was found for Black, its purely chess value was somewhat shaken. Mikhail Tal and Leonid Shamkovich wrote: 'Alekhine refrains from the relatively quiet continuation 13.♘e5, which after 13...♗xa4 (13...bxc3 14.♘xd7 ♘xd7 15.♕h5+ g6 16.♕e5! or 15...♔e7 16.♖d1 ♖a7 17.e4! favours White) 14.♘xa4 ♕d5 15.♘g4 gives White an obvious positional advantage. Objectively, this was the strongest continuation, placing in doubt Black's opening plan with 9...b4.' However, I am not convinced that after the tempting 14...♗d6 (instead of 14...♕d5) 15.♘c4 ♘xc4 16.♕xc4 0-0 White's positional advantage is all that obvious.

13...bxc3 14.♖xd7! ♘xd7 15.♘e5 ♖a7

White to play. Suggest ways to develop the initiative.

In the game, there followed **16.bxc3 ♔e7? 17.e4! ♘f6 18.♗g5 ♕c7 19.♗f4** (White's attack is already irresistible) **19...♕b6 20.♖d1 g6 21.♗g5 ♗g7 22.♘d7 ♖xd7 23.♖xd7+ ♔f8 24.♗xf6 ♗xf6 25.e5**, and Black resigned.

As well as 16...♔e7?, Alekhine also considered the variation 16...♗d6 17.♕h5+ (17.♘xd7 ♖xd7 18.♕xa6 0-0! 19.♗xd7 ♕xd7 20.♕xa5 ♗c7!) 17...g6 18.♘xg6 hxg6 19.♕xh8+ ♗f8 20.e4, assessing the position as better for White. Later we will return to this analysis.

Later, Böök pointed out Black's strongest defence: – 16...♕b8!

Analysis diagram

17.♘xd7 (17.♕h5+ g6 18.♘xg6
hxg6 19.♕xh8 ♔f7) 17...♖xd7,
and if 18.♕xa6 there follows
the counterblow 18...♕d6! with
advantage to Black. Instead of
18.♕xa6 Shamkovich recommended
18.♗a3 ♗d6 19.♖d1 ♔e7 20.♗xd7
♔xd7 21.♗xc5 with compensation
for the sacrificed pawn, but Black
did not face any special danger here.

Trying to rehabilitate my chess
hero's idea, I looked at different
ways to develop the attack, from the
last diagram:

A) 16.♕h5+ g6
16...♔e7? 17.e4
**17.♘xg6 hxg6 18.♕xg6+ ♔e7 19.e4
♗h6! 20.♗xh6**

20...♖xh6
The computer points out 20...♕g8
21.♗g5+ ♔f8 22.♗h6+ ♖xh6
23.♕xh6+ ♕g7 24.♕f4+ ♕f7
25.♕h6+ with perpetual check.
21.♕g7+!
Equality results from 21.♕xh6
♕f8! 22.♕h7+ ♕f7 23.♕h4+ ♕f6
24.♕h7+ ♕f7 etc.
**21...♔e8 22.♕xh6 cxb2 23.♕h8+
♔f7!**

Weaker is 23...♔e7? 24.♕xb2 ♔f7
25.♖d1 ♘c4 26.♕e2 ♘cb6 27.♕h5+
♔e7 28.♕g5+ ♔e8 29.♕xc5 ♕c7
30.♕h5+ ♔e7 31.♕h7+ ♔e8
32.♕g8+ ♔e7 33.♗b3 ♘c5 34.h4
♘xb3 35.axb3±.
24.♕h7+
24.♕xb2 ♕f6
24...♔f8 25.♕h6+ ♔e8 26.♖d1 ♖b7!
And White has to settle for
perpetual check.

B) 16.e4!
Later, I found out that this had
been pointed out by Suetin, who
had restricted himself to the brief
variations 16...cxb2 17.♗xb2 and
16...♕f6 17.♘xd7 ♖xd7 18.♕xa6 – in
both cases, White retains strong
threats.

B1) 16...♕b8
'16...♕b8 also solves the defensive
problem after 16.e4' –
Shamkovich.
17.♘xd7 ♖xd7 18.♕xa6

B11) 18...cxb2
18...♕d6? 19.♕c8+ ♔e7 20.♗g5+
**19.♕xe6+ ♗e7 20.♕xd7+ ♔f7
21.♕d5+ ♔f8**

22.♗xb2

The computer suggests a more convincing path: 22.♕f5+ ♔g8 (or 22...♗f6 23.♗xb2 ♕xb2 24.♖d1 with irresistible threats) 23.♗d7 bxc1♕+ 24.♖xc1 g6 25.♗e6+ ♔g7 26.♕f7+ ♔h6 27.♕xe7 winning.

22...♕xb2 23.♖d1

With a strong attack for the sacrificed material.

B12) 18...♗d6 19.bxc3! ♕c7

19...0-0 20.♗xd7 ♗xh2+ 21.♔h1 ♖xf2 22.♗e3±

20.e5! 0-0

20...♗xe5? 21.♕xe6+ ♔d8 22.♗g5+

21.♗xd7 ♗xe5 22.♕xe6+ ♔h8

23.♗e3±

In reply to 16.e4! I also looked at another defence:

B2) 16...♗d6, which after **17.♕h5+ g6 18.♘xg6 hxg6 19.♕xh8+ ♗f8**

20.bxc3 transposes to a position of which Tal wrote: 'White has two pawns for the piece and strong pressure; for example, if 20...♕e7, then 21.♗h6 ♘c4 22.♖b1 with decisive threats.'

The following small analysis does not support the World Champion's opinion: 22...♔f7! 23.♕h7+ ♔f6 24.♗g5+!? (equality results from 24.♕h8+) 24...♔xg5 25.f4+ ♔xf4 26.♕xg6 ♕g7! 27.♕xe6 ♘e3!, and the black king escapes, e.g.: 28.♖b2 (the silicon assistant strengthens White's play by means of 28.g3+! ♔g5 29.♖b6! ♕f6 30.h4+ ♔h6 31.♗xd7 ♕xe6 32.♗xe6, but even here Black is not risking anything) 28...♘e5 29.♖f2+ ♔xe4 30.♗c6+ ♔d3.

However, White has a more convincing refutation of 16...♗d6: **17.♕h5+ g6 18.♘xg6 hxg6 19.♕xh8+ ♗f8 20.♗h6! ♕e7 21.♗xf8 ♕xf8 22.♕xc3 ♘b7 23.♖d1**, and the black position collapses.

B3) The attempt to prevent the white queen appearing on h5 by means of **16...g6** is also insufficient because of **17.♕f3 ♕e7 18.♘xd7 ♖xd7 19.♕xc3! ♗g7 20.♕xa5±**.

In my opinion, this analysis shows that Alekhine's concept was justified not just psychologically, but in a pure chess sense.

B4) It remains only to add that the computer recommends meeting 16.e4 with **16...h5!?**,

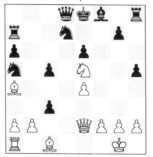

defending against the check on h5. This move did not enter my head, because of its obvious static drawbacks, but I have not found a clear path to an advantage for White here, for example:

B41) 17.bxc3 ♗d6 18.♘g6 ♔f7 19.♘xh8+ ♕xh8 20.♕d3 ♘b6 21.♕xd6 ♘xa4 22.♕f4+ ♔g6 23.♕g5+ ♔f7 24.♕f4+ with perpetual check;

B42) 17.♕d3!? ♗e7 18.bxc3 ♗f6 19.♘xd7 ♖xd7 20.♗e3 ♕c7 Preparing the knight's retreat to c6. **21.♕xa6 ♔e7 22.♗xd7 ♔xd7 23.f4** with full compensation for the sacrificed pieces, and the initiative, but Black's position remains fully defensible.

Now let us discuss the direct influence of classical ideas on the taking of decisions during the tournament battle. I became acquainted with the following game when a third-category player. Black instructively exploits the strength of a knight outpost on an open file.

George Thomas
Alexander Alekhine
Baden-Baden 1925 (10)

13...♘d5!
'This move forces the exchange of three minor pieces, and in the simplest way, increases the positional advantage Black has already achieved (Alekhine).'
14.♘xd4 cxd4 15.♘xd5 ♕xd5 16.♗f3 ♕d7 17.♗xb7 ♕xb7

18.c4
'Otherwise White is left with an incurable weakness on c2.' (Alekhine)
18...dxc3 19.bxc3 ♖ac8 20.♗b2 ♖fd8 21.♖f3 ♗f6 22.d4

'Positional capitulation, after which Black obtains a relatively easily winning position, thanks to his total control of the light squares (Alekhine).'

22...♕d5 23.♕e3 ♕b5 24.♕d2 ♖d5 25.h3 e6 26.♖e1 ♕a4 27.♖a1 b5 28.♕d1 ♖c4

The pawn structure has changed (the backward c2-pawn has become the hanging pawns on c3-d4) and the hanging pawns blockaded. The game is memorable for this final, extremely beautiful blockade position. The theme of a knight outpost on an open file could have been learned from other games (e.g. Mieses-Chigorin, Ostend 1905), but I first saw it in this game of Alekhine. Remarkably, within just days, I managed to use the same idea in a tournament of third-category players.

V. Zykov
Alexander Kalinin

Moscow 1976

The structure reached is very similar to Thomas-Alekhine (the subsequent commentary in inverted commas is from my schoolboy notebook).

13...♘d4
'Also possible is 13...♘f5.'
14.♘xd4 cxd4 15.♘xd6 ♕xd6

'As a result of the knight exchange, Black has obtained a positional advantage, consisting in more space, the exclusion of the ♗b3 from the game and the open c-file, with the backward pawn on c2.'

16.♕e4 ♖b8 17.♖fe1 ♗b7 18.♕e5 ♕c6 19.♕e4 ♕xe4 20.dxe4
'Exchanging queens does not remove the positional defects of White's position.'

20...♖fd8 21.♖ad1 ♔f8 22.f3 e5 23.♖d2

23...a5
'It was more accurate first to play 23...♖bc8, taking control of the c-file.'
24.a3

'White could have exploited his opponent's inaccuracy by 24.a4, and if 24...b4, then 25.♗c4. In that case, I would have had to play 24... bxa4 25.♗xa4 ♗a6, retaining the advantage.'

24...a4 25.♗a2 ♔e7 26.♔f2 ♖bc8 27.♖ed1 f6 28.c3?

'White wants to free himself, but commits an inaccuracy.'

28...dxc3 29.♖xd8 ♖xd8

And White's position collapsed, because 30.♖xd8 is impossible due to 30...c2.

After this case, I no longer needed any convincing of the value of studying the classics!

The following game (which Flohr regarded as one of his favourites) I first saw when I was about ten years old. The manoeuvre carried out by Black made an unforgettable impression on me!

Movsas Feigins
Salo Flohr

Kemeri 1937

What would you play?

17...♘b8!

Intending a 'long march' of the knight to e4!

18.♘d2 ♘d7 19.♗f3 ♘f6 20.♕d3 ♘e4

And Black obtained a dominating position in the centre.

In the following game, it was already easy for me to find the correct plan.

A. Minsky
Alexander Kalinin

Moscow 1984

What would you play?

White has an extra pawn on the queenside, but Black's doubled pawns in the centre also have their plusses, keeping control of the squares d5 and d4 (I should add that I was aware of the useful role of such doubled pawns from some of Botvinnik's games). The 'long march' by the knight from f6 to d4 almost played itself.

18...♘d7! 19.♘f3 f6

Strengthening the e5-square and hinting at a possible ...g7-g5.

20.♖ed1 ♘b8 21.♘d2
White plays without a plan and
allows his opponent to realise his
idea fully.
**21...♘c6 22.♘b3 a5 23.♕e3 a4
24.♘d2 ♕c5 25.♕xc5 bxc5 26.♘f3
♖fd8**
With an obvious advantage to Black.

The strategic device used in the
following game was placed into my
memory by Tal's excellent preface
to Nimzowitsch's classic book *Chess
Praxis*.

Francis Lee
Aron Nimzowitsch
Ostend 1907 (22)

Tal:
'Nimzowitsch gives a surprisingly
deep note to the move 22...♘e7
"After carrying out its work (and
the knight has worked) it is useful
to change its location. The knight is
heading to f5."

And in the first game of my match
with Larsen, the following position
arose:

Bent Larsen
Mikhail Tal
Eersel 1969

Strategically the two positions are
similar (with colours reversed, of
course). Larsen kept his knight on
d4 for a long time, but no real siege
of the isolated pawn ever emerged.
Yet after the game, he said that it
was better to blockade such a pawn
than to win it?!

I managed to use Nimzowitsch's
idea in the following game.

Alexander Kalinin
N. Besedin
Podolsk 1981

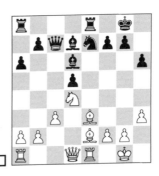

18.♗f3 ♖ad8 19.♕b3 ♗e5 20.♘c2!

Having fulfilled its blockading function, the knight is included in the attack on d5. In the process, White also creates the threat of 21.♗b6.

20...♕d6 21.♖ad1 ♗c6 22.♘b4 a5

With White threatening to double rooks on the d-file, Black decides to drive the enemy knight from its attacking position.

23.♘d3 ♗f6

Leads to material losses. On the other hand, 23...a4 24.♕b4 ♕xb4 25.♘xb4 a3 fails to 26.♗b6.

24.♗f4 ♕d7 25.♗g4 ♗a4

Nor is 25...♘f5 any better, in view of 26.♘c5 ♕c8 27.♕c2 g6 28.♗xh6.

26.♗xd7 ♗xb3 27.♗xe8 ♗xd1 28.♗xf7+ ♔xf7 29.♖xd1

And the upshot is an extra pawn for White in the endgame, with Black's pawn weaknesses remaining.

Alexander Kalinin
V. Maidla

Tallinn 1984

What would you do?

Black's position is held together by the ♗e6, which defends d7 and thus

protects the knight, which in turn covers the weakness on b6.

19.♗b3!

By accepting doubled pawns, White exchanges off the main defender of the enemy position.

19...♗xb3 20.axb3 ♘f6 21.♕d3 ♕e6 22.♘b6 ♘h5 23.g3 ♕g4 24.f3 ♕g5 25.♕d2 ♕e7 26.b4

And White dominated the key lines on the board.

It is worth mentioning that, while I was thinking over the move 19.♗b3, I recalled the association with the following game.

Mikhail Botvinnik
Nikolay Sorokin

Moscow ch-URS 1931

What would you choose?

Black is ready to solve the problems of developing his queenside by means of ...♗g4 or ...♗e6.

20.♕e3!

'This far from obvious move is the strongest in this position. With the exchange of queens, which cannot be avoided by

Black, the weaknesses in his position become more noticeable. With his development lagging, Black is already unable to oppose the pressure on the d-file. The pawn on e5 is very weak. To defend it, Black is forced to exchange bishop for knight on f3, after which he weakens not only his queenside, but also the square f7. Meanwhile, the doubled e-pawns are of no real significance.' (Botvinnik)

20...♕xe3 21.fxe3 ♗g4 22.a5 ♘c8

After 22...♘bd7 Botvinnik gives the variation 23.h3 ♗xf3 24.gxf3 ♘c5 25.b4 ♘e6 26.♗xe6 fxe6 27.♘a4! and 28.♘c5 with a dominant game.

23.♖c1

23...♗xf3

'On 23...♖e8 it was possible to play 24.h3 ♗h5 (24...♗e6 25.♗xe6 ♖xe6 26.♖d8+) 25.♘h4!, and the threat of g4 is very unpleasant.' (Botvinnik)

24.gxf3 ♘e7 25.♘d5 ♘c6 26.♘xf6+ gxf6 27.♖d7 ♖ab8 28.♔f2! ♘xa5 29.♖cc7 ♖bc8 30.♖xf7 ♖xc7 31.♖xc7+ ♔h8 32.♗d5

And White obtained a decisive advantage.

Later I found an exact predecessor game of Botvinnik's.

Mikhail Botvinnik
Isaak Boleslavsky

Moscow 1945 (11)

What should White play?

23.♗b3!

Preparing the advance c4-c5 and forcing the exchange of light-squared bishops, after which Black has to cede his opponent control of the open d-file. And again, we note that the doubled pawns are not a significant factor.

23...♖xd2

'Alas, Black cannot defend the open file, since the Bg7 must defend the e5-pawn.' (Botvinnik)

24.♕xd2 ♗xb3 25.axb3 ♕e6 26.c4 ♗f6 27.c5 ♘c8

'The continuation 27...♖d8 28.♕xd8+ ♗xd8 29.♖xd8+ ♔g7 30.cxb6 is hopeless for Black.' (Botvinnik)

28.♕d7 ♕xb3 29.♕xb7 ♗g5 30.♘xg5 hxg5 31.♕xa6

and White achieved a decisive advantage.

Sicilian Defence
Vasily Prokofiev
M. Gelin

Leningrad 1982

This game was played in a match between the school teams of Moscow and Minsk. Vasily and I played on adjacent boards and I was able to follow the development of events in his game.

1.e4 c5 2.♘f3 ♘c6 3.d4 cxd4 4.♘xd4 g6 5.♘c3 ♗g7 6.♗e3 ♘f6 7.♗c4 d6 8.f3 ♕b6

The Dragon Variation is often seen in junior events. The many tactical possibilities, together with its strategic clarity, make this opening very attractive to young players. Black's last move takes the game into less explored territory.

9.♗b5 ♕c7 10.♘d5 ♘xd5 11.exd5 a6 12.♘xc6 axb5 13.♗d4 0-0

The alternative is 13...bxc6 14.♗xg7 ♖g8, and Black straightens out his pawn structure, but pays for this with his king being in the centre in the middlegame.

14.♗xg7 ♔xg7 15.♕d4+ ♔g8 16.♘b4 ♕c4

17.c3!?

When this subtle move was played, I liked it very much. If the queens are exchanged on d4, then at the cost of doubled pawns, White gets the chance to play on the c-file.

In the game Stefansson-T.Ernst (Copenhagen 1991) there occurred 17.0-0-0 ♕xd4 18.♖xd4 f5 19.♖e1 ♔f7 20.a3 ♗d7, and White did not find it easier to exploit the enemy weaknesses on the queenside.

17...♕xd4 18.cxd4 ♗f5 19.♔d2 ♖fc8 20.♖hc1 ♖c4?

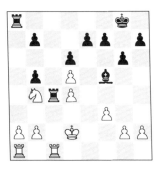

A serious mistake. The transformation of the pawn structure that this move produces turns out not to be in Black's favour.

21.♖xc4

First White doubled his own pawns, and now he undoubles his opponent's! But the c4-pawn now becomes a convenient object of attack. A great deal of importance in what follows attaches to the activity of the white king.

21...bxc4 22.♔c3 ♖c8

Or 22...b5 23.♘c6 ♔f8 24.♔b4, and Black's position is bad.

23.a4 ♗d7 24.♘c2 ♔f8 25.♘e3 e6 26.a5 ♗b5 27.♔b4 ♗a6 28.♖c1 exd5

29.♘xd5 ♖c6 30.♘b6 ♚e8 31.♖c3 ♖c7
32.♘xc4 ♗xc4 33.♖xc4 ♖e7 34.♚b5
And White soon won.

When Vasya played his 17th move,
I immediately remembered the
following game:

Vasily Smyslov
Mikhail Tal

Bled/Zagreb/Belgrade ct 1959

What would you play?

The white pawns on a5 and d5 are
ready to set up a bind on the black
queenside, but Black's pieces are
very actively placed. For example,
he threatens ...e5-e4.
There followed the unexpected
**15.♕d3!! ♖fc8 16.♖fc1 ♕xd3
17.cxd3 g6 18.♖c3 ♖xc3 19.bxc3
♖c8 20.c4**
And White developed strong
pressure on the queenside.

At the end of the round, Vasya
Prokofiev confirmed my
associations, saying that while he
was thinking about 17.c3 he also
remembered the Smyslov game!

Incidentally, the advantages of
studying the classical heritage are
not limited only to the mechanical
reproduction of remembered
devices and plans in specific
positions. The acquisition of
knowledge in this way also widens
the thinking of a chess player,
enriching his understanding of
the game and enabling him to play
better in original positions too.
The well-known Mexican
grandmaster Carlos Torre, who
had a meteoric career in the 1920s,
said the following: 'In acquiring a
knowledge of the devices and plans
used by the great masters of the
past, we should not worship them or
blindly and unthinkingly copy their
ideas. We cannot do this, because we
will never be able to re-live exactly
the same psychological process
which leads a player to play in this
or that fashion, and we should not,
because in that case, chess would
be transformed into a dry and
pointless exploitation of memory.'

The following example enabled
me in my time to learn that the
assessment of events on the board
often depends on barely perceptible
nuances of the position.

Sicilian Defence
Alexander Kalinin
Boris Alterman

Yaroslavl 1983

This game was played between
two first category players in a

103

junior event. My opponent was Boris Alterman from Kharkov, who is now a well-known Israeli grandmaster.

1.e4 c5 2.♘f3 ♘c6 3.d4 cxd4 4.♘xd4 g6

Even as a child Boris was known among his contemporaries as a Dragon expert, and he later became one of its leading practitioners. But in this last round game, which saw us fighting for third place, a draw suited Boris and so he put his faith in the quiet accelerated variation of his favourite system, allowing the Maroczy Bind.

5.c4 ♗g7 6.♗e3 ♘f6 7.♘c3 ♘g4

This knight jump, introduced into practice by Breyer, aims at exchanging a pair of minor pieces, which suits the side with less space.

8.♕xg4 ♘xd4 9.♕d1 e5

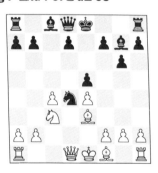

A rare move, introduced by Botvinnik. In weakening the d5-square and the d-pawn, Black counts on being able to shelter these behind the ♘d4.

10.♗e2

In the old ECO, grandmaster Filip gave the variation 10.♗xd4 exd4 11.♘d5 0-0 12.♗d3 d6 13.0-0 ♗e6

14.♕d2 ♗xd5 15.exd5 ♕d7, assessing the position not with =, but ∓. This far from impressive recommendation has some significance in what follows, however. Therefore let us take a slightly closer look at the final position. The queenside pawn advantage (a2, b2, c4, d5 against a7, b7, d6 – the pawn on d4 does not count) is hard to exploit, because the flexible position of the pawns on a7 and b7 prevent White from opening lines in that section of the board. Theory considers the main reply to 9...e5 to be 10.♘b5, with possible complications after 10...♘xb5 11.cxb5 d5!?. I only knew the fact of this recommendation and so decided not to go in for such an unfamiliar enterprise.

10...a6

Cutting out once and for all the possibility of a knight jump to b5.

11.0-0 0-0

Having completed development, I thought for a while about the subsequent plan. Theory (of which I was totally unaware) quotes the game Lein-Gipslis (Tbilisi 1966), in which there followed 12.♕d2 (logical – White wants to drive the knight from d4 by means of ♘c3-e2) 12...d6 13.♖fd1 ♗e6 14.♗f1 ♕a5 15.♘e2 ♕xd2 16.♖xd2 ♗xc4 17.♘xd4 exd4 18.♗xd4 ♖ac8 19.♗xg7 ♔xg7 20.♖xd6 ♗xf1 21.♔xf1 ♖c2, and the activity of the black rooks gave sufficient compensation for the sacrificed pawn.

However, my attention was seized by another idea.

12.♘d5 d6 13.♗xd4 exd4 14.♗d3 ♗e6 15.♕d2 ♗xd5 16.exd5 ♕d7

And we have reached a position similar to that analysed by Filip in his notes to White's 10th move.

White to move. Which plan would you choose?

However, there is one significant difference between the two positions – here the black pawn is on a6, rather than a7! As a result, White has a concrete plan of attack on the queenside – he plays a2-a4-a5 and then b2-b4-b5, exploiting the target on a6 to open the b-file. I would observe that, had I known of Filip's recommendation in ECO, I would never have thought up the idea I found at the board, thanks to my ignorance!

17.a4! ♖ae8

Black could stop the a4-pawn with 17...a5 and fix his opponent's pawn structure on the same colour squares as the ♗d3. However, in this case White would retain the possibility of creating an initiative on the queenside. With the manoeuvre 18.♖a3 followed by ♖f1-a1, ♖a3-b3-b5 and, finally, b2-b4,

he could create strong pressure on the b7-pawn. Of course, Black could regroup with ...♗g7-f6-d8 and ...b7-b6, but then the d4-pawn would be in need of defence.

I should point out that this rook manoeuvre, like a slalom skier, along the a- and b-files and deep into the heart of the enemy position, was one used by Geller in similar Sicilian structures. But in my mind, this manoeuvre is associated with the following game, which once seen is never forgotten:

Isaak Gunsberg
Mikhail Chigorin
Havana 1890

Note also the knight on e6, ideally placed behind the protection of the enemy passed pawn. Chigorin seems to have been the first master to deliberately create positions with such a blockading knight. There followed **25...♖h6! 26.♕a5 ♕b6 27.♕e1 ♖g6! 28.c4 ♖g4! 29.♗c1 ♕c6 30.♖g1 ♖h8 31.♖b2 ♕f3 32.♘f2**, and now the rook transfer to g4 allowed an effective breakthrough – **32...g5!! 33.♘xg4 hxg4 34.♕f1 ♖xh4+! 35.gxh4 g3+ 36.♖xg3 ♕xf1**, and Black won.

Let us return to our game.
18.a5 ♖e5 19.b4

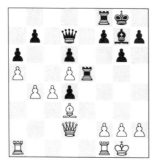

White ignores the doubled enemy rooks on the open file, and keeps his major pieces for active operations on the queenside.

This classical idea I knew from the notes to the following game, in the classic New York 1927 tournament book.

Milan Vidmar
Aron Nimzowitsch
New York 1927 (5)

19...♖ae8!

'Black's playing for a win deserves particular credit for the fact that it involves ceding the open file, a decision which many tried and tested fighters would shy away from. I, for example, from experience in recent years know of several first-class masters who, without any thought at all, would put both rooks on the d-file and exchange them off, and... then complain that chess is approaching its draw death.' (Alekhine)

And now once again we return to the text.
19...♖h5?!
The attempt to create counterplay on the kingside is hardly a good one, because the black rook could prove out of play.
20.♖ae1?!
Whilst Black has voluntarily ceded the only open file, White declines to occupy it. Incidentally, on 20...♖e5 there would follow 21.♖b1, winning a tempo.
Even so, the immediate 20.f4 was stronger, shutting the ♖h5 out of the game, and on 20...♗h6 there follows 21.♕d1, preventing 21...♖e5.
20...♗h6 21.f4
In the event of 21.♕b2 ♗f4 22.h3 ♖g5 23.♔h1 ♖h5 the game could end in a repetition of moves.
21...♗g7?
A serious mistake, leaving the ♖h5 out of play. It was essential to play 21...♖e5!, which, with White having lost pawn control of e3, would ensure Black counterplay and equal chances.

22.♖e4 ♗f6 23.♖fe1

If 23.♖b1 (preparing b4-b5) it
seemed to me that the consequences
of 23...g5 were unclear, e.g. 24.♕e2
(or 24.♗e2 ♕f5 25.♕d3 ♖h6)
24...♖h6 25..fxg5 ♗xg5 26.♖xd4? f5
with threats of 26...♖e8 and 26...♗f6.
Therefore, I decided for the moment
to put the rook on the open file and
see what my opponent would do.

23...♔g7 24.♖b1

Noticing how the position has
changed after the king moved to g7,
White now has no objection to 24...
g5.

24...g5 25.♕e2 ♖h6

After 25...g4 the black rook on h5
remains offside.

26.fxg5 ♗xg5 27.♖g4 f6?

Black could resist longer with
27...♕d8 28.♖f1 ♔h8 29.♖xd4,
though Black's position is cheerless.

28.h4!

Now after 28...♖xh4 White wins
with 29.♖xh4 ♗xh4 30.♕h5, landing
a double attack on h4 and h7.

28...♖e8 29.hxg5

29.♕d1 is also possible, because
after 29...♕e7 (with the idea of
30.hxg5?? ♕e3+ 31.♔f1 ♖h1#) the
move 30.g3 is sufficient for a win.

**29...♖xe2 30.gxh6+ ♔xh6 31.♗xe2
♕e7 32.♖b3 1-0**

One can not only draw valuable
lessons from the classical heritage
or modern super-tournaments. If
you look around you attentively,
you can find a great deal that is
interesting and instructive!
In the spring of 1986, I was a
participant in a friendly match
between the sports societies
Burevestnik and Zenit, over 100
boards. My attention was caught
by the game Dokhoian-Andrianov,
which had a highly interesting
course. I no longer remember the
position precisely, and below is just
an approximation, which conveys
the essence of what happened:

Note the knight on b4, placed
beautifully but ineffectively. More
than that, it could prove to be
completely out of the game. In the
subsequent course of the game,
the white pieces gradually drifted
towards the kingside where the
real battle was taking place, White
having effectively an extra piece.
Andrianov managed to draw, but
that is by the by – what matters is

that the strategic idea proved clear and memorable.

Within just a month or so, I managed to draw this example from my memory and use it myself.

Sicilian Defence
Alexander Kalinin
Yuri Piskov
Moscow 1986

My opponent in this game was master (now grandmaster) Yuri Piskov. Yuri can justifiably be described as my oldest friend. We studied together in the 22nd Moscow school, I in the junior class, he in the senior. Our school had two chess teams, a main one and a 'development' side, destined to replace the main team. The younger team proudly looked on their heroes from the seniors, who had already won the 'White Rook' junior event, and later the Pioneer Palace event sponsored by newspaper *Komsomolskaya Pravda*. Our main team was certainly strong – as well as Piskov, we had Mikhal Krasenkow, who became a well-known GM, and Sergey Sergienko, who is now an IM.
1.c4 e5 2.♘c3 ♘c6 3.g3 g6 4.♗g2 ♗g7 5.e3 d6 6.♘ge2 h5
We have a Closed Sicilian with colours reversed. Exploiting the fact that White has lost control of h4 by developing his king's knight to e2, Black takes the chance to push his h-pawn.

7.h4 ♗g4 8.d3 ♘ge7 9.♖b1 ♖b8 10.b4 a6
Black's last two moves are aimed at his opponent's plans to expand on the queenside. Now after 11.a4 (insisting on the advance b4-b5) there follows 11...a5! 12.b5 ♘b4 13.♗a3 c5. A similar manoeuvre (again with colours reversed) was used in the game Spassky-Larsen (Malmö 1968). I knew about this, but, as you may have guessed, my attention was seized by the position of the knight on b4.
11.a4 a5 12.b5 ♘b4 13.♗a3 c5

I would hardly have chosen this line if I had been aware that in his recently-published book on the English Opening, Bagirov had written of this position: 'White should be very careful with the move 11.a4?, not forgetting that this is met by 11...a5! 12.b5 ♘b4! 13.♗a3 c5.' The grandmaster then refers to the game Pfleger-Nunn (Germany Bundesliga 1985/86), in which White was crushed horribly: 14.♗xb4 axb4 15.♘d5 ♘xd5 16.♗xd5 0-0 17.♕c2 b6 18.♘c1 ♗e6 19.♘b3 ♗xd5 20.cxd5 e4! 21.dxe4 ♗c3+ 22.♔f1 ♕e7 23.♔g2 ♖be8

24.♗f3 f5 25.exf5 c4 26.♘d4 ♗xd4, and White resigned. Fortunately, I only found out about this after the game.

14.♕d2

Undoubtedly the move 14.♗xb4?, played by Pfleger, runs counter to Dokhoian's idea of playing on the opposite side of the board, exploiting the offside ♘b4.

14...0-0 15.0-0 b6 16.♖be1

Thus, all the white pieces are gradually moving over to the kingside. I was far from claiming any great advantage for White, but it is always easier to play when you have a concrete plan of action.

16...♗h6 17.♕d1 ♗e6 18.e4

The advance ...d6-d5 must be prevented.

18...♔h7 19.♗b2 ♕d7 20.♔h2 ♘g8 21.♘d5 f5 22.f4

The position in the diagram clearly illustrates that in the battle in the centre, White effectively has an extra piece.

22...♗xd5 23.cxd5 fxe4 24.dxe4 ♘f6 25.♗h3 ♘g4+ 26.♗xg4 ♕xg4 27.fxe5 ♕xe4 28.♘f4 ♕c2+ 29.♕xc2 ♘xc2 30.♖e2 dxe5 31.♖xe5 ♖b7 32.♖e2 ♘d4 33.♗xd4 cxd4

Black finally solves the problem of the ♘b4, but the weakness appearing on d4 allows White to continue to fight for an advantage.

34.♖e4 ♗g7

The d4-pawn drops after 34...♗xf4, but now the white tandem ♖+♘ turn out to be stronger than Black's rook and bishop.

35.♖fe1 ♖d8 36.♖e7 ♖xe7 37.♖xe7 ♖d6

Black is also in a bad way after 37...d3 38.♘xd3 ♖xd5 39.♘f4 ♖d2+ 40.♔h3 ♔g8 41.♖e6 etc.

38.♘e6 ♔h8 39.♖e8+ ♔h7 40.♘g5+

Black resigned.

I will finish this chapter with the most surprising example in my career of 'borrowing' a strategical idea.

Alexander Kalinin
Heico Kerkmeester
Wijk aan Zee 1996

Here White has a tempting possibility – 17.f4 ♕h6 18.♗xe4 fxe4 19.h4, blocking the opponent's activity on the kingside, and remaining with a good knight

109

versus bad bishop. The fact that the black bishop can execute the march e8-g6-f5-g4-f3 is of no real significance, as the bishop would be unsupported by other pieces.

I refrained from this line because of the following considerations:

A) The plan of a4-a5 followed by b3-b4-b5 will not be so effective, because White will not be able to force b4-b5;

B) This means White will have to forgo the closure of the centre with c4-c5 and attack by means of b3-b4, a2-a4 and b4-b5. But once the game opens, the weakness of the light squares around the white king might have its say. In this regard, one cannot rule out the possibility of a black piece sacrifice on e5.

Consequently, I decided not to part with my light-squared bishop.

17.♖ae1 ♗g6 18.f3 ♘f6 19.c5 ♕h6 20.h4 ♗e8 21.♕d2 ♘d7

The advance 21...g5? is refuted by means of 22.e4!.

22.♘xd7 ♗xd7 23.f4 ♕g6 24.♔h2

White has a good bishop versus a bad one, plus the superior pawn structure and space advantage on the queenside. But is his advantage enough to win? The centre and kingside are blocked, so will White be able to win by a breakthrough on the queenside alone?

24...♕f7 25.♖b1 ♖fb8 26.b4 a6 27.♖b3 ♕e8 28.♖fb1 ♖a7 29.♗f1 ♖ba8 30.a4 ♔h7 31.♗e2 ♔h6 32.♕d1 g6

It seems that the game is going to end in a draw. As soon as White plays b4-b5, Black will obtain counterplay on the a-file, and the main source of his woes, the light-squared bishop, will be exchanged. Even so, White has a plan to play for a win. It consists of the following:

A) Regrouping his major pieces on the a-file with ♖a3, ♖a2, ♕a1;

B) Transferring the king to his queenside, in anticipation of developments there;

C) Playing the break b4-b5, which will lead to the exchange of all the rooks and the light-squared bishops;

D) Breaking into the enemy camp with the king and queen via the dark squares, exploiting his space advantage and the strong pawn on c5.

I hardly need to say that I had this plan in 22.♘xd7 and 23.f4, because I had seen it all before! I had learned this plan from the Moscow master Vladimir Baikov. Playing against him in the semifinal of the Moscow championship in 1988, I suffered greatly in a similar position as Black and only made a draw with great difficulty.

33.♔g2 ♕d8 34.♔f2 ♕c7 35.♕c2 ♕d8 36.♔e1 ♗e8 37.♔d2 ♗d7 38.♖a3 ♗e8 39.♕b3 ♗d7 40.♖ba1 ♗e8 41.♔c2 ♗d7 42.♕b2 ♔g7 43.♖1a2 ♗e8 44.♕a1 ♔f7 45.b5 axb5 46.axb5 ♖xa3 47.♖xa3 ♖xa3 48.♕xa3 cxb5 49.♔b3 ♗c6 50.♔b4 ♕c8 51.♗xb5 ♗xb5 52.♔xb5 ♕c6+ 53.♔b4 ♕c8 54.♕a7 ♔f6 55.♕b6 ♕a8 56.♕d6 ♔f7 57.♔b5 ♕a7

White to play. What would you do?

Black is holding his last line of defence, not allowing the white king into b6. Zugzwang comes to White's aid. The most surprising thing is that the final winning manoeuvre is one I found when analysing my adjourned position against Baikov!

58.♕d7+! ♔f6 59.♕d8+! ♔f7 60.♕d6!

Since 60...♔f6 is impossible due to 61.♕f8#!, Black finds himself in zugzwang and is forced to allow the enemy king into his camp.

60...♕a3 61.♕d7+ ♔f6 62.♕xb7 ♕xe3 63.♕c8 ♔g7 64.♕c7+ ♔f8 65.♕e5 ♕b3+ 66.♔c6 ♕xg3 67.♕f6+ ♔g8 68.♔d7 ♕xf4 69.c6

And Black resigned.

It transpires that, when playing his 23rd move, White saw the final zugzwang in the queen ending at move 60. A record for length of plan!

And now to acquaint you with the source game.

Dutch Defence
Vladimir Baikov
Alexander Kalinin
Moscow 1988

Vladimir Baikov, a player with a subtle positional style, was a colourful figure amongst Moscow masters. Working in a car factory, he managed to find time to work out original opening and middlegame plans in his favourite opening schemes, in the style of Rubinstein, with a single thread running through the entire game. One of his examples is before you.

1.d4 e6 2.c4 f5

I remember that, when preparing for this game, I paid attention to a game Baikov-Piskov, from the previous year's Moscow championship. Yuri Piskov had won a beautiful game in the Stonewall system, and I decided to follow his example. But this was to be the first and only time in my life that I played the Stonewall!

3.g3 ♘f6 4.♗g2 c6 5.♘f3 d5 6.0-0 ♗d6 7.b3 ♕e7 8.c5 ♗c7 9.♗f4 ♗xf4

I knew that in such positions, Black should take on f4 himself (since otherwise he loses his dark-squared bishop 'free of charge'), so as later to obtain counterplay with the help of the advance ...g7-g5.

10.gxf4 0-0 11.♘bd2 ♗d7 12.b4 ♗e8 13.a4 ♘e4 14.♖a3!

The rook is simply superbly placed on the third rank!

14...♔h8 15.♘e5 ♘d7 16.♘xd7 ♗xd7 17.♘f3

And here I happily played the programmed advance ...g7-g5.

17...g5 18.fxg5 ♘xg5 19.♘xg5 ♕xg5 20.f4! ♕f6 21.♖g3

But now I realised that I had no counterplay at all, and faced a tortuous defence.

21...♖g8 22.♕d2 ♖g7 23.♖xg7 ♕xg7 24.♖f3 ♖g8 25.♖g3 ♕f6 26.♕e3 a6 27.♔f2 ♖g7 28.♔e1 ♔g8 29.♔d2 ♔f8 30.♔c3 ♖xg3 31.♕xg3

The exchange of rooks, this time on the b-file, leads us to the same type of ending as in the previous game. White will try to break through on the queenside, where his king is already stationed.

31...♗e8 32.♗f3 h6 33.e3 ♗d7 34.♗e2 ♔f7 35.b5 cxb5 36.axb5 ♗xb5 37.♗xb5 axb5 38.♕e1 ♕d8 39.♕a1 ♕c7 40.♔b4 ♕c6 41.♕a5 ♔g6 42.♕xb5 ♕c8 43.♔a5 ♕d8+ 44.♕b6 ♕a8+ 45.♔b4 ♔f6

Here the game was adjourned and White sealed his move.

I still have my notebook with my adjournment analysis, which is reproduced below: 46.♕a5 (not yet allowing the black queen any scope) 46...♕c8 47.h4 h5 (it is dangerous to allow the white pawn to advance) 48.♕a4 (forcing the black queen to cover the entry squares on the a4-e8 diagonal and preparing to attack the h5-pawn from d1) 48...♔g6! 49.♕a1 (now the white queen comes to the g-file with check) 49...♕c6! (it is essential to activate the queen to the maximum, exploiting the chance he has; 49...♔f6? is bad because of 50.♕g1) 50.♕g1+ ♔f7 51.♕a1 (if 51.♕g5 ♕a6 52.♕xh5+ ♔g7 Black has sufficient counterplay) 51...♔f6 52.♕a8 ♔g7!, a very important position of reciprocal zugzwang (52...♔f7? loses because of 53.♕a4! ♕c8 54.♕d1!, and White wins a decisive tempo, threatening to take the h5-pawn with check):

Analysis diagram

53.♕a4! (53.♕d8 ♔f7) 53...♕c8 54.♕d1 ♕a8 55.♕xh5 ♕a6 56.♕d1! ♕c4+ 57.♔a3 ♔h6 58.♕b3 ♕a6+ 59.♔b4 (or 59.♔b2 ♔h5) 59...♔h5, and Black holds the balance. After this small analytical diversion, the finish of the game becomes understandable.
46.♕d6 ♕a2 47.♔b5 ♕a7 48.h4 h5
The white pawn cannot be allowed to h5, because this cramps the black position decisively.

Compare this position with that which arose after Black's 57th

move in the previous game. They would be identical if we added white and black pawns on g3 and g6 respectively! This detail stops White playing for zugzwang, because now the move ♕d6-f8 is only check, not mate! Therefore, after several preparatory moves, Baikov tries to attack the h5-pawn.
49.♕d8+ ♔f7 50.♕a5 ♕b8 51.♔b4 ♕c8 52.♕a1 ♕d8 53.♕e1 ♕a8 54.♕e2 ♔f6 55.♕xh5 ♕a6 56.♕d1 ♕c4+ 57.♔a3 ♕c3+ 58.♕b3 ♕a5+ 59.♔b2 ♕d2+ 60.♔b1 ♕e1+ 61.♔a2 ♕xh4 62.♕xb7 ♕f2+ 63.♕b2 ♕xe3 64.c6
The last desperate attempt to play for a win. White sacrifices all his pawns, placing all his hopes on the passed c6-pawn.
64...♕xf4 65.♕b7 ♕d2+ 66.♔b3 ♕d3+ 67.♔b4 ♕xd4+ 68.♔b5 ♕d3+ 69.♔b6 ♕e3+
As often happens in such situations, diagonal checks come to the rescue of the defending side. The white king cannot escape perpetual.
70.♔c7 ♕g3+ ½-½

I would add that I have since seen Baikov lure several opponents into the same plan and win, like Baron von Munchausen shooting down an entire group of ducks with a single shot!

Creative associations play a great, if often unconscious role in decision-taking at the board. We will meet this theme again in the following pages of this book.

CHAPTER 7

Personal influences

'My main aim in dealing with all my chess pupils has been "independence above everything"!' – Alexander Konstantinopolsky

In this chapter I will speak about players of the older generation, who had a significant influence on my play. I am talking about my mentors, with whom I shared many years of contact, and of masters, meetings and conversations with whom were sometimes short-lived, but who left a long-term influence in my memory.

A young player improves as a result of tournament battles, analysis of his own games and the study of books. But no less influence on him is his 'live' encounters with mentors and masters, many of whom grew up in a different generation. The transfer of experience can occur not only through games over the board but also, it seems, quite unconsciously – in the course of a simple conversation, discussion, debate about some or other creative issue. When listening to a master's stories, young players often want to focus on concrete variations (especially if they relate to their own opening repertoire!) and the conclusions flowing from these variations. They pay rather less attention to comments from the master on more general topics. I was no exception. Only years later did I realise that the real value of discussions with strong players was not so much in concrete variations as in gaining insights into their thought processes. And, surprising as it may seem, now, when I think back to conversations with my mentors, I cannot recall a single concrete variation, but in return, I find numerous ideas still in my mind from those conversations! It is clear that our minds almost subconsciously collect universal knowledge, filtering out the unwanted chaff. But undoubtedly our improvement would be rather easier, if we knew from the beginning what were the important things to pay attention to.

I always remember with pleasure the Moscow Palace of Pioneers and our group of beginners. My first mentor, Alexander Nikolaevich Kostyev, had the ability to generate in our sessions an extremely creative and pleasant atmosphere. Knowledge of the theory and history of chess was passed to us in a very dynamic form, by means of various playing exercises and competitions. A general impression of his teaching methods can be obtained from his booklets *Chess Circles in Schools and Pioneer Camps, Chess Lessons, A Teacher Writes about Chess,* etc. [Translator's Note: Unfortunately, none of these booklets have been translated into English, so far as I am aware.] The basics of chess are taught in these simply and systematically, and it is these qualities which make the pupil want to go further and find out more about the chosen topic. I look back with particular gratitude on the homework exercises, involving commentaries on my own and classical games (I have already spoken of this in an earlier chapter). Now, as a trainer myself, I understand all too well the importance of such exploratory work, developing in the pupil the quality of independent thinking. Even then, as a child, I could feel the value of such work.

From among the playing devices used at our training sessions, I recall the blitz games 'White-Black' and the 'Test Yourself' competition. In White-Black, we would play blitz, but not with a clock. Instead, every five seconds, the trainer would call out 'White' or 'Black' and the player had to move. This meant that we always had five seconds for each move, and so the game never degenerated into the kind of 'clock race' that ordinary blitz games are wont to do. In 'Test Yourself', the trainer would show on the demonstration board a specially chosen game, but would only put up one side's moves. We then had to guess the other side's moves, each of which we would write down in our exercise books. After a few minutes, the trainer would reveal the move actually played and we would score points for having guessed it correctly. At the end of the game, we would tot up our scores and declare a winner.

To this day, I can still picture before my eyes the position from the game Schulten-Morphy (New York 1857), shown in one such event. The American champion's move 7...e3!! forever remains in my mind as a classic example of exploiting superior development. The same is true for the crushing rook sacrifice 23.♖xf6!! in the game Smyslov-K.Grigorian (Moscow 1976). Such examples sink into one's soul, probably in part because they were first seen as part of a test and required independent effort.

In general, Alexander Nikolaevich was continually inventing something new and unique. Once, he gave a simultaneous with clocks against us, 8-year old third category players, in which he stopped each game at the height of the middlegame. At the next session, the games were continued, and we were asked to record in our exercise books our analysis of the adjourned position.

Alexander Kostyev
Alexander Kalinin

Moscow 1976 (clock simul)

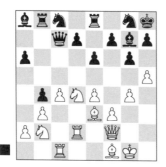

The game was stopped in this position. My analysis amounted only to the following brief note: 'Here Black can break in the centre with 22...d5 23.exd5 ♗xd5 (worse is 23...exd5 24.c5 with advantage to White), freeing his position and obtaining counterplay.'

When the game resumed, there followed:

22...d5? 23.exd5 ♗xd5 24.cxd5

The very first move made by the trainer, after the end of my so-called 'analysis', leads Black to a catastrophe! The exchange sacrifice gives White a decisive attack.

24...♕xc1 25.hxg6 fxg6 26.♘xe6 ♘d6 27.♗d4 ♖b7 28.♘d3 ♕c8 29.♘dc5 ♖f7 30.♗xa6

And Black resigned.

As the reader will have guessed, I was very poor at such 'homework'. After this episode, I realised that analysing a position was not a simple thing, but requires a serious and committed approach.

It was also instructive to see the consequences of the 'self-evident' move 22...d5. It turns out that tempting moves are far from always good.

Towards the end of the third class at school, I fulfilled the norm for a first category player and was accepted into the Smyslov chess school. Here I should say some words of gratitude to Elizaveta Ivanovna Bykova, the former women's World Champion, who asked the director of the school to accept me. In general, Elizaveta Ivanovna was a surprising woman. In the 1970s, she gave a great deal of effort to the TV series 'Chess School' and her flat was overflowing with letters from chess lovers. She answered every letter personally! My father knew the third women's World Champion and once advised her not to bother answering every letter, as many contained very naïve questions. But Elizaveta Ivanovna firmly replied that she considered herself obliged to reply to everyone who expressed any interest in chess! This became an important life lesson for me. And my father then started taking part of the correspondence home himself, to help with answering it. I remember the first time I went to Elizaveta Ivanovna's apartment. I could not wait to see the World Champion's laurel wreath, but it turned out that she had long since made soup out of it! But in return, she showed me a 'magic' white pawn, which was standing behind glass on a bookshelf. This was the pawn which had moved from b2 to b4, in Botvinnik's last game against Euwe at the 1948 World Championship tournament. It was this move b2-b4 that brought Botvinnik the world title, as the players agreed a draw in that position, securing the title. The subsequent adventures of the 'magic' pawn were recounted by Botvinnik in his memoirs: 'Some time later, the film crew told me that they had not caught the moment when I played my last move b2-b4, which brought the world title to the Soviet Union. Then they noticed that the demonstration board operator, Yacov Estrin, was wearing a suit the same colour as the new World Champion. Spectators of the film had never suspected that the 'historic' move b2-b4 which they saw played was made not by me, but by the demo board operator himself!

But the history of the b-pawn does not end there. It was taken as a talisman by Elizaveta Bykova, who was convinced that the lucky pawn would help her to become World Champion. And indeed, this happened! Not only that, but the young demo board operator, who actually touched this 'magic' pawn went on years later to become world correspondence chess champion.' Learning all this, I too could not wait to get my hands on the 'magic' pawn...

The heart and soul of the Smyslov School was undoubtedly Boris Naumovich Postovsky. The wonderful organisation of the sessions and the friendly and business-like atmosphere which prevailed at lectures were solely down to him. Boris Naumovich always stressed the importance of physical preparation and was the best personal example in this respect.

I frequently remember the daily morning exercises at Kislovodsk, followed by the long run down to the source of the mineral waters, led by him. At the waters, there would be a vigorous rubdown in the healing water and then a run back to camp. Many of the youngsters were liked squeezed lemons after this, but Boris Naumovich was always upbeat and cheerful! Postovsky's achievements are well-known as trainer of the USSR national team and then the Russian team – under his leadership, they won all important international events. It was even said of him that 'Where there is Postovsky, there is victory!'. I once played under his captaincy in the Moscow junior championships for the Burevestnik team, and sure enough, we were triumphant!

At the first session of the Smyslov school, I remember a clock simultaneous given against the youngest pupils by the master Golovko. A member of the medical service, Golovko had served in the

Second World War and finished up in the small Czech town of Pardubice, nowadays well-known to every chess fan on account of its annual chess festival. At the school sessions, Golovko acted partly as the school's doctor, reading us a series of lectures on the importance of physical preparation, rational organisation of the working day, sleep, food, etc. One can acquaint oneself with many of his useful medical and purely chess recommendations in his book *The Road to Mastery*. Our game in the simul ended in a draw and the following day, the following short dialogue took place between us:

– Sasha, why did you agree a draw in the final position?
– I thought my position was a bit worse.
– You play well, but it is important to pay attention to developing your fighting qualities!

Nikolai Grigorievich was a thousand times right – later I suffered many times from the weakness of my sporting character! But at the time, I did little to implement the advice of the experienced master.
At the first session of the Smyslov school, the pupils also had the chance to show their play to IM Mark Dvoretsky. At home, we were required to annotate two of our wins, one loss and one drawn game. When I finished showing my games, Mark Israelevich sternly asked:

– And where is your lost game?
– I haven't lost any games in recent tournaments.
– Oh well, if you haven't lost, you haven't lost!
And everyone laughed.

Now I look back on this incident with some regret. It is true that, formally speaking, I had not lost any games in the last few events, but I had several times fallen into positions where I had been lost at some point, before emerging with a draw or even a win. But I only chose to demonstrate more convincing and successful games, thereby missing the chance to hear my mistakes assessed objectively from the mouth of this remarkable trainer.
Amongst all listeners, without exception, a great impression was made by the lectures of grandmaster Razuvaev. Just at that time, Yuri Sergeevich was working on his book on Akiba Rubinstein and he demonstrated to us examples of the latter's play. The games of the great Polish player, as presented by Razuvaev, were for us a wonderful schooling in positional play. I remember Yuri Sergeevich's way of thinking. He had the ability to sum up in just a few words the essence of a position. The grandmaster thought not so much in terms of concrete

variations (although he valued these) as in general categories, based on his great experience. I also remember his advice about forming an opening repertoire: 'Do not look at everything from beginning to end, but concentrate your attention on especially instructive games, played by specialists in the line you are interested in!'

I will give you one example of how Yuri Sergeevich presented the 'mechanics' of typical middlegame positions. The grandmaster once astonished us by telling us that Vladimir Makogonov considered the minority attack in the so-called Carlsbad (QGD Exchange) structure to be an incorrect plan for White! The master from Baku (who was awarded the GM title by FIDE at the age of 80, for his past achievements!) had the following idea: 'After the move b2-b4 Black should play ...a7-a6, and after a2-a4 and b4-b5 he should play ...a6-a5!. After the exchange b5xc6, ...b7xc6, the white pawn on a4 prevents the white knight going from c3 to a4 and c5, whilst Black, by posting his bishop on b4, shelters his queenside weaknesses.'

In this book, I had wanted to show Makogonov's idea with a fragment from one of his own games, but to my surprise, I could not find a single game where anybody played the minority attack against him! I will therefore settle for showing a modern example on the same theme.

Queen's Gambit Declined
Rafael Vaganian
Alexander Panchenko
Sochi 1980 (10)

1.c4 ♘f6 2.d4 e6 3.♘c3 d5 4.♗g5 c6 5.e3 ♘bd7 6.cxd5 exd5 7.♗d3 ♗e7 8.♕c2 0-0 9.♘ge2 ♖e8 10.0-0 ♘f8 11.♗xf6 ♗xf6 12.b4 a6 13.a4 g6 14.b5

Black to play. What would you do?

14...a5! 15.♘c1
The manoeuvrability of the ♘c3 is limited, but the king's knight counts on reaching c5.
15...♘e6 16.♘b3 ♕d6
The weak square in front of the backward c6-pawn is securely defended.
17.♖fd1 ♗d7 18.♕d2 ♖ed8 19.♗e2 ♗g7 20.♖a2 ♗e8 21.g3

21...♗f8!

The black bishop finds a path to the b4-square.

22.♖b1 ♕e7 23.♖c2 ♕f6 24.bxc6 bxc6 25.♗g4 ♗d7 26.♕d1 h5

Strategically the initiative is on Black's side. White's next move proves to be a tactical oversight.

27.♕f3? ♕xf3 28.♗xf3 ♘g5 29.♗d1 ♗f5

And Black won the exchange and later the game.

Yuri Sergeevich especially stressed to us the ability to feel the geometry of the board: 'For example, place a white bishop on c1 and a black pawn on d6. We see at once that the bishop can attack the pawn immediately with either ♗c1-a3 or ♗c1-f4, but in a practical game we would probably not even consider the manoeuvre ♗c1-h6-f8. It is essential to develop your sight of the board, as this is a very important quality.'

Playing over the following game recently, I recalled the comments of this remarkable grandmaster and trainer.

Vienna Game

Sergey Makarychev
Yuri Razuvaev

Moscow 1989 (5)

1.e4 e5 2.♗c4 ♘c6 3.♘c3 ♘f6 4.d3 ♘a5 5.♘ge2 ♘xc4 6.dxc4 ♗c5 7.h3 h6 8.♘g3 d6 9.0-0 ♗e6 10.♕d3 0-0 11.♗d2 a6 12.a4 c6 13.♖ad1 ♕e7 14.♔h1 ♖ad8 15.f4

In taking on an isolated pawn on e4, White wishes to activate his pieces.

15...exf4 16.♗xf4

16...♘g4!

Finding a tactical way to transfer the knight to the blockading e5-square. White had no doubt foreseen this and prepared...

17.♘f5 ♗xf5 18.exf5 ♘f2+ 19.♖xf2 ♗xf2 20.♘e4 ♕h4 21.♕f3

Black to play. What should he do?

This is the position White had been aiming for when he sacrificed the exchange. His pieces are actively placed, the bishop on f2 is hanging, as is the pawn on d6, and the battering ram advance f5-f6 is threatened. In the event of 21...♗c5 there follows 22.♗g3 ♕e7 23.f6, destroying the protection of the black king.

21...♗e1!!

This far from obvious move allows the black forces to achieve coordination in a surprising way. By remaining deep in the heart of the white position, the black bishop prevents its opposite number from occupying g3.

22.f6

On 22.♘xd6 Black had prepared 22...♗b4! 23.c3 ♗xd6 24.♗xd6 ♖fe8 with an obvious advantage.

22...g5 23.♗h2 ♖fe8 24.♘xd6

Black to move. What would you play?

24...g4!

A subtle pawn sacrifice, which is an essential preparation for the final combination. According to the computer, a sufficient alternative

was 24...♕f2! 25.♕h5 (or 25.♕g4 ♕e2) 25...♖xd6! 26.♗xd6 (an instructive variation is 26.♖xd6 ♗a5! 27.♗g1 ♖e1, winning) 26...♕f1+ 27.♔h2 ♖e2 28.♕g4 ♗g3+ 29.♕xg3 ♕xd1, and Black wins.

25.hxg4

More tenacious was 25.♕xg4+ ♕xg4 26.hxg4 ♖e2 or 25.♕f5 ♗b4 26.c5 ♕g5, although in both variations, White's position is still bad.

25...♖xd6! 26.♖xd6 ♗d2!

An elegant blow, logically completing the manoeuvre begun by Black at his 21st move. Weaker was 26...♗g3 27.♕xg3 ♖e1+ 28.♕xe1 ♕xe1+ 29.♗g1, and White retains hopes of saving himself.

27.♕h3 ♕e1+ 28.♗g1 ♗e3 29.♕h2 ♗xg1 0-1

A game characteristic of Razuvaev's creative outlook. The action of his pieces, just like their leader, was always characterised by great internal intelligence.

One of the sessions of the Smyslov school, held at Kislovodsk, was led by international master Orest Averkin. Orest Nikolaevich was a very strong player (one only needs to recall his successful appearance at the super-strong 1973 USSR Championship final) and a remarkable trainer. In different periods he worked both with world class players (e.g. Polugaevsky) and also uncovered some hugely talented juniors (e.g. Kramnik). His lectures were characterised by great chess culture.

At this session he covered typical positions with an isolated queen's pawn. His method of presenting the material made a great impression on me. First we looked at the basic laws of such structures in king and pawn endings, then we proceeded through knight endings, bishop endings, bishop v knight endings, etc. Gradually, the same IQP structure was filled up with more and more pieces, until we ended up looking at full middlegame positions!

I also recall some specific observations by Oleg Nikolaevich. In the chapter 'Concerning the value of endgame studies', I have already mentioned his comments regarding the role of tactics in the endgame. Here is another episode.

Alexander Kalinin
Sergey Tiviakov

Kislovodsk 1983

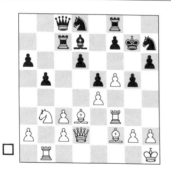

This training game was played at the school session. There followed 22.h4 f6 23.♗e2 with some advantage to White. In my notes, I pointed out that after 22...♖xc3 there is the forcing variation 23.♗xb5

23...♖xf3 24.♗xd7 ♖xf2 (or 24...♕xd7 25.gxf3 ♘c6 26.♘c5) 25.♗xc8 ♖xd2 26.♘xd2 a5 27.hxg5 hxg5 28.♖b6, which is in White's favour. Orest Nikolaevich made the following comment in my exercise book: '23...♖xb3! – all long variations can be refuted on the first move!'

In my fourth and fifth classes, I studied at the Moscow Sporting School no. 9. The chess section here was very important, because it gave the opportunity for talented kids from distant regions to get access to good trainers and to soak up the chess atmosphere of the capital. Many strong players emerged from the walls of this school, including Tamara Minogina, Yuri Dokhoian, Evgeny Bareev, Sergey Shipov and Alisa Galliamova.

My trainer for these two years was master Kimelfeld. Rudolf Iosifovich was a real chess fanatic. Cigarette permanently in hand, he was prepared to spend hours analysing a position that interested him. Undoubtedly, the master's creative outlook was passed on to his pupils, and he doted on them, always willing to help with advice and concrete action, often defending us in clashes with the school director, when we got up to mischief. Rudolf Iosifovich's opening tastes were unusual. He preferred positionally based lines, but older systems, where a knowledge of the classical heritage was useful. I used to think the master's style was somewhat 'crooked' and in my youth identified the modern opening systems as representing correct play. But my views changed after one junior event in Tallinn. On the rest day, Rudolf Iosifovich played blitz against his pupils, giving odds of two minutes against five. It was not even about the result – during play, I almost physically felt how harmoniously he deployed his forces and how in just a few seconds he found the correct squares for his pieces.

Below I present a game which is characteristic of Kimelfeld's creative outlook. It was played in the final of the Moscow championship, during the years when I was studying with him, and we, his pupils, naturally cheered for him proudly.

Bishop's Opening
Rudolf Kimelfeld
A. Lychinkin

Moscow 1979

1.e4 e5 2.♗c4
The Bishop's Opening is a rare guest in modern practice, although it was once played by Garry Kasparov, aiming to reach a position from the Italian Game, without allowing forcing variations of the Russian (Petroff) Defence.
2...♘f6 3.d3 c6 4.♕e2
White underlines his strategy of reinforcing the e4-square, which ensures him the chance to develop his pieces in a planned way.
4...♗c5 5.♘f3 0-0 6.♗g5 d5 7.♗b3 dxe4 8.dxe4 h6 9.♗h4 ♕e7 10.♘bd2 ♘bd7 11.g4!
At this moment, Black was probably regretting his move ...h7-h6. White still retains the possibility of castling queenside. Steinitz adopted a similar plan in analogous positions from the Spanish.
11...♕d6 12.0-0-0 ♘xg4
If you are suffering anyway, you might as well have a pawn to suffer for.
13.♖hg1 ♘gf6 14.♘c4 ♕e7 15.♘e3 ♗xe3+ 16.♕xe3 ♔h7

White to move. What would you play?

Now there was an immediate win with the striking 17.♖xg7+! ♔xg7 18.♖g1+ ♔h7 19.♘g5+! ♔h8 (or 19...

hxg5 20.♗xg5 with irresistible mating threats) 20.♘xf7+! ♖xf7 21.♕xh6+ ♖h7 22.♗xf6+ ♘xf6 23.♕xf6+! ♕xf6 24.♖g8#. White finds this combinative idea next move.

17.♖g3 ♕c5
Provoking White into the sacrifice.
18.♖xg7+! ♔xg7 19.♖g1+ ♔h7

20.♘g5+! ♔h8
Or 20...hxg5 21.♕xg5 ♖g8 22.♕f5+ ♖g6 23.♗xf7 mating.
21.♘xf7+ ♖xf7 22.♕xh6+ ♘h7
23.♗xf7 ♕f8 24.♕g6 1-0

For the rest of my school career, I was again studying chess at the Pioneer Palace and at Sparrow Hills in Moscow. My trainer in this period was international master Khasin. Abram Iosifovich was greatly loved and respected by his pupils. He had an interesting personality, an outward sternness concealing great warmth. Khasin was badly wounded in World War Two at Stalingrad and lost both legs. He found the strength of character to return to an active life in peacetime. He became a master of great practical strength, five times qualifying to play in the final of the USSR Championship. He is also well-known for his achievements in correspondence chess, where he became an ICCF grandmaster and played successfully for the Soviet team in correspondence chess Olympiads. His training experience was also successful, and in my opinion he was one of the best trainers in the country during the 1960s-1980s. Among his pupils are Murey, Gulko, Aksharamova, Minogina, Yurtaev, Bareev and Chuchelov.

Our studies proceeded in a very normal way, analysing our games, studying certain positions and covering specific topics. The main beneficial effects lay in the details – those assessments, recommendations, and comments of the Master, which together formed our understanding of the game. There was also the famous 'Khasin Card-index', a forerunner of modern-day computer databases of games. He copied games from magazines onto cards and sorted them by opening. When studying a particular opening variation, we could get the relevant part of the card index, containing games on the subject concerned. But the main, I would repeat, was the Master's judgements of different positions, which drew on his enormous chess and life experience. I will offer you a few instructive examples:

– In one of my games I managed to win a pawn with the aid of a

tactic. Wanting to ensure victory, I continued pressing my opponent, going for outwardly active moves. My advantage gradually dissipated and the game ended in a draw. After the game, Abram Iosifovich observed that 'after winning a pawn, the first things to do is consolidate one's position!';
– 'When playing against an isolated pawn, one should strive to exchange the minor pieces and keep the major pieces on the board';
– 'In the fight between a queen and two rooks, the advantage will be with the queen, if the coordination of the rooks is disrupted' (this observation of Khasin's was recently drawn to my attention by international master Igor Yanvarev).

The following episode deserves a small introduction. Even when I was still a kid, I got to know the following game, which has become a classic example of playing the French endgame:

Siegbert Tarrasch
Richard Teichmann

San Sebastian 1912 (14)

Tarrasch assessed the position as follows: 'White has more space, Black being cramped not only by the pawn on e5, but also by his own pawn on e6. The white knight on d4 occupies a dominating position, from which Black cannot drive it away; the black knight cannot do so.' I would add that the last factor is a direct result of the battle between White's good bishop and Black's bad one.

17...♖ac8 18.♔f2
'Although Black controls the nearest thing to an open file in the position, White in return has a significant advantage – he can centralise his king, the most important piece in the endgame. Black cannot do this.' (Tarrasch)

18...♖c7 19.♔e3 ♖e8
It made sense for Black to regroup his queenside pawns to a5 and b4 by means of 19...a5, so as to enlarge the space for his bishop.

20.♖f2 ♘b7 21.♗f1 ♘a5 22.b3 h6
Now White has a target to develop active operations on the kingside.

23.♗d3 ♘c6 24.♘xc6 ♗xc6 25.♔d4 ♗d7 26.g4 ♗c8 27.h4 g6 28.♖h1 ♔g7

29.h5

And later, by combining threats on the kingside with the possibility (after the exchange of all the rooks) of his king entering the enemy position via c5, White won.

But one day, Abram Iosifovich analysed a French Defence with us, a position very similar to that seen in the above game. The dark-squared bishops came off and Black was left with a bad light-squared bishop.

Knowing the classic example, we all thought White was winning. But to our Teacher, the black position was fully defensible: 'So what if Black has a bad bishop? In order to play for a win, White will have to open the position and then my bishop will become good!'

Such comments, expressed by a strong player or experienced trainer, are worth more to the youngsters listening than any number of concrete opening variations, because they increase one's positional understanding and stimulate independent thinking.

And several years later, relying on the ideas formulated by Khasin, Alexander Chernin managed to defend a position which had been considered difficult for Black ever since the days of Tarrasch. I present this game, together with notes from the book 'Strolls around the French Defence', which I co-authored with Viktor Kortchnoi.

French Defence
Nigel Short
Alexander Chernin
Montpellier 1985 (13)

1.e4 e6 2.d4 d5 3.♘c3 ♘f6 4.e5 ♘fd7 5.f4 c5 6.♘f3 ♘c6 7.♗e3 cxd4 8.♘xd4 ♗c5 9.♕d2 ♗xd4 10.♗xd4 ♘xd4 11.♕xd4 ♕b6

Directly from the opening, Black heads into an endgame, agreeing to the exchange of dark-squared bishops and ceding the opponent control of the d4-square. At the Montpellier Candidates, Chernin confidently defended this position in the present game against Short, and almost won with it against Timman.

12.♘b5 ♕xd4 13.♘xd4 ♔e7

Naturally, in the ending, Black prefers to keep his king in the centre. If the chance arises, he can support the break ...f7-f6.

14.g3

14...♘b8!

An important manoeuvre. The black knight transfers to c6. Aiming it at e4 instead makes no sense, as there it will just be exchanged for the opponent's bishop.

15.♔d2 ♗d7 16.♗d3 ♘c6

What does Black have by way of compensation for the weaknesses enumerated above? The fact is that he has no incurable weaknesses, and by way of trumps, he has the superior pawn structure and also control of the half-open c-file. If he can exchange the light-squared bishops, Black will stand better, because of his superior pawn structure. In addition, as we will see later, it is hard for White to find a target to bite on in the black position – there are no breaks and he can only hope for a long siege.

17.♘f3 h6

In principle, in such positions, Black tries to post his pawns on h5 and g6, i.e. on the same colour squares as his bishop! In this way, he slows up to a maximum his opponent's attack on the kingside. The moves h2-h3, g3-g4 and f4-f5 lead only to mass exchanges and, after ...e6xf5, open space for the French bishop. On the same principle, Black need not fear the white queenside break c2-c4. With the text move, Black decides to worry his opponent with the possibility of ...g7-g5.

18.h4 h5!

Black should not allow a bind to be established on the kingside with h4-h5.

19.a3 ♖ac8 20.♖he1 ♘a5 21.b3 g6

Black has achieved the optimal defensive set-up and is not ready to do anything but mark time. White is not able to break through.

22.♘d4 ♖c7 23.a4 a6 24.c3 ♖hc8 25.♖ec1 ♗e8 26.♗e2 ♗d7 27.♖a3 ♗e8 28.♗d3 ♗d7 29.♘e2 ♗e8 30.♔c2 d4 31.c4 ♘c6 32.a5 f6 33.exf6+ ♔xf6 34.♔d2 ♖d8 35.♖e1 ♖e7 36.♖aa1 e5 37.♗e4 ♗f7 38.♗xc6 ½-½

In 1985, such a treatment of the French endgame made quite an impression on the 'uninitiated', but as we have seen above, this had been an open secret on the 'unofficial' level for some time! In general, the French Defence was a great weapon of Khasin's, and it is no coincidence that his pupil Evgeny Bareev became one of the world's leading practitioners of the black side of the opening.

I will tell you of one more discussion of the French, which I had with Abram Iosifovich.

At the junior team championships of the USSR, in the match between

Moscow and Latvia, the following game was played:

French Defence
Alexander Kalinin
V. Vitols
Leningrad 1985

1.e4 e6 2.d4 d5 3.♘d2 ♘f6 4.e5 ♘fd7 5.c3 c5 6.♗d3 ♘c6 7.♘e2 cxd4 8.cxd4 f6 9.exf6 ♘xf6 10.♘f3 ♗d6 11.0-0 ♕c7 12.♗g5 0-0 13.♗h4 e5 14.dxe5 ♘xe5 15.♘xe5 ♗xe5 16.♗g3 ♗xg3 17.♘xg3
A well-known variation has been played, which in theory's opinion leads to equal chances. Even so, I was happy to head for this position, liking the fact that I had the better pawn structure (two pawn 'islands' against three).
17...♕f4 18.♗c2
The transfer of the bishop to b3, followed by concentrating the heavy pieces on the d-file, allows White to target the d5-pawn.
18...♗d7 19.♕d3 g6 20.♗b3 ♗e6 21.♖ad1 ♖ad8 22.♕d4 ♕xd4 23.♖xd4 ♖d6 24.♖fd1 ♖fd8 25.♘e2 ♔g7 26.♘f4 ♗f7 27.♔f1 h6

The game has reached a typical endgame for this variation. The attack and defence of the d5-pawn are evenly matched. Can White strengthen his position? It seemed to me that it would be favourable for White to exchange a pair of rooks, so as to be able to bring the king into the centre, without having to fear the kind of middlegame counterplay which could occur with all four rooks on the board. I soon found a way to implement this idea.
28.♖e1 ♘e4 29.♖c1 ♖c6 30.♖cd1 ♘f6 31.♖e1 ♖cd6 32.♖e7
The 'pendulum' motion has allowed the white rook to penetrate to the seventh rank and Black himself exchanges it off.
32...♖8d7 33.♖xd7 ♘xd7 34.♘d3 a6 35.f3 ♗e6 36.♔f2 ♔f6 37.♘f4 ♘b6 38.♔e3 ♗f7 39.♘d3 ♘d7 40.♘f4 ♘b6

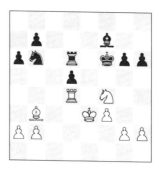

In this position, the game was adjourned and White sealed. I assessed my chances optimistically and was generally proud of my 'subtle idea' at moves 28-30. But as I stepped out of the tournament hall, Abram Iosifovich grabbed me and said 'Sasha, how can you play a technical position like this so uncertainly? I thought you knew the classics well, but it turns out you don't know the game Botvinnik-Bronstein from their 1951 match, where Botvinnik showed how to play such positions. You have messed it up and lost your advantage. Why did you exchange rooks? When playing against an isolated pawn, you should exchange minor pieces and keep the major pieces!'

Later, when adjournment analysis showed that White still had the advantage, Abram Iosifovich relented somewhat and said 'Okay, maybe it is also possible to play your way!' On resumption, Black made his opponent's task much easier than it should have been, making an obvious tactical error.

41.♘d3 ♖e6+

If 41...♘d7 42.h4 White gradually activates his kingside pawns and retains the advantage.

42.♔d2 ♖c6?

It is strange that this move should have been played straight after adjournment analysis. Black prepares the jump ...♘c4, but allows an exchanging operation favourable for White.

43.♖f4+ ♔e6 44.♘e5 ♖c7 45.♖xf7 ♖xf7 46.♘xf7 ♔xf7 47.♔d3

In the resulting position, the bishop is clearly stronger than the knight, which is underlined by White's having an outside passed pawn on the kingside.

47...♔e6 48.♔d4 ♔d6 49.f4 a5 50.a3 g5 51.fxg5 hxg5 52.h3 ♘d7 53.♗xd5 b6 54.g3 ♘f6 55.♗f3 b5 56.♗e2 b4 57.axb4 axb4 58.♗f3 ♘d7 59.♗d1 ♘e5 60.♗b3 ♘f3+ 61.♔e3 ♘g1 62.♗d1 1-0

Everything turned out successfully in the end, but Khasin's advice was not lost on me. Naturally, as soon as I got home, I looked up the Botvinnik-Bronstein game.

Mikhail Botvinnik
David Bronstein

Moscow 1951

Firstly, White builds pressure against the d5-pawn.

21.♘c2 ♖d8 22.♖d3 ♔f8 23.♖fd1 ♔e7 24.♔f1 ♔d7 25.♗g5 ♔c6 26.b4 ♗f8 27.♘e3 ♖e5

So far, events have developed like in my previous game, with the attack and defence of d5 balancing each other. But here White had at his disposal an important resource. Botvinnik could have played **28.♗xf6 gxf6 29.f4 ♖h5 30.c4! ♗xb4 31.♘xd5 ♗d6 32.♘xf6 ♖hh8 33.♘e4 ♗e7 34.♖xd8 ♖xd8 35.♖xd8 ♗xd8 36.♔e2 f5 37.♘g5** winning a pawn and gaining good winning chances.

Only here did it dawn on me that in my game, I had been laying siege not to an isolated but a passed pawn on d5! As a result, I did not have the possibility of attacking it with my pawns on the neighbouring files. This is the difficulty in applying the method of play by analogy. On the other hand, White has a queenside pawn majority and his efforts should be directed to its activation. In this context, the exchange of a pair of rooks is not so stupid, because the simplification increases the strength of White's outside passed pawn. An exact reply to the question of whether the exchange of rooks was right probably does not exist, but it is precisely this lack of a one-sided answer that is the chief lesson of this game.

Abram Iosifovich's playing attitude was characterised by tactical ingenuity and a striving to avoid stereotyped paths. He combined stubbornness in defence and a willingness to suffer for material gain with a striving to attack and willingness to sacrifice material for the initiative. The following consultation game was played by him against his pupils at a training session of the Moscow junior team. For me it was an eye-opener that our trainer was also ready to conduct the battle in a strictly positional style.

English Opening
Abram Khasin
Vasily Prokofiev, Alexander Kalinin, Vladimir Chuchelov, N. Filipsky
Podolsk 1982

___

At the time this game was played, Khasin had long since quit

over the board play, taking part only (and with great success) in correspondence chess. Even so, for this consultation his old competitive spirit was revived. He came to the game smartly dressed in a suit, white shirt and tie. During the game, the strain of battle took its toll – first the jacket was consigned to the back of his chair and then the tie...

1.c4 c5 2.g3 g6 3.♗g2 ♗g7 4.♘c3 ♘c6 5.d3 d6 6.♗d2

A subtle psychological move. Abram Iosifovich wanted to win and chose an opening that would be most uncomfortable for his opponents. Seeing that a quiet symmetrical variation had appeared on the board, his young opponents started to feel bored...

6...♖b8 7.a3 ♗d7 8.b4 b6 9.♘f3 ♕c8 10.0-0 ♗h3 11.♗xh3 ♕xh3 12.♕a4 ♕d7 13.♖ab1 ♘f6 14.♔g2 0-0 15.♘d5 ♘xd5 16.cxd5 ♘e5 17.♕xd7 ♘xd7

The game has gone into a roughly equal endgame. In what follows, the master outplays his opponents almost without any effort. There is nothing surprising in this, since, after all, it is precisely such

'simple positions' which reveal the class of someone's play. The black players content themselves with solid moves, but ones which are not united by a single idea, whilst White methodically increases the mobility of his pawn chain.
18.♖fc1 ♖fc8 19.e4 b5 20.♗e3
Preventing the manoeuvre
...♘d7-b6-a4.
20...a6 21.♔f1 ♔f8 22.♔e2 ♔e8 23.♘d2
The white knight heads for the a5-square.
23...♖b7 24.♘b3 ♖bc7 25.♘a5 cxb4 26.axb4 ♖xc1 27.♖xc1 ♖xc1 28.♗xc1 ♗c3 29.♗d2 ♗xd2

30.♔xd2
Taking the game into a knight endgame makes White's advantage clear. The opponent's queenside pawn majority is doing nothing, whilst White's forces are very active.
30...♘b8 31.♔e3 ♔d7 32.♔f4
It is obvious that White's king will find work on the queenside.
32...h6 33.d4 e6 34.dxe6+ fxe6 35.d5 exd5 36.exd5 ♔c7 37.h4 ♘d7 38.h5 gxh5 39.♔f5 ♘e5 40.f4 ♘c4 41.♘b3 ♘e3+ 42.♔g6 h4 43.gxh4 ♘g2 44.h5

♘xf4+ 45.♔xh6 ♘xd5 46.♔g5 ♔d7 47.h6 1-0

During my final years at school, I was fortunate enough to meet Alexander Konstantinopolsky, the legendary maestro (only in the 1980s did FIDE award him the grandmaster title for his past achievements) and remarkable teacher. Alexander Markovich at that time gave lessons to young players at the Moscow Burevestnik sports club. Going to my first meeting with him, I remembered that one of his pupils was... Abram Iosifovich Khasin! Konstantinopolsky's personality was attractive: he was completely without any self-importance and was surprisingly warm and kind towards all his pupils. To our great regret, Alexander Markovich only did about five or six lessons with our group, because soon his health deteriorated and he found it impossible to make the journey to the club. But even such a short acquaintance with him left a lot in my memory. Konstantinopolsky continually reminded us of the need to study the classical heritage of masters from the past. He often used the term 'chess stratagem', meaning the understanding of the connection of opening-middlegame ideas with their historical development. In general, the setting of the strategic essence of this or that opening line in its historical context was a hallmark of Alexander Markovich.

Discussions with the Master undoubtedly affected my approach to absorbing opening information. I remember that it was under his influence that I became interested in Réti's article 'Will the new opening ideas survive practical testing?' (1926), in which he developed the idea of so-called 'indeterminate' positions. At one time, I was much taken by this quote of Bronstein's from his famous book on the 1953 Candidates tournament: 'The concrete contents of opening books are interesting and can even be attractive, but constantly spending one's life with head buried in jungles of variations, never seeing the stars or the sun, is a very meagre form of chess. Modern chess has become more flexible. Large-scale, deep systems are one of the ways of ensuring stability, i.e. the ability of the opening to survive minor changes in the surroundings... One can therefore understand at first the intuitive and then a conscious striving to build deep, solid positions, in what Konstantinopolsky has called "the collision of openings".'

It is no surprise that, after embracing such an opening philosophy, I included in my repertoire the English Opening, one of the deepest and most flexible of openings, in which the 'indeterminate' set and 'collision of openings' finds its full expression. The following game is characteristic of my play at this period.

English Opening
Alexander Kalinin
Andrey Alekseev
Moscow 1985

This game with master Alekseev was played in the semifinal of the Moscow Championship. Beforehand, I had analysed the sharp variation 1.c4 e5 2.♘c3 ♘f6 3.g3 c6 4.♘f3 e4 5.♘d4 d5 6.cxd5 ♕b6 7.♘b3 a5!?, the theory of which was based on the games and analyses of my opponent and which Alekseev had played against none other than Botvinnik in the Moscow Productive Collectives Team Championship of 1968.

1.c4 e5 2.♘c3 d6
Taking the game into a type of Closed Sicilian with colours reversed.
3.g3 g6 4.♗g2 ♗g7 5.e3 ♘c6 6.♘ge2
This modest set-up was introduced into practice by the 19th century English master Howard Staunton, who used it both as White in the English and as Black in the Closed Sicilian.
6...♗e6 7.d3 ♕d7 8.h3
Botvinnik once used a similar idea with colours reversed. White prevents the exchange of light-squared bishops and, on account of the pressure against h3, is prepared to leave his king in the centre for the time being. As soon as Black plays ...f7-f5, immediate kingside castling will follow. Of course, Black can delay advancing the f-pawn, but then it is harder for him to create play on the kingside,

and White in turn can exploit this to strengthen his position on the queenside and in the centre.

8...h5 9.h4 ♘h6 10.♕a4

The idea of this move is to prepare the jump ♘c3-d5, after which the manoeuvre ...♘c6-d8 and then ...c7-c6 will become difficult.

10...♘f5 11.♘d5 0-0 12.♘ec3 a6 13.♖b1 ♖fb8 14.♕d1

Anticipating the advance ...b7-b5. The white queen has done its job and can now retreat to the rear – Black still has to spend extra time to prepare ...c7-c6 as a result of the hole on b6 caused by ...a7-a6.

14...♕d8 15.0-0 ♖a7 16.b3 ♖c8 17.♗b2

By fianchettoing both bishops, White creates the potential conditions for activating his central pawns.

17...♘b8 18.♘e4 c6 19.♘dc3 b5

Black has finally expelled the enemy knight from d5, but as a result, his pieces have ended up somewhat uncoordinated.

20.♘g5 ♗d7 21.♘e2 f6 22.♘f3 ♗e6

We have a typical 'indeterminate' position on the board. The two sides' pawn configurations have avoided direct contact in the centre, retaining the option of assuming various different outlines, from a fully blocked position to one with all lines open.

I remember the assessment of the position that was expressed by master Kremenetsky in joint analysis after the game. His view was that the compromised position resulting from the advance of the pawns in front of the black king gave White a long-term advantage.

23.♖c1

Preparing the advance d3-d4.

23...♕b6 24.♗a1 ♗h6 25.♔h2

The immediate 25.d4 does not bring any benefit because of 25...e4 26.♘d2 d5. White therefore continues regrouping his forces, taking long-range measures to reduce the effect of a possible blow on e3.

25...♖f8 26.♘fg1 ♖h7 27.d4

White's pawns start moving, creating the threats of the further advances d4-d5 and c4-c5. Black's position is already dangerous, his next move is especially unfortunate.

27...♗d7? 28.c5! dxc5 29.dxe5

And Black's bastions collapsed.

One other recommendation of Alexander Markovich's was based on his observing the many mistakes I tended to make towards the end of games – he suggested I should boost my energy by eating chocolate and drinking hot tea in the middle of the second hour of play, and also, most importantly of all, that I should play more sport – advice which, sadly, I stubbornly refused to follow!

After finishing school, I joined the training department of the Institute of Physical Culture. At that time, the leader of the chess section and of our group was International Master Boris Zlotnik. I had heard Boris Anatolyevich's lectures back when I was a kid at the Smyslov school. They were unusual, in that they were formatted as tests (for example, games with questions).

Now it is clear to me that Boris Anatolyevich had a very effective system for diagnosing the components of chess mastery. He set out his views on this in an essay entitled 'Diagnostics of the sporting mastery of chess players', which appeared in the collection *Chess – Science, Experience and Mastery*, published in 1990. He followed an analogous approach in his sessions with students. In analysing our games or those of masters, he tried to identify the key turning points in the games and to demonstrate a combined chess/psychological approach to the taking of decisions. I was struck by his ability to formulate imaginative general observations. Here are a few of these:

– 'In most games, there is only one or at most two critical moments, and taking the right decision at such decides the game';

– 'The three basic openings are the Spanish, Sicilian and King's Indian. The structures reached from these three overlap and complement one another, and are reached in more than 60% of games.'

Thus, as a great lover and expert on the French Defence, Boris Anatolyevich often told us that this opening was a mirror reflection of the King's Indian!

I remember one lesson, the subject of which was one of the variations of the Four Pawns Attack against the King's Indian. We broke up into pairs, so as to test certain conclusions. I had to take White against Boris Anatolyevich. The time control was 30 minutes per game. At a moment when White had only 5 minutes left, to Black's 15, Boris Anatolyevich suddenly declared 'Let's stop the game now and take a look at what happened. It has clearly demonstrated Sasha's strengths and weaknesses.' At that moment, I felt very strongly what those weaknesses were – I had apportioned my time irrationally and was clearly doomed from a sporting point of view.

I think Boris Anatolyevich was trying in a delicate way to point out my Achilles Heel – a low level of qualities as a fighter. We started analysing, but not a word was said about strengths and weaknesses. A typical trainer's device – let the pupil draw his own conclusions! Earlier I had thought little about chess as a battle, considering it instead as a 'pure' intellectual discipline. The years I spent studying at the training institute significantly widened my views on the game. Zlotnik, a strong player (one only has to recall his victory in the very strong blitz tournament sponsored by the Moscow evening newspaper *Vechernaya Moskva* in 1980), had a subtle feel for the internal problems of a player and tried to reveal to us the hidden chess-psychological factors that lay behind the dry outward appearance of a tournament battle.

Under Boris Anatolyevich's influence, I began to collect examples of typical strategic plans and devices. In demonstrating games, he always tried to point out the key moments and, on the basis of their chess/psychological analysis, to draw up formulae which would apply to many situations in life. As well as standard chess devices, our teacher told us, there are also less well-known and harder to formulate examples.

Here are a couple of examples.

Emanoil Reicher
Isaak Boleslavsky

Bucharest 1953 (6)

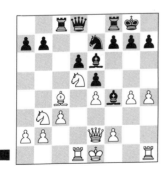

Isaak Boleslavsky played

16...♘g6 17.h5 ♘h4
leaving the ♘d5 'in peace' and attacking the opponent's weakened kingside. It soon became apparent that the lovely-looking white steed in the centre was completely harmless. Boris Anatolyevich named this device 'playing around' the ♘d5. The game ended in a quick crush of White.
18.♗d3 ♕g5 19.f3 ♗g3+ 20.♔f1 f5 21.♖g1 ♘xf3 22.♖xg3 fxe4 23.♔g2 exd3 24.♖xd3 ♗xd5 25.♖xd5 ♕h4 26.♖xf3 ♕xg4+ 0-1

Vasily Smyslov
Oleg Romanishin

Tilburg 1979 (6)

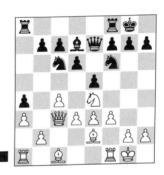

What would you play?

This position has more than one solution. Romanishin played
13...♘e8
and awarded the move an exclamation mark in *Informant*. By declining the exchange of knights, Black is ready to play ...f7-f5 and then return the knight to f6.
In the game, there followed
14.♕e1

14.b4!? axb3 15.♕xb3
14...f5 15.♘c3 ♘f6 16.♗d2 ♘a5
17.♗d1 b6 18.♘xa4
18.♗c2!?
18...e4!
And Black seized the initiative.

However, Zlotnik considered that a more promising plan for Black was 13...♘xe4!? 14.fxe4 ♘a5 15.♗d1 c5, limiting the activity of the white bishops. At the same time, he formulated an unusual rule: 'When you have the two bishops, it is useful also to have a knight on the board. The absence of knights reduces the mobility of the bishop pair!' It is very hard to give a concrete explanation for this phenomenon. But even such an abstract idea can help in practical play. Here is a fragment from one of my games, played somewhat later, when I was already an IM.

Alexander Kalinin
N. Seferian

Riazan 1996

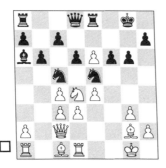

What should White play?

Black's last move was 16...g7-g6, taking the f5-square from the white knight. In the event of the straightforward 16...♘xe6 17.♘f5 White would have obtained a clear advantage. His knight can transfer from f5 to e3, followed by ♘e3-d5 or prepare the advance d3-d4. By taking control of f5, Black hopes after 17...♘xe6 to force the exchange of the white knight, or else force it back to e2. In both cases, it does not get to e3, which means it will not be easy to carry out the advance d3-d4, and the white bishops will remain passive. However, after long thought, I succeeded in finding a way to put Zlotnik's formula into effect.
17.♘f5!
The knight's striving for the f5-square turns out to be stronger than its instinct for self-preservation!
17...gxf5
If 17...♘xe6 18.♘e3 White's pawn centre becomes mobile, opening splendid prospects before the pair of white bishops.
18.exf5
The e6-pawn, which just now appeared doomed, now cuts the black position in two.
18...♗b7?
Upset and shocked, Black loses immediately. More tenacious was 18...♘b7, although after 19.♕e2 followed by g3-g4-g5 it is not easy for Black to put up any defence.
19.d4 ♘f3+ 20.♔h1 ♗e4
More prospects were offered by 20...♘xe6 21.fxe6 ♖xe6

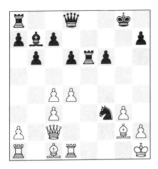

Analysis diagram

22.♕f5! (on 22.♕f2 there follows
22...♕e8! 23.♗xf3 ♖e2 24.♕f1 ♕h5!)
22...♕e7 (or 22...♕e8 23.♕g4+
♔h8 24.♖f1 ♖e1 25.♗h6) 23.♕g4+
(23.♗xf3 is unconvincing because
of 23...♖e1+ 24.♔g2 ♕e2+ 25.♔h3
♗xf3 26.♖xe1 ♗g2+ 27.♔h4 ♕xe1)
23...♔h8 24.♗f4 ♖g8 25.♕h5 ♕e8
26.♕xe8 ♖gxe8 27.♖f1, and White
should win.
21.♕e2 ♘e5 22.♗xe4 ♘xe4
23.♕xe4 ♘xc4 24.♕d5 1-0

I offer the following fragment as an
example of Zlotnik's play.

Boris Zlotnik
Vladimir Baikov

Moscow 1971

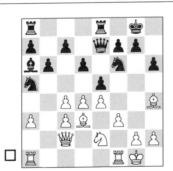

What would you do?

I remember Zlotnik's commentary,
when he showed this game at one of
his lessons:
'The game was played in the
Moscow team Olympiad. The
colours of the sports societies were
represented not just by masters
and juniors, but even by top
grandmasters. As I was thinking
about my move here, Petrosian
walked by. He glanced at the
board for just a moment and then
immediately turned away sharply.
It was obvious that the ex-World
Champion had seen something.
Concentrating on calculating the
move 15.f4, I soon realised that
Tigran Vartanovich's intuition and
tactical vision had not deceived
him!'
15.f4!
White begins an energetic and
well-calculated attack on the enemy
king.
15...exf4 16.♖xf4 g5 17.♖af1!
This temporary rook sacrifice is the
point.
**17...gxf4 18.♖xf4 ♗xc4 19.♗xf6
♕e6 20.d5 ♕d7 21.♖h4**
Black resigned. There is no
satisfactory defence against the
threat of ♖h4xh6-h8#.

Now, looking back, I can see
that my interactions with Boris
Anatolyevich significantly
broadened my chess horizons and
helped me to rapidly achieve the
master norm.

CHAPTER 8

Lessons at the chessboard

'I personally did not have a mentor or trainer in the sense that people mean the term today. Even so, I had many teachers – books and magazines, and my contemporaries and masters of the older generation, my opponents at the board. I decided what to take from each and what was not worth bothering with. And I became independent.'

Mikhail Botvinnik

This chapter is devoted to the precious lessons I learned directly at the chessboard. And we are not talking only about games against masters, but also ones against my contemporaries, from whom I learnt a great deal.

The finals of the 'White Rook' events, in which schoolchildren up to the seventh grade took part, were always a great holiday and a valuable source of instruction. I played in two such tournaments, representing the 22nd Moscow school.

The first game of mine to be published was from the first of these tournaments, although it was not exactly in a starring role!

Alexander Kalinin
Vitya Ivanov

Pervomaisk 1981

The magazine 64 gave the following commentary to this fragment:
'One is struck by one particular weakness of the youngsters, on which their trainers need to work. This is the tendency to play quickly moves that seem natural and strike them as obvious. But one of the most important components of mastery is the ability to critically assess just such apparently obvious moves. This position was reached in the game between Sasha Kalinin (Moscow) and Vitya Ivanov (Chirchik). The chances are roughly equal. White should continue 23.♖he1, but Sasha decided to 'spoil' Black's pawn structure and played 23.♗xf6?.
Now 23...♖d2! wins at once, but...
Vitya immediately recaptured – 23...gxf6?, and later even lost.'

Strangely, my second published game was played in my second White Rook final in the match between Moscow and Leningrad. It appeared in *Shakmaty v SSSR* with short, but generous notes by IM Yudovich senior.

Ruy Lopez

Alexander Kalinin

M. Elkin

Sheki 1982

1.e4 e5 2.♘f3 ♘c6 3.♗b5 a6 4.♗a4 d6 5.♗xc6+

It was my father who recommended that I employ this exchange against the Deferred Steinitz Defence.

It was prepared and analysed, including the novelty at move 14, employed in this game.

5...bxc6 6.d4 f6 7.♗e3 ♘e7 8.♘c3 ♘g6 9.♕d3 ♗e7 10.0-0-0 ♗e6 11.h4 h5 12.d5

My father's interest in this position begun with a lovely game he won in a friendly match against his regular opponent, an amateur from Zvenigorod. The game Kalinin (sr)-Sheremtievsky (Zvenigorod 1962) saw events develop as follows: 12...♗d7 13.dxc6 ♗xc6 14.♘d5 a5 15.♖h3 (Black tries to counter the striking white rook manoeuvre along the third rank by bringing his bishop to g4) 15...♗d7 16.♖g3 ♗g4 17.♘h2! (the exchange sacrifice aims to weaken a complex of light squares in the opponent's camp) 17...♗xd1 18.♖xg6 ♔f7 19.♖g3 ♗g4 20.♘xg4 hxg4

Analysis diagram

White to move. What would you play?

21.♘xc7! (the start of a nice combination, carried out from start to finish on the light squares) 21...♕xc7 22.♕d5+ ♔g6 23.♖xg4+ ♔h5 24.♕f7+ ♔xg4 25.♕g6+ ♔xh4 26.f3!, and Black resigned – he has no defence against the two mating threats on the f2- and g4-squares.

12...cxd5 13.exd5

White usually takes with the knight. The text is tied up with the development of the queen to d3 and White's subsequent play.

13...♗f7

14.g4!?

Novelty! This unexpected breakthrough on the kingside

involves the sacrifice of several pawns.

14...hxg4

In a later game A Kalinin-E Ivanovsky (Moscow 1984), played in the Moscow junior championship of Burevestnik, Black declined the sacrifice with 14...♗f8. There followed 15.g5 ♘e7 16.gxf6 gxf6 17.♖hg1 ♖g8 18.♖xg8 ♗xg8 19.♘d2 ♗f7 20.♖g1 f5 21.♗g5 ♕d7 22.♘c4 ♖b8 23.♘a5 ♖b6 24.a3 c5 25.♘c4 ♖b8 26.b3 ♘c8 27.♘e3 ♘b6 28.f3 ♕b7 29.♕xf5 ♘xd5 30.♘exd5 ♗xd5 31.♘xd5 ♕xd5 32.♖d1 ♕f7 33.♕e4 ♕b7 34.♕g6+ ♕f7 35.♕e4 ♕b7 36.♕c4 ♕c8 37.f4, and White's attack is irresistible.

15.h5

15...♘f8

This position was reached one more time in a consultation game Kalinin+Prokofiev – Babaev+Gaspariants (Chernogolovka 1982), when events developed as follows: 15...♘f4 16.♗xf4 gxf3 17.♗d2 ♖xh5 18.♖xh5 ♗xh5 19.♕h7 g6 20.♘e4 ♔d7 21.♘xf6+ ♔c8 22.♘xh5 gxh5 23.♕xh5 ♕f8 24.♗h6 ♕h8 25.♖d3 e4 26.♖b3 ♕e5 27.♕g4+ ♔d8 28.♕g8+ ♔d7 29.♕xa8 ♗g5+

30.♔b1 ♗xh6 31.♕g8 e3 32.♖b8 ♗g5 33.♕f7+, and Black resigned.

16.♘h4 ♗xh5

Yudovich sr suggested the counter-sacrifice of the exchange: 16...♖xh5!? 17.♘f5 ♖xf5 18.♕xf5 ♕d7 with mutual chances.

17.♘f5

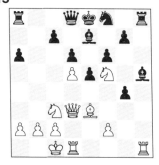

17...♔f7

On 17...g6 I had prepared 18.♖xh5! gxh5 19.f3 with strong pressure and a blockade on the light squares, in return for an exchange and two pawns!

18.♖dg1 ♘d7

Now after 18...g6 a possibility is 19.♘h6+ ♔g7 20.f3 with a very strong attack.

19.♖xh5!

The sacrifice of the rook for the light-squared bishop is one of the key ideas of the sacrifice g2-g4!

19...♖xh5 20.♗xg4 ♖h1+

An important intermediate move, allowing the black rook to leave its compromised square.

21.♔d2 g6

The alternative is 21...g5 (21...♗f8? 22.♘xg7!) 22.♘g3 ♖h6 23.♕f5, and White has an initiative that fully compensates for the material sacrificed.

22.♘g3 f5

23.♘xf5!

This latest sacrifice finally allows White to break through to the enemy king, but later he does not find a decisive continuation of the attack.

23...gxf5 24.♕xf5+ ♘f6 25.♕g6+

After a long think, White decides to force perpetual check. Neither I during the game, nor the computer, finds the quiet move 25.♘e4!, after which the black king is defenceless against the growing white attack.

25...♔f8 26.♖g1 ♖h7 27.♗h6+ ♖xh6 28.♕xh6+ ♔e8 29.♕g6+ ½-½

An instructive finish occurred in the match against the Azeri juniors.

Alexander Kalinin

O. Kurbanov

Sheki 1982

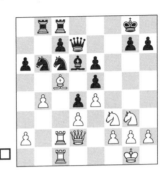

Indicate a plan of play.

White's advantage is obvious – he has unpleasant pressure down the c-file and the opponent's pawn structure is weakened. But for the time being, Black has managed to cover the vulnerable points on his queenside.

22.♕g5!

The transfer of active operations to the kingside ruins Black's defences. Tied down to defence, Black is unable to repulse threats all over the board.

22...♔h8

More tenacious is 22...h6, although after 23.♕g4 ♔h7 24.♘h5 ♘a7 25.a4 ♖a8 26.♘h4 ♘xa4 27.♗xd6 cxd6 28.♖xc8 ♖xc8 29.♕g6+ ♔h8 30.♖xc8+ ♘xc8 31.♘xg7 ♕xg7 32.♕e8+ ♔h7 33.♕xc8 White wins a pawn, obtaining a decisive advantage.

23.♘h5 ♖b7 24.♗xd6 cxd6 25.♖xc6

And Black resigned.

At the final in Sheki, I remember the play of the leader of the Chelyabinsk team, Ruslan Scherbakov, the future GM. I considered myself a 'positional' player, but Ruslan outplayed me. Later, I discovered that the youngster was already studying at the school of grandmaster Panchenko. Looking at Ruslan's games at that period, it is not hard to detect the hand of his teacher.

Réti Opening
Ruslan Scherbakov
Alexander Kalinin
Sheki 1982

1.♘f3 ♘f6 2.c4 e6 3.g3 b6 4.♗g2 ♗b7 5.0-0 ♗e7 6.b3 c5 7.e3 0-0 8.♗b2

The trainer's influence is clear even from the opening. The double fianchetto was a favourite weapon of Panchenko.

8...♘c6

Three years later, at the team event run for Young Pioneers by 'Komsomolskaya Pravda', I managed to play this position against the maestro himself. That game

continued: 8...d5 9.♘c3 ♘bd7 (this time I decided to put the knight in a more flexible position, which later allows Black to maintain pawn tension in the centre) 10.♕e2 ♖c8 11.♖fd1 ♕c7 12.♖ac1 ♕b8 13.d4 ♕a8 14.♘e5 dxc4 15.♗xb7 ♕xb7 16.bxc4 cxd4 17.exd4 ♖fe8 18.♘xd7 ♕xd7

Analysis diagram

19.d5! (this typical central break allows White to secure some advantage in the major piece ending) 19...exd5 20.♘xd5 ♘xd5 21.cxd5 ♗f6 22.♖xc8 ♕xc8 23.♕d2 ♗xb2 24.♕xb2 ♕d7 25.d6 h6 26.♕d4 ♖e6 27.h4 (the passed pawn on d6 ensures White a space advantage, but it is not easy for him to switch play to the flanks, as Black has no noticeable weaknesses and the pawn on d6 is under constant attack) 27...♖e8 28.♕d5 ♖d8 29.♖e1 ♔h7 30.♕d3+ f5 31.♖e7 ♕xd6 32.♕xf5+ ♕g6 33.♕xg6+ ♔xg6 34.♖xa7 (White has managed to win a pawn but the rook ending is a draw) 34...♖d2 35.♔g2 h5 36.♔f3 ♖b2 37.♔e3 b5 38.f3 b4 39.♖a6+ ♔h7 40.♔f4 b3 41.a4 ♖a2 42.♔g5 ♖g2 43.g4 hxg4 44.fxg4 ♖a2 draw, Panchenko-Kalinin, Irkutsk 1985.

9.♘c3 ♖c8

Black refrains for the time being from the advance 9...d5, because after 10.cxd5 exd5 (or 10...♘xd5 11.♘xd5 exd5 12.d4) 11.d4 he does not wish to allow the pressure against the hanging pawns.

10.♖c1 ♕c7 11.♕e2 ♖fd8 12.d4 d5

Now it is necessary to stop the advance d4-d5. The preliminary exchange 12...cxd4 13.exd4 and then 13...d5 allows White to develop a strong initiative: 14.cxd5 ♘xd5 (14...exd5 15.♗h3) 15.♘xd5 ♖xd5 16.♘e5 ♘xd4 (16...♖d6? 17.♗xc6 ♗xc6 18.d5!, and White wins) 17.♕e4 ♘c6 18.♘xf7! ♔xf7 19.♕xh7 with an attack.

13.cxd5 ♘xd5 14.♘xd5 ♖xd5
15.♘e5 ♖dd8 16.dxc5 bxc5

White's first achievement – Black has contracted an isolated pawn on c5.

17.♘xc6 ♗xc6 18.♕g4 g6 19.♗xc6 ♕xc6 20.♕c4 ♕d5 21.♕a6 ♕d6 22.♕xd6 ♖xd6

The resulting endgame is unpleasant for Black. Ruslan conducts the technical phase of the game in the best traditions of his teacher.

23.♖c2 f6 24.♗d4 ♖dc6 25.♖fc1 e5 26.♗c3 ♔f7 27.♗b4 ♔e6 28.♖c4 ♖a6 29.♖1c2 ♖ac6 30.♔g2 ♔d7 31.♗d2 ♗d8 32.e4 ♗b6 33.♗e3

After trying various ways of attacking the pawn on c5, White finally manages to tie his opponent up completely.

33...♖6c7 34.♔f1 ♔e6 35.♔e2 ♔e7 36.♗d2 ♔e6 37.a4 a6 38.a5 ♗a7 39.b4 ♔d7 40.♗e3 ♖b8 41.bxc5 ♖c6 42.♖d2+ ♔c7

More tenacious was 42...♔e6.

43.f4 ♖e6? 44.♖d6 ♖be8 45.f5

And Black resigned.

Alongside good technique, Ruslan's play was also marked by a willingness to switch to sharp tactical play, if this answered the demands of the position. Again, I would point out that this is a quality he 'inherited' from Alexander Panchenko.

Queen's Pawn Game
Laimonas Kudzhma
Ruslan Scherbakov
Sheki 1982

1.d4 c5 2.c3

A very solid move. Avoiding an Indian set-up (2.d5), White plays a kind of Slav with reversed colours.

2...♘f6

Black is ready to sacrifice the d5-pawn. Panchenko also liked to play this way, getting a position with colours reversed from the Réti: 1.♘f3 d5 2.c4 c6 3.g3 dxc4 etc.

3.dxc5

And the Lithuanian master goes in for the pawn grab, following up by trying to cling onto it.

3...e6 4.b4 a5 5.♕a4 ♘a6 6.♗d2 b6 7.cxb6 axb4 8.cxb4 ♕xb6 9.a3 ♗b7 10.♕a5 ♕d6 11.♕b5 ♗c6 12.♕c4

Black to move. What would you play?

White is dangerously behind with his kingside development, which allows Ruslan to go for a close-quarter fight, with a beautiful queen sacrifice.

12...♘xb4! 13.♗xb4 ♕xb4+! 14.axb4 ♖xa1 15.f3

The ♘b1 cannot be saved, e.g. after 15.♕b3 there follows 15...♗e4.

15...♖xb1+ 16.♔f2 ♗xb4 17.♘h3 ♗e1+ 18.♔g1 0-0

White's forces are completely paralysed, whilst the queen on her own cannot withstand the attack from the entire enemy army.

19.e4 ♖a8 20.e5 ♘d5 21.♕g4 ♘e3 22.♕h5 ♘xf1 23.♘g5 ♗f2+!

White resigned.

Sheki saw the first national appearance of the still young Alexey Shirov. The 9-year old Alyosha was the smallest

competitor in the event, but it was still easy to find him in the tournament hall – one only had to look for the eyes blazing under the shock of blond hair of the youngster from Riga.

Sicilian Defence
Alexey Shirov
Vladimir Isakov
Sheki 1982

1.e4 c5 2.♘f3 d6 3.d4 cxd4 4.♘xd4 ♘f6 5.♘c3 a6 6.♗g5

It is no surprise that in this sharp variation of the Sicilian, Shirov chooses the line beloved of his great countryman, Mikhail Tal.

6...e6 7.f4 ♗e7 8.♕f3 ♕c7 9.0-0-0 ♘bd7 10.g4 b5 11.♗xf6 ♘xf6 12.g5 ♘d7 13.f5 ♘c5 14.f6 gxf6 15.gxf6 ♗f8 16.♗h3 b4 17.♘d5 exd5 18.exd5 ♗xh3 19.♖he1+ ♔d8 20.♘c6+ ♔c8

21.♕xh3+

This had all been seen before in practice. Independent play begins over the next few moves.

21...♕d7 22.♕h4 a5 23.♖e3 h5 24.♔b1 ♕g4 25.♕e1! ♔c7 26.a3! bxa3 27.♖xa3 a4

28.b4! ♘b7?

In the opinion of the computer, equality could be maintained after 28...♖e8! 29.♕xe8 (or 29.♕f1 ♖b8! 30.♖d4 ♕xd4! 31.♘xd4 ♖xb4+ etc.) 29...♕xd1+ 30.♔b2 ♗h6! 31.♕xf7+ ♔c8 32.♘a7+ (after 32.bxc5 ♕c1+ 33.♔a2 ♕xc2+ Black gives perpetual check) 32...♔b8 33.♘c6+ ♔c8 34.♘a7+ with perpetual check.

29.♖d4 ♕f5 30.♕c3 ♔d7 31.♘e7 ♕f1+ 32.♔a2 ♕a6 33.b5! ♕a7 34.b6 ♕xb6 35.♖b4 ♕c7 36.♕c6+ ♔d8 37.♖xb7 ♕xc6 38.♘xc6+ ♔c8 39.♖xf7 ♗h6 40.♖g3 ♖f8 41.♖gg7 ♗xg7 42.fxg7 ♖e8 43.♘e7+ ♔c7 44.♘g6+ ♔b6 45.♖f8 ♖xf8 46.♘xf8
And Black resigned.

As we see, from his earliest years, Alexey was notable for his courage and love of attack, qualities which soon permitted him to achieve great sporting and creative successes. The young player's excellent memory is also notable. But merely remembering long variations is no great achievement! The important thing is how, in the middlegame, Alexey played in accordance with the spirit of the position, freshly and inventively – note such moves as 25.♕e1!, 26.a3!, 28.b4!.

A special role was played in developing young players during the 1970s and 1980s by the Pioneer Palace competition sponsored by the newspaper *Komsomolskaya Pravda*, in which young players had the chance to play well-known grandmasters in clock simuls. And it was not just about results, but also the chance for the youngsters to have direct, face-to-face contact with famous GMs. One can only envy the participants in the first such event, who were lucky enough to find themselves surrounded by such chess giants as Smyslov, Bronstein, Petrosian, Tal, Spassky and Karpov! Unfortunately, over the years, the ranks of the simul-givers became less star-studded, but this did not in the least reduce the value of the experience for the youngsters.

I managed to take part in two such events. In preparation, in late 1982 – early 1983, our society organised a series of clock simuls. As 'examiners', the Palace invited Bronstein, Kholmov, Balashov, Razuvaev and Chekhov. The simuls were played over seven boards, as was the case in the final tournament. It turned out that the impressions made by the training events were even greater than those from the final!

Before meeting the GMs, we were given a warm-up against our trainer, master (now International Master) Vladimir Vulfson.

Nimzo-Indian Defence
Vladimir Vulfson
Alexander Kalinin
Moscow 1982 (clock simul)

Vladimir Vulfson is now one of
the best trainers in Moscow. His
pupils in recent years have included
Boris Grachev, Alina Kashlinskaya,
Varvara Repina and Bathuyag
Mongontuul. He also worked with
us. I remember that during team
events and training sessions he kept
up our fighting spirits by playing
Vysotsky songs on his guitar.
Vulfson's playing style was
characterised by its unusual nature.
In his opening repertoire, he
included many systems that were
not particularly popular, but which
he had studied very deeply. One of
his favourite strategic devices was
sacrificing material to get a pawn
mass in motion. You can see, for
example, his article on the Dragon
Sicilian in one of the Dvoretsky /
Jussupow books. A similar strategy
was used by him in our game.
**1.d4 ♘f6 2.c4 e6 3.♘c3 ♗b4 4.e3
0-0 5.♗d3 b6 6.♘f3 ♗b7 7.0-0 ♗xc3
8.bxc3 ♗e4**

9.♘e1
Usually in this position, White
temporarily retreats the bishop to
e2, and then expands in the centre
with ♘f3-d2 (e1), f2-f3 and e3-e4.
Vulfson follows a different path,
not concerning himself with the
two bishops in a closed position.
I would add that an analogous
strategy was first used in the game
Alekhine-Reshevsky (AVRO 1938),
which continued 9.♗xe4 ♘xe4
10.♕c2 f5 11.♘e5 ♕e8 12.f3 etc.
**9...c5 10.♗xe4 ♘xe4 11.f3 ♘f6
12.d5 d6 13.e4 e5 14.♗g5 ♘bd7
15.♘c2 ♕c7 16.♘e3 ♘h5**
A provocative move, inviting the
opponent to win the pawn on d6.
**17.♗e7 ♖fe8 18.♘f5 g6 19.♗xd6
♕d8 20.♘h6+ ♔g7 21.♘g4 f6**

Thus, White has pocketed a pawn,
but his bishop is 'under arrest' on
d6. However, it is not so easy for
Black to get at the bishop.
22.a4 a5 23.g3 b5
Black has found a way to get at
the ♗d6, but has had to sacrifice
another pawn to do so.
24.cxb5 ♕b6 25.♗xe5
White gets sufficient material
equivalent for the piece, retaining
all eight of his pawns on the board!

25...fxe5 26.c4 ♕d6 27.♕d2 ♘df6
28.♘f2 ♔g8 29.♘d3 ♘d7 30.♕c3
♖e7 31.♖ae1 ♕c7 32.f4 ♖ae8 33.f5
♖f8 34.g4 ♘f4

White to move. What would you play?

35.♘xf4

This natural move allows Black to obtain counterplay, by cementing a piece on e5. More winning chances were offered by the surprising 35.♖xf4! exf4 36.e5. An unusual position has arisen. White has three pawns for the rook, and these are ready to crush the black defences. For example, a possible line is 36...♖ee8 37.d6 ♕b6 38.♕d2 g5 39.h4 h6 40.♔f2 with growing pressure for White. The final part of the game is unfortunately spoiled by mutual time-trouble errors.

35...exf4 36.♕d2 ♕e5 37.♕xf4 ♕xf4?!

37...♕d4+

38.♖xf4 g5?!

38...♘e5

39.f6? ♖ef7?

Black is the last to go wrong. By playing 39...♘xf6 or, even better, 39...♖e5, he could tame the enemy passed pawns.

40.♖f5 ♖xf6 41.e5

Here the game was adjourned and adjudicated a win for White.

Sicilian Defence
Alexander Kalinin
Valery Chekhov
Moscow 1982 (clock simul)

Valery Alexandrovich Chekhov is himself a product of the Moscow City Pioneer Palace. In 1975, he became World Junior Champion.
1.e4 c5 2.♘f3 e6 3.d4 cxd4 4.♘xd4 ♘f6 5.♘c3 d6 6.♗e2 ♗e7 7.0-0 ♘c6 8.♗e3 0-0 9.f4 e5
This variation of the Scheveningen was very popular at the time, thanks to the efforts of Garry Kasparov.
10.♘b3
At the Moscow Interzonal 1982, Geller successfully used the line 10.♘f5, but I was unwilling to enter forcing variations.
10...exf4 11.♖xf4 ♗e6
A solid continuation, although even then, the move 11...♘e8 was becoming more popular.
12.♘d5 ♗xd5 13.exd5 ♘e5 14.♕d2 ♖c8 15.c3 ♘fd7

16.♖b4!?

Trying to play the Scheveningen like Geller. The Odessa GM said that in this variation, White should attack the black queenside, since all of his pieces are pointing towards that side of the board. The enterprising rook manoeuvre is an attempt to create targets in the black pawn structure.

16...♘b6?!

In the event of 16...♕c7 White has a choice between 17.a4 followed by a5 and the manoeuvre 17.♘d4 a6 18.♘f5. However, Black has no cause to panic in any of these variations. The text move allows a sudden development of the crisis on the queenside.

17.♘a5! ♕c7 18.a4 ♘ed7 19.♘xb7 ♕xb7 20.a5 ♕xd5 21.axb6 ♕xd2 22.♗xd2 axb6 23.♖a7 d5

Or 23...♖cd8 24.♗b5.

24.♖xd7 ♗xb4 25.cxb4 ♖fd8 26.♖xd8+ ♖xd8 27.♔f2

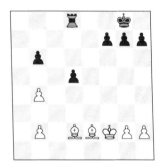

In the resulting endgame, the two white bishops prove clearly stronger than Black's rook and pawns. There followed:

27...d4 28.♗c4 ♖e8 29.b3 h6 30.♗c1 ♖a8 31.♔e2 ♖a1 32.♗d2 ♖h1 33.h3

g5 34.♔d3 ♖d1 35.♗d5 ♔g7 36.♗f3 ♖b1 37.♔xd4 ♖xb3 38.♔c4

Black resigned.

Khasin liked this game, especially the original white rook manoeuvre along the fourth rank. Maybe it had been played before, but it only became well-known after the later game Mortensen-Karpov (Plovdiv 1983).

Nimzo-Indian Defence
David Bronstein
Alexander Kalinin
Moscow 1983 (clock simul)

Meeting David Ionovich Bronstein over the board (even in a simul) was a real treat for all of us. Several generations of players had learnt from the games of the great master, and his remarkable book on the 1953 Candidates tournament.

1.c4 ♘f6 2.♘c3 e6 3.d4 ♗b4 4.e3 b6 5.♗d3 ♗b7 6.♘f3 0-0 7.0-0 ♗xc3 8.bxc3 ♗e4

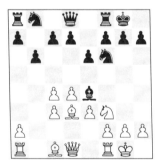

9.♗e2

Unlike Vulfson, Bronstein preserves the two bishops, even in this closed position. I think the point

148

is not so much in the much-vaunted 'advantage' of the bishops themselves as in the desire to avoid exchanges, in a position where White has a space advantage.

9...c5 10.♘d2 ♗b7 11.♗d3 ♘c6 12.e4 d6 13.d5 ♘e7

Given that the knight ends up on g6 anyway, it would have been more logical to go there via e5.

14.f4 ♘g6 15.a4 ♕c7 16.♘f3 exd5 17.exd5 ♖fe8

18.h3

After making this move, Bronstein left the board and whispered to Khasin: 'That is how Rubinstein used to play such positions, advancing the f- and g-pawns on the kingside!'

18...♖e7 19.f5 ♘e5 20.♗g5 ♘ed7 21.♖a2 h6 22.♗h4 ♖ae8 23.g4 ♖e3 24.♖g2

Note how White grants the enemy rooks control of the open file without any fight. Here it is appropriate to quote Bronstein's words, from his Zurich 1953 book: 'The understanding of positional play is constantly changing. Whereas Tarrasch taught that one should avoid weaknesses in one's own camp, create

them in the opponent's, accumulate small advantages, occupy the open lines, and not attack without first creating sufficient preconditions, nowadays we do things quite differently. Create weaknesses in your own camp, so as to distract the opponent, concede open lines, so as to preserve the rooks for other, more important tasks, show your attacking intentions, so as to hide your real long-term ideas.'

24...♘e4

White to move. What would you play?

To his great sorrow, here David Ionovich committed an error, characteristic of simul-givers, and after 25.♕c2 f6 the battle flared up with renewed strength.

The logical conclusion of White's strategic plan was 25.g5!, breaking through to the black king with overwhelming force. The resulting variations can be left to the reader, as they are prosaic and result in the collapse of Black's position.

In confirmation of Bronstein's comments about how Rubinstein handled such positions, here is an example:

Akiba Rubinstein
Aron Nimzowitsch

Berlin 1928

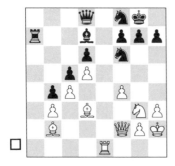

What would you play?

Razuvaev loved to use this position as a test.

28.♗xf6!

This unexpected exchange of the powerful bishop on b2 for the opponent's modest knight sharply speeds up events on the kingside.
28...♕xf6 29.♘e4 ♕h6 30.f5! ♖a3 31.♖b1 ♖a6 32.g4! f6 33.♔g3 ♗c8 34.♖e1 ♗b7 35.♕e2 ♘d7 36.♘xd6 ♖xd6 37.♕e8+ ♘f8 38.♖e7 g6 39.♕f7+ ♔h8 40.♖e8 ♖d8 41.♕xf6+ ♔g8 42.♕e6+ ♔g7 43.f6+
Black resigned.

Another unforgettable event for us all was meeting Ratmir Dmitrievich Kholmov. All of the children brought with them his book of best games, which had only recently come out, in the hope of securing the grandmaster's autograph. I still have this book in my library, and every time I open it, I recall pleasant memories of a great chess player and a remarkable person.

Sicilian Defence
Ratmir Kholmov
Alexander Kalinin

Moscow 1983 (clock simul)

1.e4 c5 2.♘f3 d6 3.d4 cxd4 4.♘xd4 ♘f6 5.♘c3 ♘c6 6.♗g5 e6 7.♕d2 h6
I loved to play this move of Botvinnik's, which brings Black such long-term advantages as the bishop pair and a strong pawn centre. But, it must be admitted, the variation is not a simple one for Black.
8.♗xf6 gxf6 9.0-0-0 a6 10.♔b1 ♕b6 11.♘b3 ♗d7 12.f4 0-0-0 13.♗e2 h5 14.♖hf1

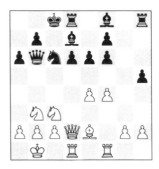

14...♗e7
Later, in several games I played the immediate 14...♔b8, not rushing to put the bishop on e7. The reason for this will become apparent.
15.♗f3
Usually in such positions, White keeps the f3-square for his rook, from where it can switch to either queenside or kingside. This manoeuvre was first seen in the beautiful game Keres-Botvinnik, (Moscow 1956), which was decided by a direct attack on the black king.

Kholmov's move conceals a cunning idea, which I did not divine.

15...♚b8

16.♕e2! h4 17.♘d5!

Thus White manages to reveal the downside of having the bishop on e7! Admittedly, I did not consider this standard blow to be dangerous for me, as I had still not fully understood the idea.

17...exd5 18.exd5 ♘e5

What could be more natural than this idea? However, there is also the other move 18...♘b4!?. In the game Guedon-M. Ivanov (Cappelle-la-Grande 1995) there then followed 19.♕xe7? ♘xc2! 20.♔xc2 ♗f5+, and it turned out that 21.♔d2 was impossible because of 21...♖he8 22.♕xf6 ♕e3#!

Correct was 19.♘d4! ♖de8 20.c3 f5 (or 20...♘xa2 21.♔xa2 f5) 21.cxb4 ♕xb4, and White's chances are somewhat preferable.

19.fxe5 fxe5

It seems as though all that White's combination has achieved is to improve the black pawn structure...

20.♗g4!

This move finally reveals the full point of Kholmov's idea. After the exchange of light-squared bishops, the black central pawns are blockaded and the ♗e7 becomes bad.

20...♗xg4 21.♕xg4 ♖df8

Here we are again reminded that the game was played in a clock simul, which Ratmir Dmitrievich played at a high tempo. There followed 22.♘d2?!, and after 22...♖hg8 23.♕e4 f5 24.♖xf5 ♖xf5 25.♕xf5 ♖xg2 Black wriggled out and even seized the initiative. Instead, the accurate 22.♖f5 ♖hg8 23.♕f3 would have led to a clear positional advantage for White.

Some time later, I saw Kholmov's idea repeated in the following game.

Jan Timman
Bozidar Ivanovic

Bugojno 1984 (4)

What would you play?

15.♘d5! exd5 16.exd5 ♘e5 17.fxe5 fxe5

Black only needs to play ...f7-f5 to secure a good position.

18.♕h6!

The point of White's idea. The threat of 19.♘xe5 allows White to win an important tempo.

18...♕c5 19.♕h5! ♖df8 20.♗f5 ♗xf5 21.♕xf5 ♗d8 22.♖f1 ♖hg8 23.g3 ♖g6 24.a3 ♕c4 25.♖d3 ♕c8 26.♘d2 ♕xf5 27.♖xf5 ♖g5 28.♖df3 ♖xf5 29.♖xf5 ♔c7 30.♘e4

And White's blockading strategy has achieved total success.

From these 'training' simuls, I will offer one more game, the text taken from the book *Tigran Petrosian's Chess Lectures*. In one chapter, he describes the course of one of the lectures at the Petrosian school, devoted to analysing the games of pupils. Below I have quoted several conceptual observations of the ex-World Champion, concerning the course of the battle. In my view, these contain more chess wisdom that any number of concrete variations.

Benoni Defence
Vladimir Chuchelov
Yuri Razuvaev

Moscow 1983 (clock simul)

At the start of the 1980s, many youngsters had just read a new book on Akiba Rubinstein, and I very much wanted to meet its author. Unfortunately, I was ill at the time of this simul and had to miss it. But the hero of the day was Vladimir Chuchelov, who scored a beautiful victory over the grandmaster.

1.d4 ♘f6 2.c4 e6 3.♘f3 c5 4.d5 exd5 5.cxd5 d6 6.♘c3 g6 7.e4 ♗g7 8.♗e2 0-0 9.0-0

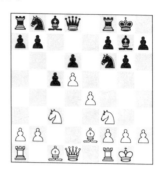

Petrosian: 'Volodya, you play these systems yourself as Black?'
Chuchelov: 'Yes, they are part of my repertoire.'
Petrosian: 'Good, but bear in mind that this is a dangerous opening. True, to win in chess, you have to play dangerous moves and play dangerous openings. That is a healthy form of risk.'

9...♗g4 10.♘d2 ♗xe2 11.♕xe2 ♘bd7 12.a4 ♖e8 13.a5 a6 14.♘c4 ♘e5

A principled continuation here is the pawn sacrifice 14...b5!? 15.♘xd6 ♖e7, leading to sharp play.

15.♘b6 ♖b8 16.f4 ♘ed7 17.♘c4 ♕c7

If 17...♕e7 18.e5! dxe5 19.fxe5 ♘xe5 20.♘xe5 ♕xe5 21.♕xe5 ♖xe5 22.♗f4 ♘g4 Black has to part with the exchange, for which, however, he has some compensation (Ivkov-Hug, Sao Paulo 1973).

18.♕d3 ♘g4 19.♔h1 b5 20.axb6 ♘xb6 21.♘a5!

Chuchelov: 'Heading to c6.'

Petrosian: 'Volodya! Never forget that pieces should not stand attractively, but usefully!'

21...c4 22.♕f3 f5 23.h3 ♘f6 24.e5 ♘fd7 25.e6 ♘c5 26.♘c6 ♖a8

27.g4!

The e6-pawn splits the black position in two and it is hard for the black pieces to come to the aid of their king.

27...♔h8 28.♗e3 ♘b3 29.♖ad1 ♖ac8

Creating the threat of 30...♘xd5.

30.♘d4 ♖f8 31.♕f2 ♘c5 32.gxf5 gxf5 33.♖g1 ♘d3 34.♕f3 ♘xb2 35.♖d2 ♘d3 36.♖dg2

Petrosian: 'Here you missed a chance to liquidate Black's 'central defender' – 36.♖xg7 ♕xg7 37.♖g2 with the threat of ♘de2 and ♗d4.'

36...♗f6 37.♕h5 ♘xf4 38.♗xf4 ♗xd4

39.♗h6!

Breaking through to the black king via the g-file.

39...♗xg1 40.♕g5 ♗d4 41.e7

Black resigned.

Petrosian: 'Well done! You played the whole game very convincingly, especially the final attack.'

The final Pioneer Palace event in 1983 took place in Vilnius. Although the composition of the GM team (Panchenko, Makarychev, Kochyev, Gavrikov and Chernin) may look modest compared with the first event, they dealt fairly well with me – I managed three draws and two defeats.

The quality of my play was not satisfactory but I remember my game with the Chelyabinsk GM.

Sicilian Defence
Alexander Kalinin
Alexander Panchenko
Vilnious 1983 (clock simul)

1.e4 c5 2.♘f3 d6 3.d4 cxd4 4.♘xd4 ♘f6 5.♘c3 ♘c6 6.♗e2 e5

The Boleslavsky System is regarded as a good reply to 6.♗e2 and I myself played it happily as Black. For this white game, I had prepared a fresh idea.

7.♘b3 ♗e7 8.0-0 0-0 9.♔h1

9.♗g5 is a mistake because of 9...♘xe4!. White plays a useful king move and also awaits developments.

9...a5 10.a4 ♘b4 11.♗g5!?

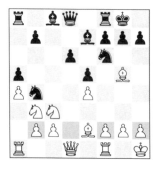

A novelty, suggested by my father. With the knight on b4, 11...②xe4 no longer works, because of 12.♗xe7 ②xc3 13.bxc3!, and so White gets to exchange his bishop for the ②f6. Admittedly, this exchange seems fairly harmless, because the other black knight is already covering the d5-square, but the point of the idea, which is intimately tied up with the plan of play for the middlegame, becomes clear a little later.

11...h6

In the training game V. Kalinin-A. Kalinin (1982) there followed 11...♗e6 12.♗xf6 ♗xf6 13.②d5 ②xd5 14.exd5 ♗f5 15.②d2 (the transfer of the pawn from e4 to d5 has shut off Black's weaknesses on the d-file, but has also emphasised the weakness of his queenside, especially after the move ...a7-a5. The white knight is heading for c4, whilst the ♖a1 can come into play via a3) 15...♖c8 16.②c4 ♖c5 17.c3 ♗e4 (the aim of Black's last few moves is to force the advance b2-b4, which sharply reduces White's chances on the queenside) 18.②e3 ♗g5 19.f3 ♗g6 (19...♗xe3 20.fxe4 was sufficient for equality) 20.②c4 ♕c7 21.②a3 ♕b6

22.②b5 f5 23.♖a3 ♗f7 24.c4 ♗e8 25.♕e1 ♖f6 (after forcing the move c3-c4, I regarded my position as completely safe and I relaxed my attention. The white knight attacks d6 and limits the activity of Black's queen. Therefore, the outwardly active text-move should have been replaced with the consolidating 25...♖c8 or the simple 25...♗xb5 26.axb5 ♗d8)
26.♗d3 ♗d7 27.♕f2 ♖h6 28.♖b3 ♕a6

Analysis diagram

29.f4! (this break was a complete surprise to me! But it is extremely logical – the black queen is cut off on the queenside and White opens lines on the other side of the board. This once again illustrates the stereotyped and insufficiently dynamic nature of my thinking) 29...♗xf4? (the sudden change in the course of events had so shaken me that the game ends in just a few moves. It was essential to play 29... exf4 30.②d4 ♗f6)
30.g3 ♗g5 31.♗xf5 ♖f6 32.♖f3, and, unable to find any retort to his opponent's overwhelming attack, Black resigned.

**12.♗xf6 ♗xf6 13.♘d5 ♘xd5 14.exd5
♗g5 15.♘d2 f5 16.♘c4 ♕c7 17.♖a3**

The diagram position clearly
illustrates the idea of the move
11.♗g5. White's pieces are extremely
flexibly placed and exert pressure
on the enemy queenside. At the
same time, it is not easy for Black to
activate his central pawn phalanx,
as the advance of either pawn leaves
a hole between them, which White
can utilise.

17...e4 18.f4! ♗f6 19.♕d2

The position starts to assume
the characteristics of a blockade.
Having achieved a promising
position, White later plays too
conservatively and decides not to
go over to concrete measures.

**19...♗d7 20.c3 ♔h7 21.♕e3 ♗e8
22.♕b6 ♗d8 23.♕xc7 ♗xc7 24.♖b3
♖b8 25.♘b6 ♖f6 26.♔g1 ♔g8
27.♔f2 ♔f8 28.♖a1 ♔e7 29.♘c4
♗d7 30.♘e3**

And here a draw was agreed.

After the display, Alexander
Nikolaevich shared his impressions
of the game with each opponent,
and this, of course, made a great
impression. All of the GM's
observations were both very
accurate and also very friendly.
Regarding our game, Panchenko
pointed out White's interesting
opening idea and the fact that the
final position was very promising
for him. Two years later, during
the next Pioneer Palace event in
Irkutsk, he greeted the members
of our team like old friends and
sometimes followed the course
of events in our games. Such an
attitude from a grandmaster,
towards the play of youngsters who
had achieved nothing in chess at
that point, is not easily forgotten.
As well as his chess talent,
Alexander Nikolaevich had a
great gift for teaching. Among
the pupils to emerge from the
'Panchenko School' were Ulibin,
Scherbakov, Rublevsky, Prudnikova,
Shumiakina and other well-known
players, all of whom, without
exception, have warm memories of
their teacher.

I would add that the Vilnius
tournament was convincingly won
by the Leningrad team, which
included such future GMs as
Khalifman, Epishin, Sokolin and
Solozhenkin.

The succeeding VII Pioneer
tournament in 1985 was held in
Irkutsk. The line-up of simul-
givers (Kasparov, Jussupow,
Psakhis, Dolmatov, Panchenko and
Novikov) was interesting, because
it included several young GMs who
had just emerged into the world
elite. The winner was the slightly

older Moscow team (captained by Jussupow), whose line-up was virtually unchanged from two years earlier. On this occasion, I went through undefeated, winning one game.

Of course, Kasparov's simul was a big event for all the teams. The future World Champion had recently played his 'unfinished' match with Karpov and was preparing for his second challenge for the world title.

Sicilian Defence
Alexander Kalinin
Garry Kasparov

Irkutsk 1985 (clock simul)

1.e4 c5 2.♘f3 d6 3.d4 cxd4 4.♘xd4 ♘f6 5.♘c3 e6

As expected, Kasparov chooses his favourite Scheveningen variation of the Sicilian.

6.♗e2 ♗e7 7.0-0 0-0 8.f4 ♘c6 9.♗e3 e5 10.♘b3 exf4 11.♖xf4

11...♘e8

Portisch's idea. Black prepares to put his bishop on e5.

12.♕d2 ♗f6 13.♖f2 ♗e5 14.♗g5 ♘f6 15.♗f3

I knew that in the game Geller-Andersson (Moscow 1982) White had fallen into a trap: 15.♖af1? ♗xc3! 16.♕xc3 ♘xe4 17.♗xd8 ♘xc3 18.bxc3 ♘xd8 19.♖d1 ♗e6 20.♖xd6 ♖c8 with an obvious advantage to Black in the endgame. The solid text move, however, shuts off White's pressure on the f6-square.

15...h6

Driving the bishop off the h4-d8 diagonal, since after 16.♗h4? there again follows 16...♘xe4!.

16.♗f4 ♗e6 17.♖d1 ♖c8 18.♕c1 ♕b6 19.♗e3 ♕c7

Black has completely consolidated his position and it is somewhat preferable, because of the strong bishop on e5. If 20.♘d5 ♗xd5 21.exd5 ♘e7 followed by ...♘f5, his position is also promising.

20.♘b5 ♕b8 21.♗f4

Trying to force a crisis by the pressure on d6.

21...d5 22.♗xe5 ♘xe5 23.exd5 ♘xf3+ 24.♖xf3 ♘xd5

On 24...♗g4 I had prepared the double exchange sacrifice 25.♖xf6 ♗xd1 26.♕xd1 gxf6 27.d6, considering that the breaking-up of the enemy king position and exclusion of the black queen from the game compensated for the material deficit. However, the computer disagrees, pointing out the resource 27...a6 28.♘3d4 ♖c5! (a draw results from 28...axb5 29.♘f5 ♖c4 30.♕f3 ♖d8 31.♘xh6+ ♔h7 32.♘f5 ♖xc2 33.♕h5+ ♔g8 34.♘e7+ ♔g7 35.♘f5+ with perpetual check) 29.♘c7 ♕d8, and White's attack fizzles out. He would have to content himself with the sacrifice of just one exchange – 26.♖f2 a6 27.♘5d4 ♗g4, although he does not have sufficient compensation. Kasparov, evidently, judged the move 24...♗g4, 'by eye', which is quite understandable in the circumstances of a simultaneous display.

25.♖df1

The position has simplified and the centre cleared of pawn tension. Here Garry Kimovich thought for about 15 minutes, in the search for a way to play for a win. The following regrouping, aiming at bringing the queen from b8 to the kingside, was the most striking event of the game for me.

25...♗d7! 26.♘5d4 ♕e5! 27.♖e1 ♕h5!

On the kingside, the queen cuts off at the roots any play on this flank by White and cooperates excellently with her own forces.

28.c3 ♘f6 29.♘d2 ♖fe8 30.♘f1 ♕h4 31.♖xe8+ ♖xe8 32.♖e3 ♖c8 33.♕e1 ♕xe1 34.♖xe1

Before the start of the tournament, Khasin had warned me that 'in so-called equal positions, where Karpov and Kasparov agree a draw, the GMs will play for a win against you!' This warning proved correct. With a bishop against a knight in an open position, Kasparov plays on.

34...♔f8 35.♔f2 ♘g4+ 36.♔e2 f5 37.♔f3

Short of time, I started running on the spot. My idea was simple – don't overlook anything, extend the game to move 45 and get a draw on adjudication. The practice of adjudication is rightly condemned and certainly conflicts with the sporting essence of the game. In this instance, such tactics can be excused only by the fact that I was certainly short of time.

37...b6 38.h3 ♘f6 39.♖e5 g6 40.♘d2 ♔f7 41.♔f2 ♖c7 42.♔f3 ♗c8 43.♔f2 ♗b7 44.♖e1 ♗d5 45.a3 ♖d7

Over the last ten moves, Black has significantly strengthened his position and his advantage is starting to assume serious proportions. However, at this moment, the logical course was interrupted by an adjudication of draw. I would add that our team put up stern resistance against our great opponent, losing only by a respectable score of 2½-4½.

The following game brought me my only win in the Komsomolskaya tournaments:

English Opening
Alexander Kalinin
Lev Psakhis

Irkutsk 1985 (clock simul)

1.c4 e5 2.♘c3 ♘f6 3.g3 d5 4.cxd5 ♘xd5 5.♗g2 ♘b6 6.♘f3 ♘c6 7.0-0 ♗e7 8.d3 0-0

9.a3
I played the opening with special interest, as two years before, I had witnessed the game Petrosian-Psakhis (Moscow 1983), in which there followed 9...a5 10.♗e3 ♗g4 11.♖c1 ♖e8 12.♘d2 ♕d7 13.♖e1 ♖a6.

Here the ex-World Champion had shocked me with the non-standard exchange 14.♗xb6! cxb6 15.♕a4 ♗g5 16.e3 h5 17.♘de4 ♗d8 18.d4 with advantage to White.
9...♗e6 10.b4 f6 11.♗b2 ♕e8 12.♘d2 ♕f7 13.♖c1 a6 14.♘ce4 ♗d5
Theory at the time was based on the game Kirov-Ornstein (Pamporovo 1981), which went 15.♘c4. It was not clear to me why it was silent about the tempting knight jump to c5.
15.♘c5 ♗xg2 16.♔xg2 ♗xc5 17.♖xc5
I refrained from 17.bxc5, to avoid shutting off the pressure against c7.
17...a5!

18.b5
Since the b4-pawn is attacked and 18.bxa5 breaks up the white queenside, I quickly pushed the pawn to b5, only then noticing the reply 18...♘d7!. This episode shows once again that unexpected intermediate moves still tended to escape my tactical vision.
18...♘d7 19.♖c2 ♕d5+ 20.♘e4 ♕xb5 21.♕a1
Strangely, White has retained a certain compensation for the pawn, thanks to the chance of organising

counterplay on the open queenside files.

21...♕d5 22.♔g1 ♖f7 23.♖fc1 ♘f8 24.♖c5 ♕d7 25.♕a2 ♕e6 26.♕b1 ♕d7

This transfer of the queen proves to be a loss of time and allows White to take the initiative.

27.♗a1

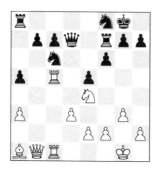

27...♖a7?

A blunder. However, even in the variation 27...♕c8 28.♖b5 ♖a7 29.a4 ♘d7 30.♕b3 White's pressure is already becoming dangerous.

28.♖xc6

And Black resigned, because after 28...bxc6 29.♕b8 ♖a6 30.♘c5 his rook is trapped.

After the game, there was a short discussion with our trainers. In response to Vulfson's question as to whether I had sacrificed the pawn or blundered it, Khasin answered for me: 'As Tolush used to say in such situations, if I win the game, that means I sacrificed it, and if I lose, then I blundered it!'
It only remains to thank all the grandmasters and masters who took part in the Pioneer Palace finals

– they gave the youngsters some memorable experiences. In addition, one should not forget the young players' successes in individual games. As we have seen, it was not easy for the GMs to deal with the well-prepared young players in such simuls, and their interesting and instructive thoughts were often mingled with serious mistakes.

In the middle of the 1980s, before any important event (such as the Pioneer Palace finals or All-Union events), the Moscow chess federation organised tournaments, in which the youngsters could test themselves against adult players. Thus, in 1984, there was a rating tournament (for Soviet ratings, that is), in which the young players faced experienced candidate masters and even several masters. The following game is memorable for me.

Nimzo-Indian Defence
Alexander Novikov
Alexander Kalinin
Moscow 1984

My opponent was a well-known trainer and a very modest man, Alexander Nikolaevich Novikov. Some of you may be aware that among his pupils were GMs Korotylev and Kosyrev, as well as ex-women's World Champion, Alexandra Kosteniuk. Although only a candidate master, Alexander Nikolaevich had a subtle positional feeling, as I learned in this game.

1.d4 ♘f6 2.c4 e6 3.♘c3 ♗b4 4.a3 ♗xc3+ 5.bxc3 0-0 6.e3 d6 7.♘e2 e5 8.♘g3 ♖e8 9.♗e2 c5 10.0-0 ♘c6

The game Botvinnik-Keres (The Hague 1948) continued 10...♘bd7 11.f3 cxd4?! 12.cxd4 ♘b6 13.♗b2 exd4 14.e4! with advantage to White. The knight move to c6 was recommended by Botvinnik.

11.d5 ♘e7

The alternative was 11...♘a5 followed by ...b7-b6 and ...♗a6.

12.♗d3 ♘g6 13.f3

In the Nimzo-Indian, I happily went in for such closed positions, but I played them badly (see my games against Vulfson and Bronstein, for example). This game proved to be the last straw and pushed me into adopting more dynamic lines in this opening.

13...♘h4

I also looked at the positional exchange sacrifice 13...e4!? 14.♘xe4 ♘xe4 15.♗xe4 ♖xe4 16.fxe4 ♘e5, establishing a blockading knight in the centre, but unfortunately, I decided against it. It was also worth considering 13...h5 14.♕c2 h4 15.♘e4 ♘xe4 16.♗xe4 ♕g5 etc. The move in the game may also not be bad, but I did not combine

it with any concrete plan and just begun running on the spot, counting on the closed position in the fight against the bishop pair. Of course, one cannot play like that!

14.♕c2 ♕e7 15.♗d2 ♗d7 16.♖ae1 ♖ad8

A typical 'developing' move, but at the same time, one that is completely pointless.

17.e4 ♘g6 18.♘f5 ♗xf5 19.exf5 ♘f8 20.g4

Now my kingside is completely tied up and, in the absence of enemy counterplay, White begins unhurriedly to seize space.

20...h6 21.♔g2 ♘6h7 22.♖h1 ♕h4 23.♖e2 ♖a8 24.♗e1 ♕f6 25.h4 g5 26.♔g1 ♕g7 27.hxg5 hxg5 28.♖eh2 f6 29.♖h6 ♖e7

The black knights have lost all mobility, but where will White break through? I soon got the answer to this question.

30.♗f2 ♖c8 31.a4 ♖cc7 32.♔g2 ♖e8 33.a5 ♖ce7 34.♕b1 ♖c8 35.♗c2 ♖ce8 36.♗e3 ♖c8 37.♔g3 ♖cc7 38.♗a4 ♖c8 39.♖6h2 ♖cc7 40.♖b2 ♖c8 41.♖hh2 ♖cc7 42.♖b5 ♖c8 43.♗c2 ♖cc7 44.♗e4 ♖ed7 45.♖hb2 ♕e7 46.♗c2 ♕g7 47.♗a4 ♖f7

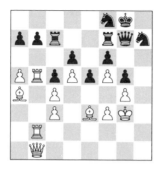

48.♕g1!
So, the breakthrough is coming at c5!
48...♕h6 49.♖h2 ♕g7 50.♗xc5!
A brilliant sacrifice – not of a piece, as it may appear, but actually of a rook!
50...a6 51.♗xd6! axb5 52.♗xb5 ♖c8 53.♕b6
Despite his extra rook, Black is completely helpless against the avalanche of white pawns, supported by two powerful bishops.
53...e4
This desperate attempt to activate his idle pieces is doomed to failure.
54.fxe4 ♘d7 55.♕xb7 ♖e8 56.♕c6 ♖xe4 57.♕c8+ ♘hf8 58.♗xd7 ♖xd7 59.♗xf8 ♕xf8 60.♕xd7?
The end of the game was played in fierce mutual time-trouble. This is the only thing that explains why White did not immediately finish his opponent off with 60.♖h8+ ♔xh8 61.♕xf8+ ♔h7 62.♕xf6.
60...♖e7?
Missing a saving chance – 60...♕b8+ 61.d6 ♖e3+ 62.♔f2 ♕b2+! 63.♔xe3 ♕xc3+ with perpetual check!
61.♕c6?
The time control was past but White played an extra move 'just in case', thereby missing a well-

deserved win. Here the players finally paused to catch their breath and before the reader we have a position we have already seen in the chapter about the value of solving endgame studies.

Black's position is desperate, as he is four (!) pawns down. After a 40-minute think, I managed to find a study-like way to draw.
61...♔g7
Preparing counterplay against the white king along the e-file. The immediate 61...♖e3+ 62.♔f2 ♕e7 fails because of 63.♕c8+.
62.♔f3
After the natural 62.d6 I had prepared the study-like 62...♖e3+ 63.♔f2 ♖e2+! 64.♔xe2 ♕e8+! 65.♕xe8 – stalemate! With the text, White prevents the entry of the enemy rook, but Black again finds a sufficient response.
62...♕b8! 63.d6 ♕b1! 64.dxe7 ♕d3+ 65.♔f2 ♕d2+! 66.♔g3 ♕f4+
And Black announced perpetual check!

I was very proud of this endgame, and at heart refrained from assessing it objectively. Only recently, after checking it with the computer, did I discover the truth. Firstly, as one might suspect, by accurate play, White can control the enemy counterplay on the e-file: 62.♕c5! ♕e8 63.♔f3 ♖e4 64.♕c7+ ♖e7 65.♖e2! (another study theme, known by the name 'the Maltese Cross'), winning.

Secondly, even in the variation 62.d6 ♖e3+ 63.♔f2 ♖e2+, White can retain winning chances by playing 64.♔f3!! ♖xh2 65.a6.

And thirdly, instead of the 'genius move' 61...♔g7? correct was 61...♕b8+! 62.d6 ♖e3+ 63.♔f2

Analysis diagram

63...♖d3!! (in my calculations, I had missed this quiet move, playing for domination), and already it is White who must find only moves to escape defeat – 64.♔e2! ♖xd6 65.♕b5! ♕d8 66.♕b2 ♕e7+ 67.♔f2 ♕d8 68.♔e2 ♕e7+ with a repetition!

Even so, although incorrect, Black's idea was imaginative. Later I created an instructional example out of this finish, which was given earlier in the endgame study chapter.

In this same tournament, I managed to achieve my first win against a master.

Sicilian Defence
Alexander Kalinin
Yuri Zotkin
Moscow 1985

1.e4 c5 2.♘f3 ♘c6 3.d4 cxd4
4.♘xd4 ♘f6 5.♘c3 e6 6.♘db5 ♗b4
7.a3 ♗xc3+ 8.♘xc3 d5 9.exd5 exd5
10.♗d3 0-0 11.0-0

In one of the earlier rounds of the tournament, Zotkin had been unable to cope with an energetic attack in the Sozin Variation, launched by my friend Volodya Ladizhansky. Consequently, this time the master chooses a quiet Sicilian variation. I had no objection to this, as at that time, I liked having a static advantage. The two bishops and IQP promise White a small, but comfortable plus.

11...d4 12.♘e2 ♕d5
A solid alternative was 12...♗g4.

13.♘f4 ♕d6 14.♘h5
The exchange of the knights opens up a path for the white queen on the kingside.

14...♘xh5 15.♕xh5 h6 16.♗d2 ♖e8
17.♖fe1 ♗d7 18.♕h4
This subtle move prepares to bring the bishop to f4 and allows the coordination of the white pieces.

18...♘e5?!
By establishing the knight in the centre, Black hoped to build his game around it, but in fact, it soon becomes an object of attack. It is

curious to note how, over the next few moves, the white pieces are drawn to the e5-square almost as if by a magnet.

19.♗f4 ♖e7

Later this position was reached in a game Tiviakov-Maliutin (Montecatini Terme 1994). After 19...♕c5? 20.♕g3 ♘g6 21.♗xg6 fxg6 22.♕xg6 ♖xe1+ 23.♖xe1 ♗f5 24.♕g3 ♗xc2 25.♗xh6 ♕f8 26.♖e5 ♔h8 27.♗d2 White obtained a decisive advantage.

20.♖e2 ♖ae8 21.♖ae1 f6

This forced weakening of the kingside brings with it far from desirable consequences.

22.h3?!

A typical move made out of 'general considerations'. Before taking decisive action, I decided to make luft for the king and only then calculate concrete variations. But Black would have faced serious problems after 22.♕g3!. Then after 22...♔h8 (playing for the weakness of the back rank fails: 22...♘xd3 23.♗xd6 ♖xe2 24.♖xe2 ♖xe2 25.h3 etc.) 23.♗xe5 fxe5 24.♕g6 Black loses a pawn. Even worse is 22...♔f8? 23.♗d2!, with

the unstoppable threat of 24.♗b4. The least evil was 22...g5, but after 23.♗d2 White's advantage is still obvious.

22...♕b6

Black's position is difficult, but he could still put plenty of difficulties in White's path. For example, interesting complications follow from 22...♕d5 23.♕g3 ♗b5 24.♗xh6 ♗xd3 25.cxd3 ♔h7 (if 25...g5 26.♔f1 ♔h7 27.♗xg5 fxg5 28.♕xg5 White has three pawns and an attack for the piece) 26.♗d2 ♘f3+ 27.♕xf3 ♕xf3 28.♖xe7 ♕xd3 29.♖xe8 ♕xd2 30.♖8e2 ♕d3, and the black queen is still keeping the enemy rook from going after the d4-pawn.

23.♗xe5

Mass exchanges on e5 will allow White to create an attacking battery on the b1-h7 diagonal.

23...♖xe5 24.♖xe5 ♖xe5 25.♖xe5 fxe5 26.♕e4

26...♕xb2?

A bad blunder. Black would end up a pawn down after 26...♕c7 27.♕d5+ ♔h8 28.♗c4 ♕c8 29.♗b3, but the game would continue.

27.♕d5+ ♔f8 28.♕xd7 ♕c1+ 29.♗f1 ♕xc2 30.♕d6+ 1-0

Another memorable event was a Scheveningen tournament, in which nine masters faced nine youngsters. Eight games against masters was an excellent school for all of the juniors. The best result amongst the masters was scored by Nikolai Andrianov. Playing in a markedly quiet manner, not avoiding exchanges and happy to go into the endgame, Nikolai scored 6.5 out of 8.

This game was an excellent example of the young player's adequate technical mastery.

King's Indian Defence
S. Kozhurov
Nikolai Andrianov

Moscow 1985

1.d4 ♞f6 2.c4 c5 3.e3 g6 4.♞f3 ♝g7 5.♞c3 0-0 6.dxc5 ♞a6 7.♝e2 ♞xc5 8.0-0 b6 9.♞d4 ♝b7 10.b4 ♞ce4 11.♞xe4 ♞xe4 12.♝b2 d5 13.f3 ♞d6 14.cxd5 ♝xd5 15.e4 ♝b7

As a result of a quiet opening, a roughly equal position has been reached. An analogous position was reached in the game Smyslov-F. Olafsson, Reykjavik 1974.

16.♜c1 ♛d7 17.♛d2 ♜ac8 18.♜fd1 ♜xc1 19.♜xc1 ♜c8 20.♜xc8+ ♛xc8 21.♛c3 ♛xc3 22.♝xc3

One after another, the pieces disappear from the board and the draw becomes increasingly obvious.

22...f5

The first attempt to disturb things a little – the symmetrical pawn structure is disrupted.

23.exf5 gxf5 24.♞b5

Forcing yet another exchange, with an absolutely static balance of the position. But Black does not offer a draw just yet.

24...♞xb5 25.♝xg7 ♚xg7 26.♝xb5

26...f4

Fixing the f3-pawn on a light square. This is Black's first, microscopic achievement in the whole game.

27.♝d3

Simpler was 27.♚f2 ♚f6 28.♚e2 ♚e5 29.♚d3 with an absolutely equal position. Now the black king aims for d4.

27...h6 28.♚f2 ♚f6 29.g3 ♚e5 30.gxf4+

By playing 30.g4, White could have established a passed pawn on the kingside, which would have limited the activity of the black king.

30...♚d4

An attempt to sharpen the situation. In the event of 30...♚xf4 31.♝e2 ♝d5 32.a3 e5 33.♝d1 ♝f7 34.♝c2! White easily holds the f3-pawn.

31.♝e2 ♚c3 32.b5 ♝d5 33.a3 ♝c4

After 33...♚b3 34.♚e3 the white king breaks into the centre.

34.♝xc4 ♚xc4 35.♚e3 ♚xb5 36.♚d4

36...♔c6

The pawn race leads to a draw:
36...♔a4 37.f5 ♔xa3 38.♔e5 b5
39.♔e6 b4 40.♔xe7 b3 41.f6 b2 42.f7
b1♕ 43.f8♕ ♕b4+ 44.♔e8 ♕xf8+
45.♔xf8 ♔b3 46.f4 etc.

37.♔e5 ♔d7

After Herculean efforts, Black has
managed certain achievements –
the better pawn structure and an
outside passed pawn. But even so,
these factors are not yet enough to
win, as the opponent has managed
to activate his king.

38.f5 b5 39.f6?

White fails to withstand the
unexpected tension, and in time-
trouble commits a serious mistake. A
draw results from 39.♔d5! a5 40.♔c5
b4 41.axb4 axb4 42.♔xb4 ♔d6
43.♔c4 ♔e5 44.♔d3 ♔xf5 45.♔e3.

39...exf6+ 40.♔xf6 ♔d6!

Shoulder-charging! Evidently,
White had counted only on 40...
a5 41.♔e5 b4 42.axb4 axb4 43.♔d4
♔e6 44.♔c4 ♔e5 45.♔xb4 ♔f4
46.♔c3 ♔xf3 47.♔d2 with a draw.

41.f4

Or 41.♔f5 ♔d5 winning.

41...a5 42.f5 b4 43.axb4 a4!

And White resigned, since the black
pawn queens with check.

The present author lost in a similar
fashion.

English Opening
Alexander Kalinin
Nikolai Andrianov
Moscow 1985

**1.c4 ♘f6 2.♘c3 c5 3.♘f3 e6 4.g3
b6 5.♗g2 ♗b7 6.0-0 ♗e7 7.♖e1 d5
8.cxd5 exd5 9.d4 0-0**

We have reached an opening *tabiya*,
on the border between a Queen's
Indian and an English. Without
waiting for the black knight to
come to a6 (when it can potentially
come via c5), White starts
immediate action in the centre.

**10.dxc5 bxc5 11.♘h4 ♕d7 12.e4
♘xe4**

The advance ...d5-d4 leads to an
unfavourable pawn structure for
Black.

**13.♘xe4 dxe4 14.♕xd7 ♘xd7
15.♗xe4 ♗xe4 16.♖xe4 ♗f6 17.♖b1**

Practically bypassing the
middlegame, the players have
gone straight to an endgame. I
considered that the isolated pawns
on a7 and c5 gave me a small
advantage.

17...♖fe8 18.♖xe8+ ♖xe8 19.♗e3

19...c4!

The exchange on h4 would be in White's favour, despite the spoiling of his pawn structure. He would retain the better chances, thanks to the superiority of his bishop over the knight and the possibility of strengthening his position by ♖c1-c4. With the text, Black prevents his weaknesses being fixed by means of b2-b3, whilst after the capture of the a7-pawn, there follows ♖a8 and then ♖xa2.

20.♖c1

Convinced I had lost my advantage, I decided to force a draw after 20...♗xb2 21.♖xc4. However, more precise was 20.♘f3, and with the subsequent ♘d2 White could possibly still claim a small plus.

20...♘e5

Deciding to keep the tension. The pawn is c4 is defended for the moment, whilst the b2-pawn could become a target.

21.f4

A nervous move, resulting from a desire to provoke an immediate crisis.

21...♘d3 22.♖xc4 ♘xb2 23.♖c2 a5 24.♘f3 ♘d3 25.a4

Not wishing to permit the advance ...a5-a4-a3, White decides to stop the pawn and fix it on a dark square.

25...h6 26.♗b6

Here I expected the continuation 26...♖e4 27.♗xa5 ♖xa4, and a draw could be agreed. However, Black continues to maintain a small degree of tension.

26...♖a8

27.♖d2?

Black's determination reaps its reward – in an equal position, the opponent commits a serious mistake! After 27.♘d2 ♖a6 28.♘c4 ♘b2 (Black could get into difficulties after 28...♖xb6 29.♘xb6 ♗d4+ 30.♔f1 ♗xb6 31.♖c6!) 29.♘xb2 ♖xb6 30.♘c4 ♖b4 or 27.♗d4 ♘e1 28.♘xe1 ♗xd4+ 29.♔f1 ♖b8 30.♖c4 the position would be absolutely equal.

27...♘b2 28.♖d5 ♗c3

It is all over – the a5-pawn is invulnerable, whilst the a4-pawn inevitably falls. Black went on to realise his advantage easily.

So, what was the cause of White's defeat in the last two games? I think the real cause is not so much weakness in endgame technique as psychology. The young players did not have sufficient self-belief, and the desire to secure a quick draw at some moment resulted in impulsive actions. At the same time, the master's play was characterised by quiet self-assurance and belief in his own strength, determination to keep trying to win until the very last moment, and attention to detail.

Among the eight youngsters in this event were two future GMs (Oleg Korneev and Vladimir Chuchelov). But the best result (5.5/8) was posted by the nowadays unknown Sergey Rokhmanov. In those years, he showed high sporting and creative results and he was expected to have an interesting future in chess. Unfortunately, after leaving high school, Sergey gave up playing in tournaments.

Ruy Lopez
Sergey Rokhmanov
Alexey Kuzmin
Moscow 1985

1.e4 e5 2.♘f3 ♘c6 3.♗b5 a6 4.♗xc6 dxc6 5.0-0 ♛d6 6.d4 exd4 7.♘xd4 ♗d7 8.♗e3 0-0-0 9.♘d2 ♘h6 10.f3

10...g5
The future GM and Karpov second, Alexey Kuzmin, was an excellent Spanish player even in those days. Thus here, instead of the theoretical 10...f5 11.♛e2 ♛g6, he plays a fresh idea, advancing the g-pawn.
11.c3 ♛g6 12.b4 f5 13.a4
Both sides carry out their plans purposefully. As usual in such positions, the white b-pawn is advancing towards its targets on a6 and c6, which will allow him to tear open lines in front of the black king's bastion.
13...f4
Maybe Black should not have pushed his pawns so energetically. It was worth considering 13...♗g7, completing his development and maintaining the tension in the centre.
14.♗f2 g4 15.♗h4 ♖e8 16.b5 c5 17.♘e2
Because of the vulnerability of the f4-pawn, Black cannot play ...a6-a5 to prevent lines being opened on the queenside.
17...gxf3?
This leads to the destruction of Black's central position. He should have strengthened the central squares with 17...♗d6, e.g. 18.bxa6 bxa6 19.♘c4 gxf3 20.♖xf3 ♛xe4 21.♛xd6 ♛xf3 22.gxf3 ♖hg8+ 23.♔f2 ♖xe2+ 24.♔xe2 cxd6 25.♘xd6+ ♔c7 26.♘e4 ♖g2+, maintaining approximate equality.
18.♘xf4 ♛d6
On 18...♛g4 there could follow 19.bxa6 bxa6 (19...♛xf4? 20.a7) 20.♛xf3 (20.g3 f2+!) 20...♛xf3 (20...♛xh4? 21.e5 c6 22.e6) 21.gxf3 ♗g7 22.♘d5 ♗e6 23.♗f6 with advantage to White.
19.♘d5
The computer recommends the move 19.♛xf3, the tactical basis of which is the variation 19...♛xd2 20.♖ad1 ♛a2 21.♖xd7! ♔xd7 22.♛h3+ ♖e6 (if 23...♔d6 the

decisive blow is struck by 24.e5+!)
23.e5!, and, despite the extra rook,
Black is completely paralysed.

19...♘g4

19...fxg2? is bad because of 20.♖f6.

20.♘xf3

An excellent alternative is 20.♗g3.
The point is that after 20...fxg2
White is not obliged to accept the
queen sacrifice (21.♗xd6 gxf1♕+
22.♕xf1 ♗xd6 with compensation
for Black), but can prefer the
stronger 21.♖e1! ♕h6 22.♘c4 with
an irresistible attack.

**20...c4 21.♔h1 ♖xe4 22.♗g3 ♕c5
23.bxa6 bxa6 24.♗xc7**

The smoke has cleared somewhat
and it is clear that the black king's
position is hopelessly weak.

24...♗e6

In the event of 24...♘f2+ 25.♖xf2
♕xf2 a nice finish is possible:
26.♘b6+! ♔xc7 27.♕xd7+ ♔xb6
28.♖b1+ ♔a5 29.♖b5+ axb5
30.♕xb5#.

25.♘f6!

The decisive blow!

25...♕xc7

The black king perishes after
25...♘xf6 26.♕d8+ ♔b7 27.♖ab1+
♔c6 28.♕b8 etc.

26.♘xe4

And White soon realised his large
material and positional advantage.
This game clearly shows that in a
sharp battle, as opposed to quiet
technical games, the youngsters had
nothing to fear from the holders of
higher titles.

My own performance in this event
was rather dull. This was not just
because of the high number of
draws, but more because in half of
them, peace was agreed long before
the resources of the position had
been exhausted. It became obvious
that a lack of fighting qualities was
my Achilles Heel.

Discounting my losses, there was
only one genuinely instructive game.

Sicilian Defence
Alexey Kuzmin
Alexander Kalinin
Moscow 1985

**1.e4 c5 2.♘f3 d6 3.d4 cxd4 4.♘xd4
♘f6 5.♘c3 ♘c6 6.g3**

The Panov system, one of the
most solid set-ups in the Sicilian.
In my opponent's repertoire,
sharp Sicilian variations co-exist
peacefully with its more positional
lines.

6...e6 7.♗g2 ♗d7 8.0-0 ♗e7 9.♘ce2

Preparing a press with the move
c2-c4.

9...0-0 10.c4 a6 11.b3 ♖c8 12.♗d2

An interesting development of the
bishop. White intends to meet the
advance 12...b5 with 13.cxb5 ♘xd4
14.♘xd4 axb5 15.♗b4!.

12...♛c7 13.♖e1 ♛b8 14.♖c1 ♖fd8 15.♗c3 ♗e8

The manoeuvre ...♖fd8 followed by ...♗e8 reminds me of the game Zukertort-Steinitz (Match 1886), which started as a QGA!

16.♛d2 ♞d7

Black continues to manoeuvre, since he cannot sharpen the game – 16...d5? 17.exd5 exd5 18.♞f5 etc.

17.♞xc6 ♖xc6

Retaining the possibility of playing ...b7-b5. At the same time, after 18.e5 ♞xe5 Black is guaranteed compensation for the exchange.

18.f4 ♖cc8 19.♞d4 ♞c5 20.f5

Black cannot defend the pawn on e6 and must cede control of the d5-square.

20...e5 21.♞c2 b5 22.♗a5 ♖d7 23.♞b4 f6 24.cxb5 axb5 25.♞d5

So, the white knight has reached the key square d5. When this position arose, I was not very optimistic, but gradually I realised that Black has reasonable counterchances. The bad bishop can come out via e7-d8-b6, whilst the 'eternal' knight on d5 can be targeted with ...♗f7. Meanwhile, White also has his minuses – a

passive bishop on g2, a vulnerable e4-pawn and a weak complex of dark squares.

The further course of the game supported the assessment of rough equality.

25...♗d8 26.♗b4 ♗b6 27.♔h1 ♗f7 28.♖c2 ♛b7 29.♞xb6 ♛xb6 30.♖ec1 ♛b7 31.♛e3 ♖cd8

The doubled rooks on the closed file serve as an indirect answer to the threat to take on c5.

32.h4 ♞a6 33.♗a5 ♖b8 34.♛b6 ♛xb6 35.♗xb6 ♔f8 36.♖c8+ ♔e7 37.♖xb8 ♞xb8 38.♗f1 ♖b7 39.♗a5 ♗e8

And here a draw was agreed.

Once I saw the game Tarrasch-Paulsen (Breslau 1889):

I was very surprised by the fact that Louis Paulsen went in for this position and Tarrasch failed to win it. But after my game with Kuzmin, I started to understand the problem of the 'eternal' knight on d5. I would only add that Paulsen's ideas are the basis for the modern Sicilian variations with ...e7-e5, such as the Boleslavsky and Sveshnikov systems.

I will conclude my discussion of the match-tournament with two more dynamic games.

Nimzo-Indian Defence
Vladimir Vulfson
Vasily Prokofiev

Moscow 1985

1.d4 ♘f6 2.c4 e6 3.♘c3 ♗b4 4.f3 d5 5.a3 ♗xc3+ 6.bxc3 c5 7.cxd5 ♘xd5 8.♕d2

As I have already mentioned, Vulfson liked offbeat variations and tried to give them his own twist. The variations with 4.f3 later became popular through the efforts of Malaniuk and Shirov, but the move 8.♕d2 remains rare. White's usual attempts at an advantage involve the move 8.♕d3 (which can lead to an exchange of light-squared bishops after 8...cxd4 9.cxd4 b6 10.e4 ♗a6) or 8.dxc5 (breaking up his own centre, but opening lines for the bishop pair). With the text move, White demonstrates his willingness to retain both static plusses – the two bishops and the pawn centre.

8...cxd4 9.cxd4 f5 10.g3

But this move still does not appear on the pages of theoretical manuals. White gradually prepares the advance e2-e4.

10...f4 11.♘h3 0-0

An interesting continuation. By sacrificing a pawn, Black outstrips his opponent in development.

12.♘xf4

In a subsequent round, White attempted to improve the variation

with 12.gxf4 ♕h4+ 13.♘f2 ♘xf4 14.e3 ♘d5 15.♕c2 ♘c6 16.♕e4 ♕h6 17.♗d2 ♗d7 18.h4 ♘f6 19.♘g4 ♕h5 20.♘xf6+ ♖xf6 21.♗e2 ♖e8 22.f4 ♕h6 23.h5 ♘e7 24.♖g1 ♗c6 25.♕d3 ♘d5, but here too, Black had nothing to complain about (Vulfson-Kalinin, Moscow 1985).

12...♘xf4 13.gxf4 ♕h4+ 14.♔d1 ♗d7 15.a4

Black to move. What would you play?

15...e5!

A nice breakthrough at the strongest point of the enemy defences. By sacrificing a second pawn, Black creates a strong attack against the enemy king.

16.fxe5 ♘c6 17.♗b2

On 17.f4 there follows 17...♘xd4! 18.♕xd4 ♖ad8 19.♗d2 ♗c6 20.♕c4+ ♗d5, and White stands badly.

17...♗e6

The immediate 17...♘xe5! was a superior alternative.

18.♖g1?

A serious mistake. White could hold the defences of his king with 18.♖a3! with unclear play.

18...♗b3+ 19.♔c1 ♘xe5?!

An incorrect form of the right idea. Black could get a decisive advantage

with the intermediate 19...♕f2
20.♖h1, and only now 20...♘xe5.
20.♗c3
Hopeless is 20.dxe5 ♖fd8 etc.
20...♖ac8 21.dxe5 ♖fd8

22.♕e3?
It is surprising, but even in
this desperate position, the
computer does not lose its head.
Its recommendation 22.♖g4! ♕f2
23.♖xg7+! ♔xg7 (23...♔h8? 24.♖d7)
24.♕g5+ ♔f8 25.♗b2 leads to a
position of dynamic equality!
22...♕b4
The computer prefers a variation
with geometric motifs: 22...♖d1+
23.♔b2 ♖xa1 24.♖g4 ♕e7! 25.♖b4
♖a2+! 26.♔b1 ♗e6, and White has no
defence against the threat of 27...♖a3.
**23.♖xg7+! ♔h8 24.♔b2 ♖xc3
25.♖xh7+ ♔xh7 26.♕xc3 ♖d2+
27.♕xd2 ♕xd2+ 28.♔xb3**
White has sufficient material
equivalent for the queen, but his
forces are scattered.
**28...♕d5+ 29.♔c2 ♕c4+ 30.♔b2
♕d4+ 31.♔b1 ♕d2!**
Several precise steps by the black
queen have completely paralysed
White. There followed:
**32.e6 ♔g7 33.e7 ♔f7 34.e8♕+
♔xe8 35.e4 a6 36.h4 ♔e7 37.e5**

♕e1+ 38.♔a2 ♕b4 39.♖c1 ♕xa4+
40.♔b2 ♕b4+ 0-1

Sicilian Defence
Alexey Kuzmin
Vasily Prokofiev
Moscow 1985

**1.e4 c5 2.♘f3 d6 3.d4 cxd4 4.♘xd4
♘f6 5.♘c3 e6 6.f4 ♘c6 7.♗e3 e5
8.♘f3 ♘g4 9.♕d2 ♘xe3 10.♕xe3
exf4 11.♕xf4 ♗e6 12.0-0-0 ♗e7
13.♘d5 ♗xd5 14.exd5 ♘e5 15.♗b5+
♔f8 16.♖hf1**
This position had already been seen
in practice. The game Ligterink-
Andersson (Amsterdam 1979)
continued 16...♘xf3 17.♕xf3 ♗f6
18.♖de1 ♕b6 19.♕e2 ♗e5 20.c3 g6
21.♕f3 f5 22.♗d7 ♔g7 23.g4 ♕d8
24.♗e6 ♕g5+ 25.♔c2 fxg4, and
Black managed to consolidate his
position, albeit with some difficulty.
16...♗f6?
The youngster had prepared an
improvement, exploiting the fact
that the black knight is indirectly
defended. However...

**White to move. What would you
play?**

17.♘xe5!

Over the board, Alexey Kuzmin finds a lovely refutation of his opponent's idea. Sacrificing the queen for two minor pieces, White organises a chase of the enemy king.

17...♗g5 18.♘xf7 ♗xf4+ 19.♖xf4 ♕a5

In the event of 19...♕b6 White decides with 20.♘h6+ ♔e7 21.♖e1+ ♔d8 22.♘f7+ ♔c8 23.♘xh8 ♕xb5 24.♖e7 ♔d8 25.♖xg7 ♕e8 26.♘f7+ ♔c7 27.♔d2!, and Black is completely helpless, as the reader can check for himself.

20.♘h6+

But not 20.♘xh8+? ♔g8, which throws away the win. However, the computer prefers the quiet move 20.♖df1!.

20...♔e7 21.♖e4+ ♔d8 22.♘f7+ ♔c7 23.♖e7+ ♔b6 24.♘xd6 ♕b4 25.♖xb7+ ♔c5 26.♗c4 ♕xb7 27.♘xb7+ ♔xc4

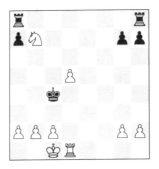

28.a4! ♖ab8 29.b3+ ♔b4 30.♖d4+ ♔a3 31.a5

A nice king hunt has ended – there is no defence against mate. Black resigned.

Incidentally, I also learnt a great deal not only from my games but also from encounters with my colleagues. I remember the Profsoyuz junior championship of 1982, which took place in Yaroslavl. I shared a room with a candidate master from Lvov (now a GM and recently trainer of the Ukrainian team), Yuri Kruppa. Yura was older than me and significantly stronger in chess terms. Even so, we interacted as equals and analysed games together. I was struck by the sporting correctness of my new friend, his subtle understanding of chess and his unfailing kindness in his dealings with people. I met Yuri again two years later at the Burevestnik event in Dnepropetrovsk. The Ukrainian was very taken at that time with Rubinstein's games, and this was clear in his own play. The following two games were played in the true classical spirit.

Queen's Gambit Declined
Yuri Kruppa
Sergey Tiviakov
Dnepropetrovsk 1984

Black here was a very young Sergey Tiviakov. The Krasnodar player was the youngest in the event and he found it hard going. But Sergey showed fighting qualities unusual for his age, as well as a self-critical attitude and the ability quickly to absorb new knowledge. Within a couple of years he was among the top juniors in the country and, ten years later, among the world's leading GMs. In a recent interview, Boris Postovsky, a long-time trainer of the Krasnodar youngster, said that Sergey kept a book called *My Lost Games*. I have to admit with shame that I had no such book...

1.d4 d5 2.c4 e6 3.♘c3 ♘f6 4.♗g5 ♗e7 5.♘f3 0-0 6.e3 ♘bd7 7.♕c2

Rubinstein's favourite weapon in the Orthodox QGD.

7...c5

The main line, leading to simplifications. The great Polish master scored several memorable wins in the variation 7...b6 8.cxd5 exd5 9.♗d3 ♗b7 10.0-0-0!? etc.

8.♖d1 ♕a5 9.cxd5 ♘xd5 10.♗xe7 ♘xe7 11.♗d3 ♘f6 12.0-0 cxd4 13.♘xd4

13...e5

In one of the games of the Capablanca-Lasker match of 1921, Black tried to neutralise the minimal white advantage with the less radical 13...♗d7.

14.♘b3 ♕b4 15.♘e4 ♘xe4

In the game Lutikov-Klovans (Riga 1954) Black was unable to cope with his problems after 15...♘ed5?! 16.♗c4 etc.

16.♗xe4 f5 17.♗d5+!

In an open position, it is psychologically difficult to swap bishop for knight. The alternative 17.♗f3 e4 18.♗e2 ♗e6 19.♕c5 a5 poses Black fewer problems.

17...♘xd5 18.♖xd5

Black's problems stem from the advanced position of the e- and f-pawns. Now he had the chance to solve this problem by tactical means: 18...♗e6! 19.♖xe5 ♖ac8 20.♕b1 (20.♘c5 ♗f7) 20...♗c4 21.♖d1 (21.♖e1 ♗d3) 21...♗xb3 22.axb3 ♕xb3 23.g3 ♖c2 (23...♖c7 24.♖d3) 24.♖b5 ♕xb5 25.♕xc2, although in the major piece ending, White's chances are still preferable, thanks to his control of the central files and the weakened position of the black king (...f7-f5).

18...♕e7?! 19.♖c1 ♕f6 20.♕c3 e4?

Black cannot stand the pressure and commits a serious mistake, giving his opponent control of the main avenues on the board. It was essential to play 20...♖e8 21.♘c5 b6 22.♘d7 ♕e6 23.♖cd1 ♗xd7 24.♖xd7 ♖ac8 25.♕d3 with the better chances for White.

21.♕xf6 ♖xf6 22.♘d4 ♖f7 23.♖d8+ ♖f8 24.♖xf8+ ♔xf8 25.♖c7 b6

White to play. Indicate a plan to realise the advantage.

26.h4!
Preparing a march by his king, along the dark squares into the enemy position. Black is completely helpless.
26...♔g8 27.♔h2 g6 28.♔g3 a5 29.♔f4 ♗a6 30.♔e5 ♗f1 31.g3 b5 32.a3 ♖b8 33.♘c6 ♖a8 34.♘e7+ ♔h8 35.♘d5 ♖e8+ 36.♔f4 ♖f8 37.♔g5 ♗c4 38.♘f6 ♗g8 39.♖b7 b4 40.axb4 axb4 41.♖xb4 ♔g7 42.♘xg8 ♔xg8 43.♖b7 ♖d8 44.b4 ♖d2 45.b5 ♖xf2 46.b6 ♖b2 47.♔f6 1-0

It is possible that it was this very games which persuaded Sergey Tiviakov to switch his opening repertoire against 1.d4 to something more aggressive. In later years, he successfully used asymmetrical variations of the Nimzo- and Queen's Indian defences, introducing many new ideas into them.

Queen's Pawn Game
Yuri Kruppa
Alexander Kalinin

Dnepropetrovsk 1984

1.♘f3 ♘f6 2.d4 e6 3.e3

This was another of Rubinstein's favourite 'dishes', this time in reply to the Queen's Indian Defence. 'In the resulting symmetrical positions, Rubinstein managed to secure the advantage, in a manner known only to him.' (Nimzowitsch)
3...b6 4.♗d3 ♗b7 5.♘bd2 d5 6.b3 ♗d6 7.♗b2 ♘bd7 8.♘e5 0-0 9.f4 ♘e4 10.♘xe4 dxe4 11.♗b5 ♘b8 12.0-0 f6 13.♘g4 f5 14.♘e5 ♕e7 15.a3 c6 16.♗c4 ♘d7 17.b4 ♘xe5 18.dxe5 ♗c7

In analysis after the game, Yura, knowing my fondness for the classics, expressed his surprise at my willingness to enter this position, saying that 'Rubinstein long ago demonstrated the dangers for Black'. White's advantage consists in the more active position of his bishops (for example, the ♗c4 exerts unpleasant pressure against the e6-pawn) and the difference in the positions of the pawns on c2 and c6, which means that White may be able to sacrifice an exchange on d6.
19.♕e2 ♖ad8
With this move, Black begins a rather harmless doubling of his

rooks on the open d-file, where he has no penetration squares. But, having no other obvious useful plan, I decided to neutralise the above-mentioned idea of the opponent's, involving the exchange sacrifice on d6.

20.a4

Starting to soften up the enemy queenside. Note that White does not put his rooks on the only open file, preserving them for 'higher tasks'.

20...♖d7 21.a5 ♖fd8 22.♗d4 c5 23.bxc5 bxc5 24.♗c3 ♗c6 25.g4

Creating tension on the kingside as well.

25...♖f8 26.gxf5 ♖xf5 27.♗b5

The exchange of light-squared bishops is aimed at winning the pawn on e4, which has lost its support.

27...♗xb5 28.♕xb5 ♖d5

As is always necessary, White's strategy is combined with tactical alertness – the enemy counterattack by 28...♖h5 29.♖ad1 ♕h4 is beaten off by means of 30.♖d2! ♖xd2 (30...♖d8 31.♖xd8+ ♕xd8 32.♕xc5) 31.♕e8#; or 28...♖h5 29.♖ad1 ♖xh2 30.♖xd7 ♕h4 31.♖d8+! ♕xd8 32.♔xh2 ♕h4+ 33.♔g2 ♕g4+

34.♔f2 ♕f3+ 35.♔e1 ♕xe3+ 36.♔d1 ♕xc3 37.♕e8#!

29.♖ad1

The direct 29.♕c4 ♕h4 30.♕xe4 fails to 30...♗xe5.

29...♕d8 30.♖b1 ♖h5 31.♗e1 ♖h3 32.♕c6 ♖xe5?

After being under unpleasant pressure for the whole game, and being short of time, I was unable to withstand it and deceived myself. It was still possible to defend with 32...♕d7.

33.fxe5 ♕g5+

Hoping for 34.♔h1 ♖xh2+ 35.♔xh2 ♗xe5+, which, however, still leads to a win for White, after a lot of checks: 36.♔h3 ♕xe3+ 37.♔g2 ♕g5+ 38.♔f2 ♕h4+ 39.♔e2 ♕g4+ 40.♔e3 ♗d4+ 41.♔d2.

34.♗g3 ♖xg3+ 35.♔h1 1-0

This game, in my view, is typical of Yuri's play in those days, characterised by a high level of chess culture and great will to win. Returning to the subject of the Profsoyuz event at Yaroslavl in 1982, I would point out that Yuri Kruppa led from the first round until the start of the last – but the winner was the 13-year old Boris Gelfand! By beating the leader in the last round and catching him up on normal points, Boris won on tie-break. His talent for, and preoccupation with, chess was obvious at once. When thinking about his move, Boris would usually not be looking at the board. I thought this was strange at the time, but later I came to understand that he found it easier to calculate variations when not distracted by the sight of the pieces on the board! Boris' play was typified by its dynamism and striving for the initiative. His opening repertoire reflected this general approach – as Black, he played sharp lines of the Sicilian and King's Indian. I was also staggered by his endgame technique. He never avoided transposing into an ending, if he thought this met the demands of the position. The following game is characteristic in this way.

Sicilian Defence
Boris Gelfand
A. Lukyanov
Yaroslavl 1982

1.e4 c5 2.♘f3 d6 3.d4 cxd4 4.♘xd4 ♘f6 5.♘c3 e6 6.♗e2 ♗e7 7.0-0 ♘c6 8.♗e3 0-0 9.f4 e5 10.♘db5
Played in accordance with theory's last word at the time. Geller's idea 10.fxe5 dxe5 11.♘f5!? only became known a few months later.
10...a6 11.fxe5 dxe5 12.♕xd8 ♗xd8 13.♘d6 ♘d4 14.♗d3 ♗c7
In the stem game Dolmatov-Dorfman (Frunze 1981) there followed 14...♗e7 15.♘c4 ♗c5 16.♘a4 ♗a7 17.♘ab6 ♖b8 18.c3 with advantage for White. The text is an attempt to strengthen Black's play.
15.♘f5 ♘xf5 16.exf5 e4 17.♗e2 ♗e5
More precise was 17...b5 followed by ...♗b7, quickly bringing the queenside forces into battle.

The grouping of pieces in the centre seems to insure Black against any unpleasantness. However, within just a few moves, White succeeds in turning the pride of Black's position – the e4-pawn – into a real weakness.
18.♖ad1 b5
On 18...♗d7 there follows 19.♘xe4. Better was 18...♗xc3 19.bxc3 ♗d7 20.g4 ♗c6 21.c4 ♖fe8, but in this case too, White's chances are preferable.
19.♗d4
The exchange of dark-squared bishops opens the white king's path to e3.
19...♗xd4+ 20.♖xd4 ♗b7 21.g4 h6 22.♔f2 ♖fe8 23.♔e3 ♖ac8 24.h3 ♔f8 25.♖fd1 ♖c5 26.a4!
After achieving excellent centralisation, White breaks up the opponent's queenside.
26...bxa4 27.♖xa4 a5 28.♖c4 ♖ec8 29.♖d8+ ♖xd8 30.♖xc5 ♖a8 31.♗c4 ♘e8 32.♘xe4
And White went on to realise his material and positional advantage.

Gelfand spoke instructively in an interview in 2008: 'I was not afraid to enter the endgame. I was nine years old, but I already knew certain endings (from Capablanca's games and some rook endings). Of course, I had not yet read any of Dvoretsky's books, which brought this subject to its highest level, but I knew the main principles of the endgame. Later, in 1994, I was astonished at the play of grandmaster Tony Miles – in a game against me, he broke all the rules, moving his king somewhere and then moving it back again... I recalled that at age nine, I knew an endgame which even a GM did not know! And he was such a classy player. Perhaps this is why I always found him easy to play against – I won three games against him, all quite one-sided.'

A few months after the Yaroslavl tournament, Gelfand took part in the Sokolsky Memorial. This debut in an adult master tournament was a hard one for him (14-16th places, on 5 out of 15), but gave the young player precious experience. In 1990, a book was published in Minsk, which gave a selection of games from all the Sokolsky Memorial tournaments and this book featured some of Gelfand's analytical work in respect of the 1982 event. Boris analysed in detail a far from error-free game (one that he lost) against IM Cherepkov. At one moment, he writes: 'After a fierce battle, in which both sides missed wins, the game was adjourned in an interesting rook endgame. The analysis and resumption of this ending brought me great benefit.'

It is not surprising that Boris' talent and capacity for work soon saw him achieve a sharp advance. As early as 1983, the 14-year old schoolboy won the next Sokolsky Memorial with 11.5/16, and in 1984 and 1985, he was adult Byelorussian champion. Returning to the Profsoyuz junior event in Yaroslavl, I must say that it was a wonderful school for the young players. As well as the games themselves, there was the whole arrangement of the event – we played on the stage at the city chess club in front of spectators, with the games shown on demonstration boards. An especially impressive thing was the regular chief arbiter, Yakov Rokhlin, a legendary figure in Soviet chess. Just imagine – during the Moscow international tournaments of the 1920s and 30s, he had rubbed shoulders with such giants as Lasker and Capablanca! I took part in two of these events in 1982 and 1983. In the latter, the winner was the Uzbekistan representative, Grigory Serper, now a well-known GM in America. Grisha was noteworthy for his great concentration during a game – throughout the four hours of play he hardly ever left the board. Already he was noted for his excellent technique and high level of chess culture. It is interesting that Grisha was interested in chess composition and showed us several of his studies. Unfortunately, I did not make a note of any of them, but my own subsequent interest in studies was to a considerable extent prompted by Grisha's example. Grigory's main opening weapon against 1.e4 was various lines of the Sicilian Dragon, although he was also by nature a positionally-inclined player. Undoubtedly, the young player's confidence in sharp Dragon battles was helped by his analytical work.

But now let us look at a game between two future GMs, in which Grisha had to fight against his own favourite variation.

Sicilian Defence

Grigory Serper
Viacheslav Zakhartsov

Yaroslavl 1983

___

1.e4 c5 2.♘f3
The game Ogorodov-Serper from the same tournament featured the line 2.♘c3 ♘c6 3.g3 g6 4.♗g2 ♗g7 5.d3 d6 6.♘h3 e5 etc. Later, Grisha successfully played the same set-up as White in the English, thus obtaining his favourite Dragon-type position, but with an extra tempo, which allowed him to avoid the very sharp lines he often had to face as Black.

2...d6
Against me, Grisha played the Accelerated Dragon, allowing the Maroczy: 2...♘c6 3.d4 cxd4 4.♘xd4 g6 5.c4 ♗g7 6.♗e3 ♘f6 7.♘c3 0-0 8.♗e2 d6 9.0-0 ♗d7. Later, I played very directly and showed a lack of knowledge of many of the key ideas in such positions. I remember that after 10.♘c2 a5 11.a4 ♘b4 12.f3?

(with a space advantage, White should avoid exchanges by means of 12.♘d4) 12...♘xc2 13.♕xc2 ♗c6 14.♘d5 ♘d7 15.♖ab1 ♘c5 16.b3 e6 17.♘c3 ♕f6 18.♖bc1 ♖fd8 19.♖fd1 ♕e7 20.♗f1 ♖ac8 21.♘e2 b6 I willingly exchanged dark-squared bishops – 22.♗d4?.

Analysis diagram

The error in this exchange was shown long ago in the classic game F.Olafsson-Simagin (Moscow 1959). Grigory reacted in the standard fashion – 22...♗xd4+ 23.♘xd4 e5!, obtaining an obvious advantage, thanks to White's remaining 'bad' bishop. I only avoided real trouble because of a slight hesitation by my opponent at one moment: 24.♘e2 ♕g5 25.♕c3 f5 26.exf5 gxf5 27.♖c2 f4 28.♔h1 (a good defensive manoeuvre – the g1-square is freed for the knight, defending the kingside and preparing the exit of the bishop to d3) 28...♖d7 29.♖cd2 ♖cd8 30.♘g1 ♘e6? (White would face serious problems after 30...e4!) 31.♗d3 ♖g7 32.♗e4, and White managed to emerge unscathed.
3.d4 cxd4 4.♘xd4 ♘f6 5.♘c3 g6 6.♗e3 ♗g7 7.f3 0-0 8.♕d2 ♘c6 9.0-0-0

In the game Prokofiev-Serper, a few rounds earlier, White had chosen 9.g4 (this move was popular at the time, thanks to several wins by Karpov at the London Tournament in 1982) 9...♗e6 10.0-0-0 ♘xd4 11.♗xd4 ♕a5 12.♔b1 ♖fc8 13.h4?! (he should have chosen the prophylactic 13.a3) 13...♖xc3 14.♕xc3 ♕xa2+ 15.♔c1 ♗xg4!. The whole of this combination had also appeared previously in one of Vladimir Simagin's games. After 16.fxg4 ♕a1+ 17.♔d2 ♘xe4+ 18.♔e1 ♘xc3 19.♖xa1 ♗xd4 Black took the game into a favourable ending.
9...d5 10.exd5 ♘xd5 11.♘xc6 bxc6 12.♗d4 e5 13.♗c5 ♗e6 14.♘e4
Despite the opposite castling, in this variation the game has a fairly positional character, based around the battle for control of the central squares.
14...♖e8 15.h4 h6 16.h5 g5 17.g4 ♕c7 18.♗d6 ♕b6 19.♗c5 ♕c7

20.♕d3!?
This move is one you still won't find in the databases to this day. The unusual queen manoeuvre to a3 allows the strongest white piece to take up an active (controlling c5 and d6) and also invulnerable position.

20...♖ed8 21.♕a3 a5 22.♗d6 ♕b6 23.♗c5 ♕c7 24.♗c4 ♖d7 25.♖d2 ♖ad8 26.♖hd1 ♔h8 27.c3 ♔h7 28.♕b3
Having supported the advance of its army to threatening positions, the queen finds a new way to show its agility.
28...♖b8 29.♕c2 ♔h8

30.♗f2! ♗f8
In meeting the threat of 31.♘c5, Black allows a blow on the other flank.
31.♗xd5 ♖xd5 32.♘f6 ♔g7 33.♘xd5 cxd5
Often such exchange sacrifices allow Black to get adequate counterplay, thanks to his powerful pawn centre. But in this position, his centre soon comes under mass attack and collapses.
34.♗g3 ♖b5 35.♖e1 ♗d6 36.♖de2 e4 37.♗xd6 ♕xd6 38.fxe4 ♗xg4 39.♖d2 ♗xh5 40.♕d3 ♖c5 41.exd5 ♗g6 42.♕d4+ f6 43.♖e6 ♕f8 44.d6 ♖c8 45.♖f2 1-0

The combined actions of the white pieces in this game made a great impression on me.

CHAPTER 9

The fight against weaknesses

'*By means of chess, I developed my character.*' – Alexander Alekhine

During my time at school and the first year of university, I did not manage to get a master norm, and there were many reasons for this. I was insufficiently self-critical, my work was not systematic enough and my sporting qualities left something to be desired. I could see my weaknesses but did not undertake systematic work to eliminate them. In my case, it was army service which rescued me and developed my character, even though I served in relatively decent conditions in a sports outfit. I had little tournament practice, in two years playing only in two Moscow armed forces championships and a few team matches. But in compensation, I had time to think and could, as it were, look at my chess career from the side.

In the Moscow armed forces championship of 1987, I took first place, but no masters were playing in the event. The following year, with two masters among the field, I occupied only fifth place. The quality of my play in this latter event was poor. In the absence of practice, all my weaknesses came to the surface and seemed especially obvious. My play was dry and lacking in imagination. For the first time in my life, I thoroughly and self-critically annotated all of the games from this event. I did the analysis blindfold, because in the conditions of army service it was impossible to work at the board itself. But every cloud has a silver lining – blindfold analysis proved to be an excellent method of training for my poor calculation of variations. It was then that I decided to fight systematically against my weaknesses and become a master.

After demobilisation, I returned to study at the university and re-establishing contact with Zlotnik helped me greatly in strengthening myself psychologically. I fought against my main weakness, the dryness of my play, in a well-established and old-fashioned manner. Without further ado, I followed the advice of Kotov, who faced a similar problem in his own day.

Reading once again his books *Think Like a Grandmaster* and *Play Like a Grandmaster* (which I had been familiar with since childhood), I began training my calculation technique and annotating the games of masters notable for their dynamic and sharp styles of play, then comparing my analysis with that of the players themselves or other authorities. All the work of preparing such training exercises was undertaken by my father, and I had only to devote all my energy to penetrating their secrets. I also occupied myself with a study of the subject of sacrifices for the initiative, using Spielmann's *The Art of Sacrifice* and Shamkovich's *Sacrifices in Chess*.

By way of a curiosity, here is one inaccuracy found in published analysis.

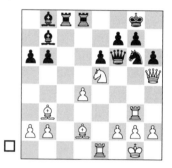

What would you play?

This position was cited by Kotov in one of his books, as an example of unsystematic thinking (with White jumping from one move to another in his calculations) and the importance of first delineating all the candidate moves, which should be considered during one's calculations. I had tried to solve this position as a ten year old, but got hopelessly confused. So, a new try! First, according to Kotov, we should identify the candidate moves. It is clear that White must proceed energetically, because by playing ...♗b7-d5, Black will consolidate to a large degree. Therefore the moves identified were 1.♘xf7, 1.♘xg6, 1.♖xg6, 1.♗xh6 and 1.♘g4. I started by looking at 1.♘xf7, because the blow against f7 seemed

the most logical in a position with an IQP, especially with the crossfire of white pieces against e6. I was greatly surprised when I realised that, in fact, there was nothing to calculate! The simple and short variation 1.♘xf7! ♗xg3 (or 1...♔xf7 2.♖xe6) 2.♘xh6+ ♔f8 3.hxg3 leaves no doubt as to White's victory. I was even more surprised when I realised that the move 1.♘xf7! was not even considered in the book! Kotov does not give the names of the players in this game and it is not in the databases. Only recently did I see the game in the book by Levenfish on the IX USSR Championship: it is the game Riumin-Belavienets (Leningrad 1938). The analysis in Kotov's book just quotes that by Levenfish. However, despite this work to make my style more active, the results were not obvious in my first event after leaving the army. At the all-union junior tournament in Kramatorsk (1989) I played for the Moscow team. Of course, it was interesting to test myself in a tournament where the first board line-up was fantastic (Ivanchuk, Gelfand, Dreev, Shirov, Akopian, Bologan, etc.), but even on my fifth board there was a solid set of opponents (I will mention only future GMs Scherbakov, Alexandrov and Sulskis).

I played solidly, sharing 2-3rd places on my board (first place was taken by the Leningrad player Alexei Ivanov – a future IM and champion of Northern capitols in 1991, who soon after gave up competitive play), but again made too many draws (+2=6) and did not play a single really decent game.

A few months earlier, a similar picture emerged at the semi-final of the Moscow adult championship (a whole range of masters played in the tournament, but there was no master norm available). I shared 3-4th places, but again had few decisive games (+3-1=11!), and the level of constructive ideas in my play did not give rise to great optimism. I was especially disappointed with my game against the master Dmitry Losev, during the course of which I could not guess a single one of my opponent's moves!

King's Fianchetto

Alexander Kalinin

Dmitry Losev

Moscow 1988

1.c4 g6 2.d4 ♗g7

This subtle move order was a favourite of Losev. In those days, he even used a not entirely sound gambit line, involving a piece sacrifice – 3.♘c3 d6 4.e4 ♘c6 5.♗e3 e5 6.d5 ♘d4 7.♘ge2 ♗g4?! 8.f3 ♗xf3 9.gxf3 ♘xf3+ 10.♔f2 ♕f6 etc. Not wishing to allow such lines, I decided to hold back the e-pawn.

3.♘f3 d6 4.♘c3 ♗g4 5.♗g5 h6 6.♗h4 c5 7.d5 ♕a5 8.♕d2 ♗xc3!?

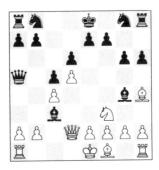

This exchange of the fianchettoed bishop was a surprise to me.

9.bxc3 ♘d7

One of the possible routes for the black knight is via b6-a4, hassling the doubled white pawns.

10.h3 ♗f5

Exchanging the second bishop (10...♗xf3 11.exf3) would open too many lines for White.

11.♕b2

Beginning to prepare expansion in the centre with ♘f3-d2 and e2-e4.

11...g5 12.♗g3 ♘gf6 13.♘d2 ♘b6 14.f3 ♗d7 15.♖c1 0-0-0 16.e4 e5 17.♖b1

Limiting the mobility of the ♘b6 and creating threats of a sacrifice on c5 or e5, which does not work at once: 17.♘b3 ♕a6 18.♗xe5? ♘a4!

17...♖de8!

An excellent prophylactic move. On e8 the rook not only fulfils defensive functions, strengthening the squares e5 and c5, but, as soon becomes clear, it can also support the actions of its own army.

18.♘b3 ♕a6 19.♗f2 ♘a4

Now the c5-square is invulnerable. By placing his knight on a4, Black consolidates his entire queenside.

20.♕d2 ♘h5 21.g3 ♕b6

The black queen returns to action via d8, using the square vacated by the queen's rook.

22.♗d3 ♕d8 23.♘a1?

A stereotyped decision. White intends to transfer the knight to e3, not seeing the hidden dynamic resources concealed in the position. The prophylactic 23.♔f1 was essential.

Black to move. What would you play?

23...f5!

Breaking up the 'petrified' central position!

24.exf5 e4! 25.♗xe4 ♗xf5 26.0-0 ♗xe4 27.fxe4 ♕d7 28.♔h2 ♖xe4

Even stronger was 28...♘f6.

29.♖be1 ♖he8 30.♖xe4 ♖xe4 31.♖e1 ♘f6

Black's advantage is obvious, as the white pawns are weak and his pieces have lost coordination. Only my opponent's traditional time-trouble enabled me to save the game.

I would like to say a few words about master (now International Master) Losev. A pupil at the Moscow city pioneer palace, Dmitry passed a typical development for a young player at that time. He was a pupil at the Botvinnik school, and took part in the pioneer palace tournaments sponsored by *Komsomolskaya Pravda*.

Although having an attractive attacking style and an original manner of playing, he also had one serious weakness – he was permanently in time-trouble, which reduced the level of his sporting results.

However, results are not the main thing for players such as Dmitry. He is attracted by the creative side of the game, and tries in every game to produce something special. More than a quarter of a century has passed since my first game against Dmitry and to this day, though now a veteran, he remains a romantic.

The following game, played quite recently, is a nice addendum to the previous one and to our creative portrait of the Moscow master.

Various Openings
Alexey Piskun
Dmitry Losev
Moscow 2010

1.d4 g6 2.c4 ♗g7 3.♘c3 d6 4.♘f3 ♗g4 5.g3 ♕d7 6.♕b3 ♘c6 7.♗g2 ♘h6

Black's original treatment of the opening has a sound basis – piece pressure on the enemy centre.

8.d5 ♗xf3 9.exf3 ♘d4 10.♕d1 ♘hf5 11.0-0 h5 12.♖e1 0-0-0 13.♕d3 h4 14.♗g5 hxg3 15.fxg3 ♖h5 16.♘e4 ♖dh8 17.h4 ♖5h7 18.♗h3 ♔b8 19.♔g2 f6 20.♗d2

Black to move. What would you play?

Black's non-standard play is crowned with a beautiful combination.

20...♘xh4+! 21.gxh4 ♕xh3+!! 22.♔xh3 ♖xh4+ 23.♔g3 ♖h3+ 24.♔g2 ♖h2+ 25.♔f1 ♖h1+ 26.♔f2 ♖8h2+ 27.♔g3 ♘f5+

White resigned.
This time Dmitry Losev did succeed in creating something special!

Returning to the Moscow 1988 semifinal, I would add that I only

once managed anything like such a combination, and then largely by accident.

Alexander Kalinin
Evgeny Dragomaretsky
Moscow 1988

The players are pursuing active operations on both sides of the board. Black has clearly won the battle on the queenside – he has the b-file in his hands, and the pawns on a2 and c3 are weak. White has concentrated his forces against the enemy king, but Black's defences have no vulnerable points.

20...♕a4?!

It should be pointed out that at this point in the tournament, master (later IM) Evgeny Dragomaretsky led the event with 7/7! No doubt this series of wins had weakened his sense of danger. Black's last move proves too optimistic – it prepares the rook's entry to b2, but underestimates the opponent's possibilities. By continuing 20...♗xf5 or 20...♖fe8, Black could eliminate at the roots any threats to his king.

21.♘e7+ ♚h8 22.♕h4

Suddenly a well-known mating mechanism is in the air – 23.g5 followed by 24.♕xh7+! ♚xh7 25.♖h4#. A second threat is ♖af1 and then ♘g6+.

22...♕e8?

This instinctive queen retreat, covering Black's tactical weaknesses, proves the decisive mistake. I will not confuse the reader with a mass of variations, but will only point out that 22...♘e3 maintains the balance.

23.e5!

Including the ♗g2 in the attack crushes Black's defences.

23...dxe5 24.♗e4 f5

If 24...h6 then 25.♖f6 decides.

25.gxf5 exf4 26.fxe6 h6 27.♘g6+ ♚g8 28.♘xf8 ♕xf8 29.♗d5 1-0

Such things often happen – you work hard in a certain direction, but don't seem to make any real progress. One can only keep faith that purposeful effort will eventually pay off.

In his time, Botvinnik, who gave the classical definition of a combination ('A combination is a forced variation with a sacrifice') pointed out: 'Several masters like to regard themselves as players of a combinative style. Well, now we have an objective way of testing this claim.' For all the subtlety of this statement, it still does not apply to me – there were not enough sacrifices in my games at the time, and not enough dynamics. Then I decided on a radical measure – striving for dynamic play in my games, without regard to the sporting result!

The following fragments are interesting for the fact that, at the critical moments, there were other, quieter continuations, that were in no way worse, and maybe even better, than those chosen in the game. However, I bravely went in for sacrifices, in order to gain the necessary experience.

Handszar Odeev
Alexander Kalinin

Moscow 1989

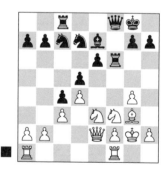

After starting out as a Sicilian (with 3.♗b5+) the game has assumed the contours of a French Defence. Black has a backward pawn on e6 and the e5-square is in White's hands. Even so, the assessment of the position is close to dynamic equality – Black's pieces are well-placed and exert pressure on the f-file.

17...♖f4?!

At the cost of the exchange, severing White's contact with the e5-square.

The quiet 17...♗d6 is tempting. After 18.♘e5 ♗xe5 19.dxe5 ♖f7 20.f4 ♘c5 21.f5 ♘d3 (21...♘e4 22.fxe6 ♘xe6 23.♘xd5) 22.♖f3 White's position is somewhat preferable. But instead of 19...♖f7 the move 19...♖f4!? is interesting, sacrificing the exchange in more favourable circumstances than in the game.

18.♗xf4 ♕xf4

The exchange sacrifice allows Black to show up the minuses of the advance of the pawn to g4, weakening the protection of its own king, and also gives Black control of the key square e5. It is also important that the black dark-squared bishop no longer has an opponent. The computer is not too ecstatic at Black's decision, but even

now, I am not inclined to attach too much significance to this. In the game there followed:

19.h3 ♗d6 20.g5

Preparing a knight jump to g4.

20...e5

It was worth considering 20...♘f8 21.♘g4 ♘g6.

21.dxe5 ♘xe5 22.♘xe5 ♗xe5 23.♘g4 ♗d6 24.♕e3 ♕f5 25.f4 ♘e6 26.♘e5 ♖f8 27.♖ad1 ♘xf4+ 28.♕xf4 ♕xf4 29.♖xf4 ♖xf4 30.♖xd5

And here a draw was agreed, on account of the complete equalisation of the position.

Alexander Kalinin
Grigory Bogdanovich

Moscow 1989

With his last move (12...e7-e5) Black activated his central pawns, which in fact can seem to be very vulnerable. Thus, White has the advantage after 13.♕h4 d4 14.♘xe5 or 13.♕c1 d4 14.e3, as the reader can convince himself. I, however, was immediately attracted by the idea of a positional queen sacrifice.

13.♘xe5!? ♘xe5 14.♕xe5 ♘e4 15.♕xg7+

The idea of this sacrifice was undoubtedly prompted by the following famous example:

Rashid Nezhmetdinov
Oleg Chernikov

Rostov-on-Don 1962

There followed
12.♕xf6! ♘e2+ 13.♘xe2 exf6
14.♘c3 ♖e8 15.♘d5 ♖e6 16.♗d4
♔g7 17.♖ad1 d6 18.♖d3
After sacrificing the queen for two pieces, White develops extremely strong pressure against f6.
18...♗d7 19.♖f3 ♗b5 20.♗c3
♕d8 21.♘xf6 ♗e2 22.♘xh7+ ♔g8
23.♖h3 ♖e5 24.f4 ♗xf1 25.♔xf1 ♖c8
26.♗d4 b5 27.♘g5 ♖c7 28.♗xf7+!
♖xf7 29.♖h8+! ♔xh8 30.♘xf7+
♔h7 31.♘xd8 ♖xe4 32.♘c6 ♖xf4+
33.♔e2 and Black resigned.

15...♔xg7 16.♘xe4+
The alternative is 16.♘xd5+ f6
17.♗xe4 ♕c8 18.♖d3 etc.
16...f6 17.cxd5
White has two minor pieces and two pawns for the queen, with his pieces actively placed, pressure against f6 and a passed pawn on the

d-file. It is clear that the sacrifice has justified itself – White has a firm grip on the initiative.
17...♕d7 18.♖d3 h6 19.♖c1
By continuing 19.♖f3 ♕xd5 20.♘xf6
♖xf6 21.♗xf6+ ♔g8 22.♗c3 ♕c5
23.♖e3 ♗xg2 24.♔xg2, White could seize the f6-square and even obtain a small material advantage. But I did not want to part with the strong d5-pawn.
19...♖ac8 20.♖xc8 ♕xc8 21.♖d2
♕f5 22.h3
Preparing the battering ram advance g4-g5. In the event of 22... h5 this threat is renewed by 23.♗f3.
22...♗xd5 23.g4 ♕e6 24.♘xf6 ♗xg2

White to move. Justify your choice by calculating variations.

Now a draw results from 25.♖d7+
♖f7 26.♘d5+ ♔h7 27.♖d8 g5
28.♖h8+ ♔g6 29.♖g8+ ♔h7 30.♖h8+
with perpetual check. White correctly realised that he can count on more, but he failed to cope with the specific task of working out precisely how.
25.♘d7+ ♔f7 26.♘xf8 ♕e4
This is the move I had overlooked! Now the knight on f8 is under attack, whilst after ...♗xh3 the

white king can come into trouble. I only considered 26...♔xf8 27.♔xg2, which leaves White with a minimal material advantage and some winning chances.

27.♘d7??

The result of being completely upset at the unexpected turn of events. By continuing 27.♘h7! ♕c6 (a problem-like mate arises after 27...♗xh3 28.♖d7+ ♔e6 29.♘f8#!) 28.h4 ♗d5 29.♘f6 White obtains an obvious advantage.

27...♗xh3 28.♘e5+ ♔e8

White resigned.

In the following example, the queen sacrifice proved more successful from the sporting point of view.

Alexander Kalinin
Alexander Trofimovsky

Moscow 1989

The game saw a nowadays popular variation of the English Attack against the Sicilian. Admittedly, Black's queenside castling looks rather committal. His last move (12...d6-d5), is clearly intended to justify it. Now White had available a

simple and strong line: 13.exd5 ♘b8 (13...♘b6 14.♗xb6 ♕xb6 15.♗c4) 14.♕f2 ♘xd5 15.♘xd5 ♖xd5 16.♖xd5 ♗xd5 17.♗d3 ♘d7 (or 17...♘c6 18.♗b6 followed by 19.♖d1) 18.♗f5 ♔b8 19.♖d1 ♗e6 20.♗xe6 fxe6 with a comfortable advantage thanks to the opponent's damaged pawn structure. But again, I preferred a positional queen sacrifice.

13.♘xd5 ♘xd5 14.exd5 ♘f6
15.dxe6!? ♖xd2 16.♗xd2 fxe6
17.♗a5 b6 18.♗xa6+ ♔b8 19.♗c3

This is where I ended my calculation. For the queen, White has a rook, minor piece and pawn. But the two active bishops, together with Black's pawn weaknesses and exposed king, give White a definite positional advantage.

19...♘d5 20.♖d3 ♗e7 21.♘d2
♗b4 22.♖xd5 ♗xc3 23.♖d3 ♗xd2+
24.♖xd2 ♕c6 25.♖hd1 ♕a4 26.♗d3
♕xa2 27.c3

As a result of the exchanges which have occurred, Black's material advantage has even increased a little, but it soon becomes clear that White has achieved a decisive domination on the light squares and the d-file. It is important that

Black cannot exchange rooks, because 27...♖d8? loses to 28.♗b1.

I played the rest of the game easily, since the main ideas were well-known from the game Spassky-Zhukovitsky (Leningrad 1957), which I had seen as a child.

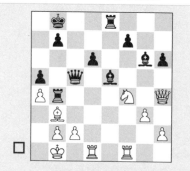

What would you play?

31.♘xg6! ♖xh4 32.♘xh4 f6 33.♘f5
The sacrifice of the queen for rook and minor pieces has given Spassky control of the light squares. The rest of the game shows the cooperation of the light-squared bishop and two rooks.

33...h5 34.♖d5 ♕c7 35.♖b5 b6 36.♘e3 ♗d4 37.♘d5 ♕d8 38.♖f4 ♗c5 39.♖xf6 ♖e2 40.♖f7 ♖f2 41.♖h7 ♖xh2 42.♘xb6 ♗xb6 43.♗d5 ♔c8 44.♖b7 ♕e8 45.♖5xb6 ♕e1+ 46.♔a2 ♖xc2 47.♖a6 ♖c7 48.♖b8+ ♔d7 49.♖f8 ♕b4 50.♖f7+ ♔d8 51.♖f4 ♕d2 52.♖f8+
And Black resigned.

Spassky's instructive play makes the end of our featured game clear without commentary.
27...♖c8 28.♗e4 ♕a1+ 29.♔c2 ♕a4+ 30.♔b1 ♕b3 31.♔c1 ♕a4

32.h5 ♕a1+ 33.♔c2 ♕a4+ 34.♔b1 ♕b3 35.♔c1 ♕a4 36.♖d6 ♕a1+ 37.♔c2 ♕a4+ 38.♔b1 ♕b3 39.♔c1 ♖c7 40.♗c2 ♕b5 41.♖xe6 ♔a7 42.♖ed6 ♕c5 43.♗e4 b5 44.♔c2 ♕f2+ 45.♔b3 ♖c4 46.♖d7+ ♔b8 47.♖xg7
Black resigned.

Finally, an example of a direct attack on the king.

Sicilian Defence
Davit Kodua
Alexander Kalinin
Moscow 1989

1.e4 c5 2.♘f3 d6 3.c3 ♘f6 4.♗d3 g6 5.h3 ♗g7 6.0-0 0-0 7.♗c2 ♘c6 8.♖e1 e5 9.d4 cxd4 10.cxd4 exd4 11.♘xd4 ♘xd4 12.♕xd4

This position is well-known to theory. The natural continuation 12...♗e6 promises Black good piece play and completely compensates for the weakness of the d6-pawn. However, I was attracted by a more artificial idea, involving the creation of tension around the white king's position.
12...♘g4!? 13.♕b4

More solid is 13.♕d1 ♘e5 (unclear play results from the piece sacrifice 13...♕h4 14.hxg4 ♗e5 15.g3 ♗xg3 16.♕f3 ♗h2+ 17.♔g2 ♗xg4 18.♕e3 ♖ac8 19.♖h1 (weaker is 19.♘c3 ♖c5! 20.♖h1 ♖h5) 19...♖xc2 20.♖xh2 ♕e7 21.♘c3 f5 etc.) 14.♘c3 ♕h4 with mutual chances.

13...a5

Here the piece sacrifice 13...♕h4 is incorrect – 14.hxg4 ♗e5 15.f4 a5 16.♕d2 ♗xf4 17.♕xf4 ♕xe1+ 18.♕f1 ♕xf1+ 19.♔xf1 ♗xg4 20.♘c3 with advantage to White. With the text, Black tries to break the contact between the white queen and the ♖e1.

14.♕b5

If 14.♕d2 I was intending to continue 14...♘e5 15.♕d1 ♗e6 16.♘c3 ♕h4, and the appearance of the black queen on h4 creates the possibility of a piece sacrifice on h3.

14...♕h4

At first, I looked at another way of sacrificing a piece: 14...♘xf2!? 15.♔xf2 ♕h4+, but after 16.♔f1 f5 17.e5 or 16...b6 17.♗d3, Black's chances are unclear. But I should have checked 16...♗d4!? (I did not consider this resource at the board) 17.♖e2 (on 17.♕e2 a strong reply is 17...b6 with the idea of 18.♗d3 ♕f6+ 19.♕f3 ♗xb2) 17...♗xh3 18.gxh3 ♕g3! 19.♖d2 ♕xh3+ which gives Black an attack and a guaranteed draw.

15.hxg4

On 15.♕e2 Black can play 15...♘e5 16.♘c3 ♗e6 or 15...♗d4!? 16.hxg4 ♗xg4 17.♕f1 ♖ac8. In taking the knight, White thought the game would inevitably end in a draw.

15...♗e5 16.g3

Otherwise the white king will have to march into the centre 'free of charge'.

16...♗xg3 17.fxg3 ♕xg3+ 18.♔f1 ♕f3+ 19.♔g1 ♕xg4+ 20.♔f2 ♕h4+ 21.♔e2 ♗g4+ 22.♔d2

22...d5!

An important psychological moment. Black gives up the possibility of forcing a draw by perpetual and continues to attack the white king, two pieces down. The centralised white king and his undeveloped queenside are fully sufficient justification for this.

23.exd5

The computer recommends 23.♘c3. Since the move in the game fails to 'cement' the d-file, this is a logical suggestion. After a short think, the computer offers the assessment 0.00, but this requires careful analysis. For example, after 23...dxe4 24.♖xe4 ♕f2+ 25.♘e2 ♗f3 26.♖e3 ♖ad8+ 27.♗d3 ♖d5 28.♕b3 ♖fd8 White's pieces are tied up, but does Black have a win?

23...♕h2+ 24.♖e2 ♕h6+ 25.♔d1 ♕h1+

The queen has found a square, where she will not be attacked after the exchange on e2, and so Black gains a tempo to play ...♖fe8.

26.♔d2 ♗xe2 27.♕xe2 ♖fe8 28.♕f2 ♕h6+

The continuation 28...♕xd5+ 29.♗d3 ♖ad8 30.♕g3 seemed unconvincing to me and so the black queen again begins a zigzag manoeuvre.

29.♔d1 ♕h5+ 30.♔d2 ♕g5+ 31.♔d1 ♕xd5+

32.♗d2

In the event of 32.♘d2 Black wins with 32...♖ad8 33.♗b3 ♕h1+ 34.♔c2 ♖c8+ 35.♔d3 ♕h3+ 36.♔d4 (36.♘f3 ♕f5+ 37.♔d2 ♖cd8+; 36.♕f3 ♖cd8+ 37.♔c4 ♕c8+ 38.♔b5 ♖e5+) 36...♖cd8+ 37.♗d5 ♖xd5+ 38.♔xd5 ♕d3+ 39.♔c5 ♖c8+ 40.♔b6 ♕a6#.

32...♖ac8

The continuations 32...♕h1+ 33.♗e1 ♖ad8+ 34.♘d2 or 32...♖ad8 33.♔c1 allow White to defend.

33.♘c3 ♕h1+ 34.♗e1 ♖cd8+ 35.♗d3 ♖xd3+ 36.♔c2 ♖f3 37.♕h4 ♖h3 38.♕f6 ♖h2+

Of course, not 38...♖xe1 39.♕d8+ ♔g7 40.♕d4+ ♔h6 41.♕d2+ ♖he3 42.♕xe3+!.

39.♔b3 ♖xe1 40.♕d8+ ♔g7 41.♕d4+ f6 42.♕d7+ ♔h6

And after a few moves White resigned.

At this period, I also pursued dynamic lines in analysis, looking for sacrificial resources in various lines. Here is an illustrative analysis, relating to an opening of some theoretical significance.

At some moment, I became interested in the following line of the King's Indian Attack:

1.♘f3 ♘f6 2.g3 b6 3.♗g2 ♗b7 4.0-0 e6 5.d3 d5 6.♘bd2

Here Black has the cunning move order

6...♘bd7

Rather than 6...♗e7 7.e4!, and the e4-pawn is immune because of the variation 7...dxe4 8.dxe4 ♘xe4? 9.♘e5 ♘d6 10.♗xb7 ♘xb7 11.♕f3! with a double threat against b7 and f7.

7.e4

7.♖e1 ♗c5! (the advance 8.e4 is again hampered by the possibility after 8...dxe4 9.dxe4 of the knight jumping to g4), which became fashionable after the game Portisch-Karpov, Moscow 1977.

Instead of the preparatory move 7.♖e1 my attention was grabbed by the pawn sacrifice 7.e4.

7...dxe4

If Black declines the pawn, then the position of his knights on f6 and d7 is not ideal, because of the advance e4-e5.

8.dxe4!?
Previously White had only ever tried 8.♘g5, which leads to mass exchanges on e4 and an equal game.
8...♘xe4 9.♘xe4 ♗xe4

The critical position. The pawn sacrifice has allowed White to open lines in the centre, whilst the black king is still two moves away from castling.
10.♗g5 ♕c8
The move 10...f6, weakening the e6-square, is one Black prefers to avoid, of course. In one of my casual games (the only time I managed to use the idea 8.dxe4!?) there followed 10...♗e7 11.♕d4 ♗xg5? (essential was 11...♗xf3 12.♗xe7 ♕xe7 13.♗xf3 ♖ad8 14.♕xg7 ♕f6 15.♕xf6 ♘xf6 with a small advantage for White in the endgame) 12.♕xe4 0-0 13.♖ad1 ♗e7 14.♘g5!, and Black lost material. White also retains the initiative after 10...♘f6 11.♕e2 followed by ♖ad1.
11.♕e2 ♗xf3
White succeeds in attacking the e6-square in the variation 11...♗b7

12.♘d4 ♗xg2 (12...♘c5 13.♘c6) 13.♘xe6! or 11...♕b7 12.♘d4 ♗xg2 13.♘xe6!.
12.♕xf3
At first, I planned to pursue the initiative by means of 12.♗xf3 ♖b8 13.♗h5! (this original way of creating threats with the bishops was known to me from the game Keres-Kotov, Budapest 1950, which arose from a Sicilian Defence) 13...g6 14.♗g4

Analysis diagram

14...♗e7 15.♗xe6! ♗xg5 16.♗xd7+ ♔xd7 17.♖ad1+ ♔c6 18.♕f3+ ♔b5 19.♕d3+ ♔a5 20.b4+, and the black king is mated.
Many years later, after checking the analysis with a computer, it turned out that Black can escape from this tricky situation with 14...h6!. For example: 15.♗xe6 (after 15.♗f4 ♗g7 White has sufficient compensation for the pawn, but no more) 15...hxg5 16.♗g4+ (now 16.♗xd7+ ♔xd7 gives nothing) 16...♔d8 (after 16...♗e7 17.♖fe1 ♕d8 18.♖ad1 f5 19.♗f3 ♔f8 20.♕e6 ♗d6 21.♖xd6 cxd6 22.♕xd6+ ♔g7 23.♖e7+ ♔h6 24.h4! White develops a very strong attack) 17.♖fe1 ♗d6 18.♖ad1 b5! (18...f5 is not good

because of 19.♖xd6! cxd6 20.♕e7+ ♔c7 21.♖e3 with advantage) 19.♕e3 f6 20.♕e6 ♖b6 – White has excellent compensation for the sacrificed piece, but nothing decisive is obvious.
So I had to seek new ways to develop the initiative. The text move was analysed in 2006.

12...♖b8 13.♕c3
Preventing Black from quietly completing the development of his kingside.

13...f6

White to play. How should he continue the attack?

14.♖fe1!
Attacking the Achilles Heel of the black position.

14...♔f7
A quick collapse follows 14...fxg5 15.♖xe6+ ♔f7 16.♗d5 etc.

15.♖xe6!
An effective blow! The slower 15.♗h3 ♘e5 allows Black to hold.

15...♔xe6 16.♖e1+ ♔f7
A forced mate results from 16...♘e5 17.♖xe5+ (here White has many ways to win) 17...fxe5 18.♕c6+ ♗d6 19.♕d5+ ♔f5 20.♕f7+ ♔xg5 21.♕xg7+ ♔f5 22.♕f7+ ♔g5 23.h4+ ♔h6 24.♕f6+ ♔h5 25.♕g5#.

17.♕b3+ ♔g6 18.♗e4+ ♔xg5
19.♕e3+ ♔h5 20.g4+ ♔xg4
21.♕g3+ ♔h5 22.♗f3+ ♔h6
23.♕h4+ ♔g6 24.♕h5#

This analysis has remained unknown to this day. I did share my discoveries with some of my pupils, but to the best of my knowledge, none of them have managed to play it either. However, a similar motif after 1.♘f3 ♘f6 2.g3 b5 3.♗g2 ♗b7 4.0-0 e6 5.d3 d5 6.♘bd2 ♘bd7 7.e4! dxe4 8.dxe4 ♘xe4 9.♘xe4 ♗xe4 10.♕e2 ♗c6 etc. was played in a game Vasyukov-Alexandrov (Moscow 1996), but here it is easier to decide on the move 7.e4, because the position of the pawn on b5 significantly compromises Black's position.

Finally in December 1989, my efforts paid off. In the USSR Central Chess Club tournament, I fulfilled the master norm and showed a decent quality of play. My confidence grew after my third round game with master Evgeny Maliutin, in which I managed to hold up in a tense calculating battle, where I was on the defensive.

Ruy Lopez
Evgeny Maliutin
Alexander Kalinin
Moscow 1989

Maliutin is an IM, Moscow men's champion in 1991 and a favourite pupil of Kimelfeld. Evgeny has a combinative style of play, avoiding all stereotype and routine. The talented youngster was prevented from achieving great sporting successes by excessive sensibility. In the summer of 1989, Zhenya and I played for the Moscow team at the All-Union youth games in Kramatorsk. His play on top board created a real furore – 5/5! Amongst his examiners were Gelfand, Dzhandzhava and Komarov! The turning point came with his sixth round game against Ivanchuk. After losing this, Evgeny was so upset that he lost his last three games as well. The aforementioned game against Ivanchuk was the background to our game at the Central Chess Club tournament.

1.e4 e5

At this time I played exclusively the Sicilian Defence, but knowing my opponent's fondness for the Exchange Spanish, I decided to go for that. 'Transposing into a quiet endgame, which I myself like to play, will dampen down my opponent's combinative imagination', I thought. I would add that it was never a problem for me to play a new opening, because when studying master games, I did not restrict myself to those which featured my own favourite openings. On the other hand, such experiments should be kept to a minimum, since any move of the opponent which is different from the lines one has prepared can shake one up.

2.♘f3 ♘c6 3.♗b5 a6 4.♗xc6 dxc6 5.0-0 f6 6.d4 exd4 7.♘xd4 c5 8.♘b3 ♕xd1 9.♖xd1 ♗g4

In the classic game Fischer-Portisch (Havana 1966) Black unexpectedly faced difficulties after 9...♗d6 10.♘a5! b5 11.c4 ♘e7 12.♗e3.

10.f3 ♗e6 11.♘c3

The idea of Black's ninth move can be illustrated with the variation 11.♗f4 c4 12.♘d4 0-0-0 13.♘c3 ♖xd4 14.♖xd4 ♗c5 15.♗e3 ♗xd4 16.♗xd4 ♘e7 with equality.

11...♗d6 12.a4

The usual continuation here is 12.♗e3 b6 13.a4 ♔f7 14.a5 c4 15.♘d4 b5 with roughly equal chances. The cunning move order in the text was Maliutin's novelty.

12...0-0-0 13.♗e3 c4

After 13...b6?! 14.a5 ♔b7 15.e5! Black's position is quite unpleasant.

14.♘d4

The game Maliutin-Ivanchuk (Kramatorsk 1989), on which I had based my preparations, continued as follows: 14.♘a5? (trying to surround the c4-pawn) 14...♘e7 15.♘d5 ♗xd5 16.exd5 c3! 17.bxc3 ♗e5, and Black obtained the advantage.

14...♗d7

This position seemed to me to be completely harmless for Black. But here, like lightning from a clear sky, there followed...

15.♘cb5!!

After the game, Zhenya told me that this unexpected sacrifice had been suggested by Ivanchuk in their post-mortem in Kramatorsk! It turned out to be far from simple to neutralise White's beautiful idea.

15...♗c5!

If the sacrifice is accepted – 15... axb5 16.axb5 – the following variations are possible:

A) 16...♔b8 17.♖a5! (17.♖a2 ♗xb5! 18.♘xb5 ♗xh2+) 17...b6 18.♖a2 ♗xb5 (or 18...♗b4 19.♘c6+) 19.♖da1;

B) 16...♗e8 17.♘e6 ♔d7 18.♘xd8 ♔xd8 19.♗c5 (19.♗f4) 19...♔e7 (19...♗xb5 20.♗xd6 cxd6 21.♖xd6+ ♔c7 22.♖d5±) 20.♗xd6+ cxd6 21.♖a7±

16.♘f5! ♗xe3+ 17.♘xe3 ♘e7

Taking on b5 is again impossible, because of the undefended rook on b8.

18.♘d4 c5

The only way to defend the c4-pawn (18...b5? 19.axb5 axb5 20.♖a8+ ♔b7 21.♖xd8 ♖xd8 22.♘e6±).

19.♘e2 ♗e6 20.♘f4 ♗f7 21.♘fd5! ♘xd5!

After 21...♗xd5 22.exd5 ♔c7 23.a5 ♖d6 24.♖d2 ♖hd8 25.♖ad1 Black's position looks dangerous, because White retains the possibility of advancing the kingside pawns, supported by the king.

22.exd5 ♔c7

23.a5!

Announcing the c4-pawn's death sentence!

23...♖he8! 24.♖a3! ♖e5 25.♖c3 g5!

Not 25...♗xd5? because of 26.f4 ♖h5 27.g4±.

26.♘xc4

On 26.♘g4 there could follow 26...♖exd5 27.♖xd5 ♖xd5 28.♘xf6 ♖d1+ 29.♔f2 h6 30.♘g4 ♖d2+ 31.♔f1 (or 31.♔g3 h5 with the idea of ...h5-h4) 31...♗e6 (weaker is 31...♗g6 32.♘e3) 32.♘xh6 ♔d6 (less precise is 32...♔c6 33.♖e3 followed by ♖e2) 33.♘g4 ♗xg4 34.fxg4 ♔d5, and the active position of the rook guarantees Black against any unpleasantness.

26...♖exd5 27.♖xd5 ♗xd5!

If 27...♖xd5 an interesting knight raid becomes possible – 28.♘e3 ♖e5 29.♘g4 ♖f5 30.♘h6!, and White wins.

28.♘e3 ♔c6 29.b4 c4!

The final subtlety, leading to a completely equal game.

30.♘xc4 ♗xc4 31.♖xc4+ ♔b5

Draw.

The following episode had an important psychological

significance for me. In the middle of the tournament, I had to face the master (now IM) Alexey Gorbatov with the black pieces. On the eve of the round, Alexey, generally noted for his principled and uncompromising sporting behaviour, for some reason suggested we play out a draw. In former times, I would gladly have grabbed this attractive (in all respects) offer of a pre-arranged draw, but now I decided to fight for a win with either colour and against any opponent.

Such 'audacity' fired Alexey up. He conducted the game in energetic attacking style, choosing the Four Pawns Attack against the King's Indian. I only drew with great difficulty. But for me, this was much more than just half a point – I saw that I could overcome my weaknesses and fears! Incidentally, in this tournament, for the first time in my life, I won more games than I drew (+6-2=5), and none of the draws were peaceful ones!

The following two games against masters proved memorable from the creative standpoint.

Nimzo-Indian Defence
Sergey Krasnov
Alexander Kalinin
Moscow 1989

1.d4 ♘f6 2.c4 e6 3.♘c3 ♗b4 4.♘f3 b6 5.e3 ♗b7 6.♗d3 0-0 7.0-0 c5

The lessons learned from the games given earlier against Vulfson, Bronstein and Novikov had their effect – I had taken up a new weapon against 1.d4, which was more suited to my tastes. After 8.♘a4 cxd4 9.a3 ♗e7 10.exd4 d6 11.b4 ♘bd7 the game could transpose into channels more reminiscent of the Sicilian, which was my repertoire against 1.e4.

8.a3
White cannot hope for an opening advantage with such a move. One only has to compare the text with the variation Black sometimes chooses at move seven: 7...♗xc3 8.bxc3 ♗e4 9.♗e2 c5, and now if White were to play the strange move a2-a3, then we would reach the position in the game. This white a-pawn is better on a2, keeping control of the b3-square and leaving a3 free for the queen's bishop.

8...♗xc3 9.bxc3 ♗e4 10.♗e2 ♘c6 11.♘e1
The game Najdorf-Smyslov (Zurich 1953) continued 11.♘d2 ♗g6 12.♘b3 ♘e4 13.♕e1 ♘d6, and here the players repeated moves with 14.♕d1 ♘e4 15.♕e1 ♘d6 16.♕d1, draw.

11...d5
Thanks to his good development, Black can play actively in the centre, not fearing the opening of lines for the opponent's bishops.

12.cxd5 exd5 13.♘d3 c4 14.♘e5 ♘a5
Objectively speaking, it was stronger to play 14...♘xe5 15.dxe5 ♘d7 16.f3 ♗d3 17.♗xd3 cxd3

18.♕xd3 ♘xe5 19.♕d4 ♘c6 with
some advantage to Black. But I did
not want to simplify the position
too much.
**15.f3 ♗g6 16.♖a2 ♘b3 17.e4 ♘xc1
18.♕xc1 dxe4 19.♗xc4 exf3**
Forcing the white rook to leave the
first rank, which tells, for example,
in the variation 20.♖xf3 ♖c8
21.♖af2 b5! 22.♗xb5 ♕xd4, although
the position arising after 23.cxd4
♖xc1+ 24.♖f1, is still pretty equal.
20.♖xf3 ♖c8
With the threat of 21...♖xc4 22.♘xc4
♕d5 23.♕f1 b5.
21.♕f1
Preparing to meet 21...♗e4 with
22.♖f4 ♗d5 23.♗xd5 ♕xd5 24.c4. As
we have already seen, it is perfectly
possible to play 21.♖af2, whilst after
21.♘xg6 hxg6 22.♕f1 there would
follow the same continuation as in
the game.

**Black to move. What would you
play?**

21...b5! 22.♗xb5 ♖xc3!

This small combination destroys
White's pawn centre. I clearly
remember how, during the game, I
immediately recalled a delightful

combination I saw as a child, from
the game

**Eivind Poulsson
Ivan Farago**
Gausdal 1976

What would you play?

With two unexpected blows, Black
destroyed the enemy centre:
**16...♘xd4!! 17.♘xd4 ♖xc3!! 18.♕xc3
♗xd4 19.♕c2 ♗xa1 20.♗a3 ♕g5
21.♗e4 ♖c8**
And Black won.

Later, there was an interesting
discussion around the variation
17.cxd4 (instead of 17.♘xd4):
**17...♗xf3 18.gxf3 ♗xd4 19.♗a3
♗c3! 20.♕e3**
After 20.♕e2 ♕g5+ 21.♔f1 ♕xh5
White is in a bad way.
And now after 20.♕e3 Farago,
annotating the game in *Informant*,
gave the variation 20...♗xa1 21.♖xa1
(or 21.♗xf8 ♗c3! 22.♖c1 ♕xf8
23.♗a6 ♕b4! 24.♗xc8 ♗d2 25.♕e4,
and the opposite-coloured bishops
ending is lost for White) 21...♖c3,
winning for Black.
However, after 22.♗xf8 ♖xd3
23.♗e7! ♖xe3 24.♗xd8 it is Black

who must look for a way to save himself! Maybe the move 20...♗xa1 was simply a misprint. The correct decision is:

20...♗xe1!

21.♖xe1 ♖c3 22.♗xf8 ♖xd3 23.♗e7 ♖xe3, and now the ♖e1 is under attack.

But modern computers have also corrected this variation. After

21.hxg6!

(instead of 21.♖xe1?)

21...♗c3

in the variation 21...hxg6 22.♖xe1 ♖c3 23.♕h6 ♖xd3 24.♗b2 ♖d4 25.♖e4 e5 26.♗xd4 exd4 27.♖h4 Black is suddenly mated!

22.gxh7+ ♔h8 23.♖c1 ♕f6 24.♗xf8 ♖xf8 25.f4

Black has only a small advantage.

23.♘c6 ♖xf3

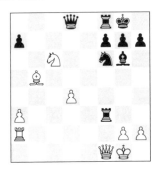

24.gxf3!?

If 24.♕xf3 ♕d6 (less accurate is 24...♕d7 on account of 25.♖e2, after which, with the queen on d6, not exposed to discovered checks, there follows ...♗h5) followed by ♗e4 Black establishes control over the light squares in the centre of the board. By agreeing to a weakening

of his king's cover, White takes control of e4, counting on consolidating his position with the help of the manoeuvre ♕f1-c4-c5.

24...♕d6 25.♕c4 ♕f4 26.♖f2

More precise was the immediate 26.♕c5 ♖e8 27.♘e5 (27.♘e7+? ♖xe7 28.♕xe7 ♕g5+ and 29...♕xb5) 27...♖d8 28.♘c6, and the black rook has to hide in the corner to escape the attacks – 28...♖a8!?.

26...♕g5+ 27.♔f1 ♕e3 28.♕c5 ♖e8 29.♘e5 ♖d8 30.♘c6

Not allowing the black rook to join the attack and continually harassing it.

30...♗d3+

The alternative was 30...♖a8!?. The rook finds a safe square and the ♗g6 is preserved for the attack, supporting a tactical raid by the knight to g4 or e4. Later Black could strengthen his position with ...h7-h6. But my hand simply could not bear to put the rook into the very corner.

31.♔g2 ♖e8 32.♘xa7?

In serious time-trouble, and since 32.♘e5 is impossible because of 32...♗xb5, White sends his steed to the opposite side of the board, seizing a pawn in the process. However, the temporary removal of the knight from the epicentre of the action proves fatal.

White had two alternatives of roughly equal merit: 32.♗xd3 ♕xd3 33.♘e5 and 32.♘e7+ ♖xe7 33.♗xd3 ♖e8. In both cases, in view of the insecure cover of the white king, Black's position looks the more attractive, but I have not managed to prove a concrete advantage.

Black to move. What would you play?

32...♘e4! 33.fxe4 ♕xe4+ 34.♔g3 ♕g6+ 35.♔f3

It may appear that Black has to give perpetual check, but...

35...h5!

A problem-like move. Now it transpires that after 36.♗xe8 there follows 36...♕e4+ 37.♔g3 ♕g4#!

36.h3 h4!

There is no defence against the two mates on e4 and g3, so White resigned.

Grünfeld Indian Defence

Alexander Kalinin

Ilya Frog

Moscow 1989

1.d4 ♘f6 2.c4 g6 3.♘c3 d5 4.♘f3 ♗g7 5.cxd5 ♘xd5 6.e4 ♘xc3 7.bxc3 c5 8.♖b1 0-0 9.♗e2 cxd4 10.cxd4 ♕a5+ 11.♗d2 ♕xa2 12.0-0 ♕e6

The black queen hurries to quit the danger zone at once. Nowadays, this move is rarely played.

13.♕c2 b6

The queen moves to d7, d6 or c6 are more popular.

14.♗c4 ♕d7 15.♕a2

On a2 the queen is ideally placed, exerting pressure on the a-file (♖xb6 is already a threat) and the diagonal a2-g8.

15...♗b7 16.d5 ♕d8 17.e5 ♘d7 18.♖fe1

18.e6 fxe6 19.♘g5 ♘c5 20.dxe6 leads only to a premature forcing of the position.

18...a6?

This preparation for driving the white bishop off the key diagonal by means of 19...b5 20.♗b3 ♘c5 proves to be too slow. It was essential to play 18...♘c5, slowing up the advance of the enemy central pawns.

19.♗g5

Now the breakthrough 19.e6 fxe6 20.♘g5 looks more soundly based, e.g. 20...♘c5 21.♘xe6 ♘xe6 21.♖xe6 ♔h8 22.♖exb6 ♗c8 etc. However, fearing to cash in my chips too cheaply, I decided to continue strengthening the position. In connection with the threat of d5-d6 Black has to go for a weakening on his kingside.

19...h6 20.♗h4 g5

White to play. Calculate the consequences of the bishop sacrifice on g5.

21.♗xg5

As the American GM Reuben Fine once said, 'in some positions, a combination is as natural as a baby's smile.' Events now develop by force.

21...hxg5 22.♘xg5 ♘xe5

If 22...e6 the blow 23.♘xf7! is decisive.

23.♖xe5! ♗xe5 24.♕c2!

24.♕e2? is premature because of 24...♕d6 25.♕h5 ♕g6.

24...f5 25.♕e2

White does not reach his goal after 25.d6+? e6! 26.♘xe6 ♕xd6 or 26.♗xe6+ ♔g7.

25...♗f6

Black is not helped by 25...♕d6 26.♕h5 ♖f6 27.♕h7+ ♔f8 28.♕h8# or 25...♗xd5 26.♕h5 ♖e8 27.♖xb6, and White wins.

26.♕h5 ♗xg5 27.♕xg5+

Black manages to defend after 27.♕g6+ ♔h8 28.♖b3 e6 29.♖h3+ ♗h4 30.♕h6+ ♔g8 31.♖xh4 ♕xh4 32.♕xh4 ♗xd5 etc.

27...♔f7

In the event of 27...♔h7, White decides things with 28.♖b3.

White had reached this position in his preliminary calculations, when considering the sacrifice on

g5. As a minimum, he is guaranteed a draw (28.♕xf5+ ♔e8 29.♕g6+ ♔d7 30.♕e6+ ♔e8 31.♕g6+), but I felt that there should be a win. I did not calculate any further, instead trusting my intuition and preferring to save time and energy for the decisive stage of the game. Once the position arises on the board, then one can find the correct solution.

28.d6+! e6

If 28...♔e8 29.♕g6+ ♔d7 30.♕e6+ ♔e8 31.♖d1 the black king perishes in the centre of the board.

29.♕xf5+ ♕f6

Or 29...♔g7 30.♕g4+ ♔h8 31.♖b3 ♖f7 32.♖h3+ ♖h7 33.♕d4+ winning for White.

30.♕h7+ ♔e8

It turns out that after 30...♕g7 Black is mated – 31.♗xe6+ ♔f6 32.♕f5#!

31.♕xb7 ♖d8

The check on f2 is just a pinprick and leads to Black's immediate defeat.

32.♕xb6

With this, White's combination can be considered over. Despite the rough material equality, Black's position is bad because of the tragic position of his king.

32...♕f4 33.♕c6+ ♔f7 34.♕c7+ ♔g8

The black king ends up running all round the board after 34...♔g6 35.♗d3+ ♔h5 36.♕h7+ ♕h6 37.g4+ ♔g5 38.h4+ ♕xh4 39.♕g6+ ♔f4 40.♖b4+ ♔e5 41.♖e4+ ♔xd6 42.♕xe6+ ♔c7 43.♖c4+ mating.

35.♗xe6+ ♔h8 36.♕c3+ ♖f6
Or 36...♕f6 37.♕h3+ ♔g7 38.♖b7+,
and White wins.

37.f3
By securing the f2-square, White
creates the threat of bringing the
rook into the attack along the
fourth rank.

37...♖xd6
Black has finally managed to
eliminate the d6-pawn, but now the
opponent's heavy artillery breaks
through into his position.

38.♖b8+ ♔g7 39.♕c7+ ♖f7
Black has to go into a hopeless
endgame. He loses at once after
39...♔h6 40.♖h8+ ♔g5 41.♕g7+ ♖g6
42.h4+ ♕xh4 43.♕e5#.

40.♕xf7+ ♕xf7 41.♗xf7 ♔xf7
42.♖a8
Time-trouble is over, and with it,
the game – Black resigned.

In working on this book, I checked
my old analyses with the computer.
It turned out that White's
combination was only good enough
for a draw.

In this position, Black has an
unexpected way to save himself:

25...♗xh2+!! It is easy to miss such a
move, since Black is sacrificing the
only piece that defends his king.

A) 26.♔xh2 ♕d6+ 27.♔g1 ♖f6
28.♖b3 (according to the computer,
a draw results from 28.♖xb6! ♕xb6
29.♕xe7 etc.) 28...♖h6 29.♖g3 ♔f8
30.♘e6+ ♔e8 31.♘g7+ ♔d7 32.♘xf5
♖ah8!, and Black takes over the
initiative;

B) 26.♔h1 ♗f4 27.♕h5 ♗xg5
28.♕xg5+ (equality also results
from 28.♕g6+ ♔h8 29.♖b3 e6
30.♖h3+ ♗h4 31.♕h6+ ♔g8
32.♖xh4 ♕xh4+ 33.♕xh4 ♗xd5)
28...♔f7, and thanks to the open
position of his king on the h-file,
White has to settle for perpetual
check – 29.♕xf5+ ♔e8 30.♕g6+
♔d7 31.♕e6+ ♔e8 32.♕g6+ etc.
In searching for an improvement
in White's play, let us return to the
position after 19...h6.

A tempting alternative to the
bishop retreat to h4 is the attempt
to break up Black's defences with
another version of the piece
sacrifice: 20.d6! hxg5 21.e6! with a
very strong attack.
It is important to note that,
despite my success, after the

tournament I analysed all of my games thoroughly and critically, identifying many mistakes not only in the games I lost, but also in my wins. I will show just two instructive moments from my notes of that period.

Alexander Kalinin
Igor Lempert

Moscow 1989

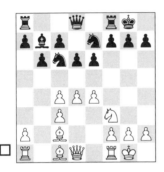

What would you play?

In this game, I did not show sufficient ingenuity in developing the initiative.

The white bishops are pointing at the residence of the black king. Well-known combinational motifs are already in the air – 10.e5 dxe5 11.♗xh7+ ♔xh7 12.♘g5+, which, however, leads only to unclear consequences, e.g. 12...♔g6 13.♕g4 f5 14.♕g3 f4 15.♕g4 ♕c8!? etc. Let us consider other ways to develop the initiative:

A) 10.c5 ♘a5 is a blow in the air;

B) I was also not convinced by the consequences of the energetic 10.d5 ♘a5 11.dxe6 fxe6 12.♘g5 ♕d7 (less accurate is 12...♕c8, intending

to meet the jump 13.♕g4 with 13... e5, on account of 13.e5 ♘f5 14.♖e1 h6 15.exd6! hxg5 16.d7 ♕d8 17.♖xe6 with an attack for White) 13.♕g4 ♗a6 14.♕xe6+ ♕xe6 15.♘xe6 ♖fc8;

C) Seizing space on the kingside with 10.h4 (with the idea of 11.e5 dxe5 12.♗xh7+) 10...e5 11.h5 h6 12.♘h2 (taking the g6-square from the black knight and preparing f2-f4) looks rather slow;

D) The manoeuvre I chose also looks rather heavy: 10.♘g5 h6 11.♘h3 with the idea of opening the white queen's path to the kingside and playing f2-f4. There followed 11...♘a5 12.♗d3? (stronger was 12.♕g4 ♔h8! – after 12...♘g6 13.f4 ♕h4 14.♕xh4 ♘xh4 15.g3 ♘g6 16.f5 exf5 17.exf5 ♘h8 18.c5 White obtained the advantage – 13.♕h5 ♘g8 with chances for both sides) 12...♘g6 13.f4 f5!, and the activity of the white bishops and his pawn centre is limited.

But the correct idea went undiscovered! White should combine the different ideas for central pawn breaks into one whole: **10.d5! ♘a5 11.e5! dxe5**

Other possible variations are 11... exd5 12.♗xh7+! ♔xh7 13.♘g5+ ♔g6 14.♕g4 f5 15.exf6 ♔xf6 16.♕e6# or 11...♘f5 12.♘g5 with advantage to White, since after 12...h6 there follows 13.dxe6.

**12.♗xh7+! ♔xh7 13.♘g5+ ♔g6
14.♕g4**

14.♕d3+? ♘f5 15.g4 ♘xc4! 16.gxf5+ exf5 17.♕xc4 ♕xd5 etc.

14...f5 15.♕g3 f4 16.♕g4

and here the inclusion of the d5-pawn in the attack proves decisive – Black has no satisfactory defence against 17.♘xe6+. Therefore Black would have to settle for the line 10.d5 ♘e5 11.♘xe5 dxe5 12.♗a3 with a clear positional advantage to White, whose bishops obtain much more scope.'

Alexander Kalinin
Vassili Burlov

Moscow 1989

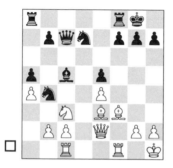

What would you play?

We have reached a position characteristic of the Scheveningen Variation of the Sicilian. Here White committed a serious positional error.
19.♗g4?
And after
19...♗xe3 20.♕xe3 ♕c5 21.♕g3 ♘b6 22.b3 ♖ad8 23.♖f5 ♘c6 24.♖cf1 ♕e7
Black had no problems.

'It was wrong to exchange dark-squared bishops. After 19.♗g5! nothing can stop White playing

♘b5, c2-c3 and ♗g4. In this case, the white bishops develop unpleasant pressure, whilst the ♗c5 is firing into the air. Sooner or later, Black would have to decide on the move ...f7-f6, which weakens a whole complex of light squares. The emotional advance made in this period, assisted by the analytical work carried out, a critical attitude to my own play and a continuing fight against my weaknesses, laid the basis for my successful tournaments in the years 1990/91. I managed to fulfil the norms for the IM title (although I was not officially awarded the title until 1994), and scored my first wins against GMs.

Unfortunately, later I suffered an experience which occurs with many young sportsmen. Tournament successes deceived me into being less critical towards myself, and weakened my resolve in my independent work in the period. The chance that the opening of the country's borders gave to play in foreign open tournaments was not used by me rationally, and in running from one tournament to another, I had no time to think seriously about my play. Soon I stopped annotating games altogether. In such situations, as Botvinnik warned, a player just becomes a journeyman, and a new phase of sporting and creative crisis approached rapidly...

In place of an epilogue

Work on this book is already approaching its end. Opening a number of the magazine *64-The Chess Observer* (№2/2013) some time ago, I immediately noticed three articles, one after another. Their tone was sharply different from what the 'press' has been telling for decades already, about the increasing strength of computer preparation, especially in the opening.

From Kramnik's interview, regarding the tournament at Wijk aan Zee 2013:

'If you take players of 2800 and compare them with players of 2730 or lower, then in recent times, the gap between them has grown for some reason. However, I do not have the impression that we in the top five or ten are playing more strongly than previously. It is simply that the lower group have dropped off somewhat. This may be the result of too much computer reliance. I looked through some games and realised that it was not a question of blunders (these happen to us all). I was much more shocked by some of the really serious positional mistakes. I think that this results from people increasingly looking at positions from a computer viewpoint. Games proceed nowadays move by move, almost in isolation from each other. People forget that chess has its general principles, which one is advised not to break. I think that all players of 2700 nowadays have become victims of the computer, whereas the very top players have managed to achieve the right symbiosis.'

From the notes by Leko to the game Leko-Caruana (Wijk aan Zee 2013) after the moves 1.e4 e5 2.♘f3 ♘c6 3.♗b5 a6 4.♗a4 ♘f6 5.0-0 ♗e7 6.d3 (! – Steinitz's favourite continuation A.K.):

'Possibly the biggest discovery of the past year! In the past this was regarded as a harmless weapon, but nowadays, among the top players, it is seen as a way to reach a complicated, fighting position.'

From the theoretical survey by Alexey Kuzmin, devoted to the Wijk aan Zee tournament of 2013:

'Strictly speaking, in the forming of the article on new opening ideas, the games of Magnus Carlsen should not be included. Surprisingly, the

world number one, who wins practically every tournament he plays
in, does not really have a properly worked-out opening repertoire. The
phrase "his opening preparation could be better" is definitely applicable
to Carlsen. But, on the other hand, what more can one want – he scored
"+7"!... Carlsen does not often delight his admirers with startling opening
discoveries, unless, of course, one counts his whole approach to the
problem and his choice of openings.'

As they say, 'what goes around comes around'...

Index of games, fragments and studies